Duncan McNab is a former policeman and private investigator. He's worked as a journalist covering current affairs
for both the ABC and the Nine Network. His first book,
The Usual Suspect – The Life of Abe Saffron, was published
by Pan Macmillan in 2005.

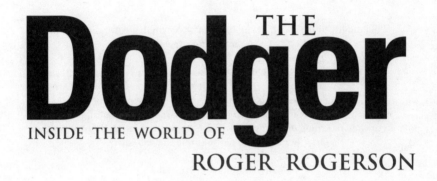

THE
Dodger
INSIDE THE WORLD OF
ROGER ROGERSON

DUNCAN McNAB

MACMILLAN
Pan Macmillan Australia

First published in 2006 in Macmillan by Pan Macmillan Australia Pty Ltd
1 Market Street, Sydney

National Library of Australia
Cataloguing-in-Publication data:

McNab, Duncan.
The dodger: inside the world of Roger Rogerson.

ISBN-13: 978 1 4050 3751 8
ISBN-10: 1 4050 3751 2.

1. Rogerson, Roger. 2. Ex-police officers – New South Wales – Biography.
3. Detectives – New South Wales – Biography. 4. Police misconduct –
New South Wales. 5. Police corruption – New South Wales. I. Title.

363.2092

Typeset in 14/15.5 pt Granjon by Post Pre-press Group
Printed in Australia by McPherson's Printing Group

CONTENTS

ACKNOWLEDGMENTS

Firstly to Lyn Tranter and her team at Australian Literary Management, who do a fine job of keeping we writing types busy and on the straight and narrow (most of the time, anyway). Thanks also to Pan Macmillan for their continuing enthusiasm, insight and support. Writing is fun, editing is hard work.

Both my research and memory were stimulated and supported by two terrific books, John Dale's *Huckstepp – A Dangerous Life* and Tom Noble and Neddy Smith's *Neddy: the Life and Crimes of Arthur 'Neddy' Smith*.

Finally, my thanks to the numerous bods I've chatted with over the years about Roger Caleb Rogerson.

PROLOGUE

A police force inhabits a world of its own – a world where good and bad co-exist comfortably. So, it's not surprising that the first 'detective' in New South Wales was actually a convicted crook.

Israel Chapman was transported to Sydney in 1818 for the crime of 'highway robbery'. In the colony he found himself working in positions of increasing trust, and on 21 November 1821 he was granted a conditional pardon. As a free man, the poacher decided to turn gamekeeper. His first job was with the Sydney Police.

For reasons that are lost in time, Chapman found himself out of a job after a short period. However, he was a skilled networker, with influential friends who interceded on his behalf and soon had him back on the beat.

While history suggests that Chapman's success as a copper was due to his diligence, I suspect that he was both very bright and very charming. He soon found himself with plenty of contacts in the underbelly of Sydney and he quickly became a very successful sleuth.

In 1827, Chapman announced that he was leaving the police force because of the poor pay and conditions. The government swiftly offered him more money and the new position of 'police runner'. The name was taken from the famous Bow Street Runners, the very effective body of investigators established in 1749 by Henry Fielding,

London's Bow Street magistrate and author of *Tom Jones*, among other works of fiction.

The following year, Chapman again resigned. He went back to England, where he took a wife. In 1833 he returned to Sydney, where he was reappointed by the Sydney Police. He finished his career as an inspector in the then far-flung outpost of Campbelltown, some 50 kilometres southwest of the city.

The next great step for criminal investigation in New South Wales was taken on 1 March 1862 with the addition of a specialist Detectives Force to the NSW Police Department. It was led by Sub-Inspector Charles Edward Harrison, and supported by twelve 'detectives' who were primarily involved in tracing people from England who had disappeared in the colony. In many cases, foul play was suspected.

Business was brisk. In February 1851, Edward Hargraves, who had recently returned from the gold rush in California, found gold at Summer Hill Creek, near Bathurst. The government made a public announcement about the find on 22 May, and prospectors who had been about to set sail for California decided instead to head for Bathurst. When gold was also found in Victoria later that year, the rush was on in Australia.

With all that prosperity came business for retailers, hoteliers and, of course, crooks. Bushranging became a growth industry. And so did policing. The newly minted detectives joined the troopers in chasing the likes of Ben Hall and the Kelly Gang around the New South Wales countryside, with some success.

The Criminal Investigation Branch (CIB) was formed on 19 November 1879, its founding father the then premier and colonial secretary of New South Wales, Sir Henry Parkes.

The CIB, headquartered at 109 Phillip Street, Sydney, comprised fourteen men under the command of an inspector. The CIB grew steadily in size but was little changed in structure until 1929 when the head of the Detective Branch, Superintendent W. J. Mackay, returned from a lengthy overseas tour with some very modern ideas about techniques of criminal investigation.

To sharpen up the Branch (as it was known to those working in it), he introduced specialist squads and new sections. This was the CIB I joined in 1979 after two years in uniform. I remained there until making good my escape in 1986. It would soldier on in this format until the late 1980s, when Commissioner John Avery pretty much dismantled the Branch, believing it to be hopelessly corrupt and beyond redemption.

The man associated most closely in the public's mind with the demise of the CIB joined the NSW Police Force in 1958 and soon became a detective. He was a boy from Bankstown, in Sydney's southwest. Through the 1960s and 1970s he was the CIB pin-up boy, the detective's detective. By the mid-1980s, he signified everything that was wrong with the CIB. His name was Roger Caleb Rogerson.

1

A BOY FROM THE SUBURBS

There was little about the upbringing of Roger Caleb Rogerson that pointed to his future reputation as Australia's most notorious police officer.

On Friday, 3 January 1941, Mabel Rogerson (nee Boxley) gave birth to her first child, a son. Australia was at war. The headlines of the day announced, 'Norway under the Nazis – submission turns to hatred' and 'Australian forces attack Bardia'. Britain was being bombed, and inevitably there was 'Suspense in the Balkans'. And in Sydney, life was bustling along as usual. Within a few months the family would transplant from seaside Bondi to the fast-growing suburb of Bankstown.

At the start of the twentieth century, Bankstown had been on the cusp of a population explosion. The census of 1901 counted 1246 people living in the suburb, of whom 661 were male and 585 female. It was a nice balance for those looking to find a mate, build a house and settle down to raise a family. A century later, Bankstown is a snapshot of multicultural Australia, with immigrants from Asia and the Middle East as visible a presence as the well-established Anglo-Saxon families. The 1901 census noted that most of the locals were Church of England, along with a sizeable Roman Catholic minority, a smattering of miscellaneous Protestants and one, perhaps rather lonely, Jew. There wasn't a Muslim or Buddhist in sight.

On 14 April 1909, the railway service from Sydney's Central Station to Bankstown was opened, and by the following year the population had surged to 2000. The railway became the focal point of the community, encouraging the development of a shopping hub.

In the decade leading up to the 1920s, Sydney's southwest was the fastest-developing area in the state. The local population grew by 307 per cent. Industries previously located close to the city centre began to take advantage of the new transport infrastructure, cheaper and plentiful land, and the rapidly swelling population that was in search of local work. The growing appeal of Bankstown attracted the Rogerson and Boxley families.

Owen Rogerson, nicknamed 'Roger', was from Hull, in England. A hardworking, plain-speaking Yorkshireman, he had sailed to Australia aged nineteen in 1920 looking for a new life far removed from the bleak industrial cities and mines of his homeland. He brought with him iron-working skills as a boilermaker and engineer. Work was easy to find, and he soon managed to put away a few pounds. It was time to do a little adventuring.

After poking about in the warm and sunny northern reaches of the continent, Owen and a travelling companion decided to invest their cash in a peanut farm situated beside the Roper River. The farm prospered, and all went well until Owen's mate was struck down with malaria. The two men sold their property and headed south to Sydney in search of better medical treatment and a kinder climate.

While knocking about in Sydney's east, in 1939 Owen met

and quickly fell hard for Mabel Boxley, a pretty church-going girl some fourteen years his junior. She lived with her parents in Bondi and worked as a dressmaker. A whirlwind courtship and marriage followed, and Owen moved into the Bondi home with his new bride and her parents. Such domestic arrangements weren't unusual at the time, and Owen found in his in-laws both a family and friends.

When Mabel's father developed asthma, medical science could offer little relief. His doctor thought the bracing sea air of Bondi was probably a cause of his breathing difficulties and suggested that somewhere drier and warmer might be more suitable. The availability of acreage and the offer of work in the rapidly expanding southwest of Sydney appealed, and the family sold up in Bondi and moved to Bankstown, to a property on what is now Stacey Street, the main road linking Canterbury Road with the Hume Highway. The property would later be subdivided and a street on the subdivision named after the Boxleys. The modest Owen Rogerson missed out on immortality. The family name was destined for a worse fate.

His skills in working with iron ensured that Owen Rogerson was always in employment. It was a matter of pride in the family that he was working on the Sydney Harbour Bridge on the day the last rivet was driven home. Later, during the Second World War, his attempt to join the fight was denied because of his essential work on warships. This work often took him to sea off Sydney in cruisers, destroyers and corvettes of the Royal Australian Navy, working on the big guns that comprised the main armament.

Owen Rogerson, a passionate advocate for the rights of the working man, became a member of the Communist Party of Australia, which had been formed on 30 October 1920. These were in the salad days of communism, before the bastardry and brutality of Joseph Stalin became common knowledge and the dreams of the idealists were shattered. It wasn't until the late 1940s and the beginnings of the Cold War that the Communist Party was on the nose. The general secretary of the party, Lance Sharkey, said that the formation of the party was 'one of the decisive revolutionary acts of the Australian working class'. Workers were drawn to the party, he went on, which was 'grounded in the working man's experiences of the Labor movement of the preceding 50 years' and 'to carry on the fight for the working class'. It was music to the ears of a young man who had grown up in the tough working-class towns of northern England.

Owen's identification with and support for the Communist Party hit a hurdle when, on 4 March 1949, Sharkey, still the general secretary, said in a speech: 'If Soviet forces in pursuit of aggressors entered Australia, Australian workers would welcome them.' The idea of Soviet troops trampling around Australia didn't sit well with the populace, who were still recovering from the Second World War. For a government coming to grips with the start of the Cold War, it was a heaven-sent comment. In the dying days of the Chifley government, Sharkey was prosecuted for sedition.

With the arrival of the Menzies government on 19 December 1949, Sharkey's prosecution became even more vigorous. He was convicted by a jury of his peers. An appeal to the High Court failed, with the learned judges finding five to one against him. Back in New South Wales, Justice Dwyer gave Sharkey a rousing dressing-down, and sentenced him to three years' hard labour – the maximum sentence under the law of the day. This began the slow and lingering death of the Communist Party in Australia, as party members moved their allegiances to the union movement and the Australian Labor Party.

The casual observer might think that when Roger Caleb Rogerson was named in 1941, his parents were guilty of a gross lack of imagination ... or had a nasty sense of humour. In fact, 'Roger' came from his father's nickname, and 'Caleb' was a family name handed down from his grandfather. Rogerson would later grumble, '*Roger Rogerson*'s a silly bloody name ... Of all the millions of names you could be called, picking "Roger".' Owen Rogerson would give his Christian name to his second-born son some fourteen years later.

Bankstown in the early 1940s was buzzing with activity. In 1940, 630 acres (255 hectares) of land had been resumed by the government to build an aerodrome. The project had been on the books since 1929 to serve as a secondary airport for Mascot and one that could be used for pilot training – a safer alternative to having the inexperienced darting about in the airspace above a commercial airport. The arrival of the Second World War gave the government a distinct hurry-up. By December 1940, the airport had become the Royal Australian Air Force Station – Bankstown. The hangars that dotted the field housed Avro Ansons and Airspeed Oxfords – not the cutting edge of aircraft design, but handy for training. Hawker de Havilland soon established a production facility alongside the field, building the much better Mosquito fighters.

Nearby, on what is now Marion Street, a secret underground air force operations base was built on Black Charlie's Hill. The hill was named after a farmer who had lived there in the early 1900s in a mud-brick, igloo-style hut he had built. Every evening at nine o'clock, he would fire a gun. After his death, local legend had it that he haunted Marion Street.

The secret operations base was three storeys deep and

5

built of reinforced concrete some five feet (one-and-a-half metres) thick. When the war ended, the base was completely forgotten until it was stumbled upon in 1971. The walls were found still covered in maps of the Pacific; there were bedrooms, bathrooms, dining rooms and a code room, and 50 telephones that still worked. The site was filled in and then covered in villa-style housing typical of the period.

The influx of military personnel for what was rapidly becoming one of the key defence establishments for Sydney saw the building of an RAAF hospital, and that social necessity, a VD clinic. Years later the clinic would become the Royal Aero Club.

Despite the rapid development of the area, many local landholders still made their living from market gardens, orchards and poultry farms. Housing styles were a blend of weatherboard, brick for the more affluent, and a new building product that was cheap, easy to use and durable – fibro. 'Asbestos', the less kind would call it these days. The introduction of fibro spawned a generation of dull, flat-sided, three-bedroom boxes that typify the housing of southwestern Sydney.

The Boxley–Rogerson selection was still a few acres that had yet to succumb to unsubtle developers. It was acreage where young Roger would tend to the horse that was still used to cart materials about, and learn to drive in an old truck long out of registration and not roadworthy. By the time Owen Rogerson junior came along, the rest of Bankstown had given way to suburban sprawl.

Growing up at 31 Stacey Street, Bankstown was a very pleasant experience for the young man who was destined to become Australia's best-known copper. He had loving, supportive parents and grandparents, who had very high moral and ethical standards. They were perfect role models and mentors for a young bloke growing up in Sydney's working-class southwest. As another notable local boy, former Australian prime minister Paul Keating, said at the opening of a park named in his honour in April 2000, 'Bankstown represented all that was good about Australia. The people had no inherited wealth. They effectively sold their labour.'

Thanks to Roger's mother's strong Christian commitment, the local Church of Christ was on the agenda for weekly visits. But Roger went along more out of a sense of duty to his mother than out of any true passion for the Church.

Even in his teens the young Roger was the sort of kid that drew others to him. Piercing blue eyes that lit up a room, sandy-coloured hair, and a knockabout, rather roguish, sense of humour made him the centre of attention. Although not an attention seeker, he found himself naturally comfortable in the role into which he was cast. At church he was a strong singer and a dab hand at the organ, should he be called upon to play. In an era when television had yet to light up the nation's living rooms, the piano was often the focus of family and social gatherings. Young Roger would take a seat at the keyboard, and sing heartily in a pleasant tenor.

Roger was proving to be a very bright young lad. When it was time to start secondary school, he was sent to one of the better public schools in the district, Homebush Boys High. One of his schoolmates from class 2A of 1955 recalled, 'He was a fair-haired lad in school uniform. He looked like butter wouldn't melt in his mouth!' Unlike many of the working-class kids in the area, he stayed on past the earliest leaving age. His father wanted him to follow in his footsteps. Owen reckoned his bright and personable young son could

7

go a long way in the engineering trade, and had the potential to make a great unionist. University, for a kid from Bankstown in the 1950s, was a dream but not an option. Of course, there would always be a secure job for life with the public service if he sat for and passed the entrance exams. Roger, however, had other ideas.

A young man with a sharp and enquiring mind, a knack for listening and engendering trust, and an innate curiosity could easily be entranced by the prospect of a slightly swashbuckling career in the NSW Police. A cousin of Roger's had already slipped into the uniform of a police cadet. For someone with Rogerson's stable and supportive home life, it also presented opportunities for adventures otherwise denied him.

Despite the objections of his parents, who were aware that the police had long felt antipathy towards communists, non-practising as well as practising, Roger submitted his application to become a cadet in the NSW Police Force. His parents accepted that their son would make his own decisions.

2

ON PROBATION

On 28 January 1958, just after his seventeenth birthday, Roger Caleb Rogerson had his hair trimmed to the regulation cut demanded by the NSW Police Force and slipped his shoulders into the uniform of a police cadet. Cadet Rogerson then reported for duty at Police Headquarters in Central Lane, in the city. During his time as a cadet he'd also work at Regent Street and Campsie.

Up until the introduction of 'junior trainees' in the early 1980s, there were two methods of entering the NSW Police. The first was by becoming a cadet. Cadets had no powers of arrest, and usually ended up as dogsbodies at either police stations or at Police Headquarters.

They first became part of the police culture in 1933. It wasn't an immediately popular move, with the rank and file thinking it had the potential to create an elite of potential commissioned officers. The first intake was of twelve young men, with eighteen more being added a few months later. Their remuneration was the princely sum of two pounds a week. Cadets had to be between fifteen and eighteen years old, not less than five feet eight-and-a-half inches

(173 centimetres) in height, with weight in proportion, and to be of 'fit and proper character'.

Training focused on 'keeping cadets mentally and physically alert' and embodying 'a high standard of discipline, dress and bearing'. This translated as making the tea, filing, cleaning and directing traffic at school crossings. The genuinely unlucky had the task of operating the old-style telephone switchboard, a contraption of lights, cords, holes and levers which could still be found in many police stations into the early 1980s. A few days a week, the cadet would attend the Police Academy in Redfern for classes in the law, Pitman's shorthand and typing. On turning nineteen, he would be sworn in as a probationary constable. Although only one step up in the hierarchy of the police force from the generic 'cadet', he now had a name, full powers of arrest, a gun, baton and handcuffs.

The other method of entry was after age nineteen as a trainee. This involved ten weeks of intensive training at the Academy, then being sworn in as a probationary constable. There wasn't a lot of love lost between the two types of entrants. Trainees were known as 'ten-week wonders', while it was said of cadets, 'You can always tell a cadet, but you can't tell them much.'

Both cadets and trainees were required to undergo some basic checks and enquiries, such as whether they had a criminal record or were known to associate with persons of ill repute. If they rode with the Bandido bike gang in their spare time, for example, that could count against them. If they were related to a former or serving police officer, that was considered to be highly desirable. They were then interviewed by a local police officer and their domestic circumstances investigated. It wouldn't do to be found to be living in a squat, or being a scruffy hoodlum, a homosexual (still a problem until the mid-1980s), or even a cross-dresser, however discreet.

Trainees also had to satisfy the recruiters that they were academically adept. 'Adept' was considered to be any score above 50 per cent on a spelling test and composition exercise. Unsurprisingly, generations of police were notoriously bad spellers who often found comfort in 'policese', rather than competent composition. They would write their reports in lumpy, ghastly prose, usually intoning the likes of, 'The offender decamped in a northerly direction.'

A cadet's wage was little more than a pittance, so a car was out of the question. Free rail travel, thanks to the uniform, got Roger Rogerson into the city for his daily toil.

Police Headquarters was a purpose-built complex between George Street and Pitt Street, at the rear of that venerable sandstone pile known as the Central Court of Petty Sessions. The two buildings shared both a car park and an underground complex of cells that allowed prisoners to be brought straight into the court from the security of the police station, and vice versa. The place had a fetid smell of unwashed and unhappy humanity. Decades after I first entered the complex as a young copper, that smell comes fresh to my mind whenever I think of the stained walls, clanking doors, huge old keys, and big books that had to be filled out painstakingly by hand. Away from the cells, it was usually quiet.

Rogerson and his fellow cadets would arrive for their shift, do as they were told and go home. Everyone would go quietly about his or her business.

The Academy to which Roger and the other cadets repaired for their formal indoctrination into the culture and ways of the NSW Police Service was a four-acre (1.6-hectare) chunk of Redfern, bounded by Bourke Street to the east and Baptist Street to the west. It was built after the Mounted

Police, and their horses, got their marching orders from barracks at Belmore Park (near Central Railway) in 1901. After a short sojourn at the Royal Agricultural Showground at Moore Park, they moved into their new premises in Redfern in June 1907. Originally, the 'Depot' housed training facilities, the police recruiting officer and staff, and a barrack sergeant whose job it was to keep the trainees under control. In 1954, the police commissioner, Colin John Delaney, changed the facility's name to the Police Training Centre.

On the Bourke Street frontage was an imposing three-storey building containing classrooms, a library and administration offices. This structure, together with the stables and offices built over two storeys on the Baptist Street side, effectively kept the public's prying eyes from the serious business of police training. The northern boundary featured another three-storey building and gym, and a similar structure on the southern boundary housed classrooms. Over the years, the northern building would be used by a few of the specialist squads as their operational base. Their discreet comings and goings, often in rather odd disguises and vehicles, would provide entertainment for the inquisitive trainees.

In January 1960, Roger Rogerson was sworn in as a probationary constable. With a Bible held in his right hand, standing with his fellow cadets on the lush green grass of the Academy's parade ground, he swore allegiance to the Queen. He promised to discharge his duty as a constable 'without favour or affection, malice or will'. Along with his allegiance to the Queen he offered a shorthand speed of over 120 words per minute, useful for taking down lengthy statements by prisoners and witnesses. He was also a 'proficient' typist.

Such skills were highly prized in the police force, even when I joined nearly two decades later. This was well before the days when computers moved out of university laboratories and on to people's desks. The typewriter in a police station was a manual device. Most cops typed very slowly, using just a couple of fingers. Ross Nixon, a former assistant police commissioner responsible for criminal investigation, would later say of Roger Rogerson, in response to a question put to him at an Independent Commission Against Corruption (ICAC) hearing, 'Yes, he was an excellent detective at that time. He was also a very good shorthand typist which made him very valuable.'

On the day he was sworn in, Rogerson and his compatriots were handed their first official notebook in which to record their daily duties and make 'contemporaneous notes'. He was given a leather-clad baton to slide into a pocket on the outside right-hand leg of his trousers, and a gun. In the 1960s, police firearms were standardised with the introduction of the Smith & Wesson .38 six-shot revolver; it was utterly reliable, and reasonably accurate if used at close range. Women police and senior officers often carried the smaller five-shot version.

Rogerson's first posting as a freshly minted constable in his navy-blue serge uniform was close to home at Bankstown. Like any other constable at the start of his career, he was a blank canvas. At that time, Sydney was broken up into geographical 'divisions' that contained a couple of police stations and usually were controlled by an inspector or chief inspector. Above the divisional level were districts, arranged in alphabetical order and presided over by a superintendent. Within those structures was a divisional detective sergeant responsible for matters involving the detectives. Keeping an eye on him and his men was a detective inspector who operated at the district level. It was a very structured chain of command that ran along military lines.

Mentoring of young police was a hit-or-miss affair, not the structured induction that is part of today's police force. Rogerson would have had a selection of good cops, crooks, thugs and drunks from which to choose his role models. Pick a style, or mix and match. He soon proved himself to be a bright, ambitious and hardworking young constable. These were highly desirable traits simply because it meant the old lags could pile their responsibilities and the mountains of paperwork that were a copper's stock in trade on to their young workmate. He, of course, had simply to grin and bear it.

Work for a uniformed copper such as Rogerson revolved around a morning shift starting at 7 am, the afternoon shift from 3 pm and the night shift from 11 pm. When special events were held in the area, such as on New Year's Eve, or when there were major union strikes or pub strikes and beer shortages, special shifts would be called on to deal with any potential problems. The usual business of suburban policing was pretty mundane: point duty on busy intersections, traffic accidents, domestic disputes generally fuelled by too much alcohol and not enough common sense, the elderly dying alone in squalid housing, and petty local grievances.

A bit of excitement might come courtesy of a shoplifter around the corner in the retail hub of Bankstown, or from a burglary at one of the local factories, or from an armed robbery at a bank. These more serious matters were quickly handed over to the local detectives, whom the young probationary constables regarded with some awe.

Days or even weeks later, the detectives would turn up at the station with a crook in tow to be charged with the crime. In the eyes of the young and ambitious Constable Rogerson, it was a mystery, an art and an inspiration, and confirmed for him his future career path.

Aside from the routine of police work, the paperwork that accompanies every action, and the muttering of the police radio, VKG, in every room and car, the young constable got a glimpse of what could be called 'the dark side'. In most busy stations such as Bankstown, the dark side was never too far from the surface. On receiving notification by phone or radio of a vehicle accident or of a person having been found dead in their home (usually referred to as a 'dead'un'), it would be standard practice for at least one constable to place a discreet phone call to a 'mate' in the towing or funeral director ('bodysnatcher') business. If the 'towie' or 'body-snatcher' got the job, the constable would earn a spotter's fee.

The more experienced and dodgy cops found the elderly to be an excellent source of revenue. Even pensioners kept a stash of cash in the house. Underwear drawers were popular hiding places, as were envelopes taped to the back of the bedroom chest of drawers or hidden under a carpet square in the lounge. Relatives never knew how much or where the old dear had the cash stashed. Those with no next of kin might also lose jewellery, heirlooms and anything else of value that was easily concealed in a policeman's tunic or pants. The dead got bugger-all respect. A very bright and observant lad, Roger Rogerson was aware from his earliest days on the force that many among his superiors and supposed mentors were supplementing their salaries thanks to these illicit perks of the job. What he also saw was that those not involved turned a blind eye.

For most of its existence the NSW Police Force ran on liberal doses of alcohol; coppers of the time had a talent for finding a drink. It wasn't unusual for officers on duty in the station answering the phone, charging and printing prisoners, and dealing with the public to take a furtive drink from a can or bottle of beer kept in a paper bag in the station fridge. A mate would keep watch, ready to give the cry 'Whale in bay' if an inspector or superintendent hove into view. Of course, everyone would know what was going on, but the façade had to be maintained. The higher-ranking officers would inspect the occurrence and telephone message pads to make sure everything had been filled out correctly, sign them, nod and leave. Drinks would then resume.

If a constable was on foot patrol or in a vehicle, it was a lot easier. Hoteliers and local businesses would often keep a cool one on hand for the passing constabulary. Colourful Sydney identity Abe Saffron recalled that when running his parents' business in the Haymarket, he always kept a cold beer in the icebox for the local constable to refresh himself while directing traffic nearby. The more libidinous senior coppers also had a girl or two locally, so the young constable would wait patiently in the car listening to the police radio for their call sign, or an emergency, while his superior had a quick 'leg over'.

The other perk a young copper such as Rogerson could expect was the 'police discount'. The rag trade had yet to be hit by imports. Items of clothing would usually be made by businesses run by émigré Russian or Hungarian Jews and staffed by displaced European or Asian migrants. The heart of the rag trade was in the Regent Street patrol, where Roger had spent time as a cadet, or just across the tracks in Surry Hills, an area looked after by the lads of No. 3 Division headquartered in the justifiably notorious Darlinghurst Police Station. Two decades later, Rogerson would find himself growing in notoriety while stationed there. Coppers could buy clothing for themselves and their young families at healthy discounts. Food was also nicely discounted, if not free, in those days before McDonald's did its famous half-price deal for police. Those restaurants and takeaway outlets not offering a discount could expect to receive surly treatment from the boys in blue.

On the rare occasion that a probationary constable found himself involved in the investigation of a serious crime, the detectives running the case would draft a statement for the young bloke to use at court. The statement would be well crafted, non-negotiable, and reflect what the detectives wanted the court to hear. It would also support their case, and might contain a few admissions the constable would swear on the Bible that he had overheard. This was the constable's introduction to the arcane arts of the 'load' and the 'verbal'. Start 'em young.

Towards the end of his first year as a constable, young Rogerson joined his peers back at the Academy for the compulsory six weeks of secondary training. It was time to catch up with old mates, compare their experiences and to 'further consolidate the principles of their earlier courses, and to introduce a number of allied subjects calculated to widen the knowledge of the probationer'. This meant studying slabs of police procedure and statute law, and spending some serious time on the pistol range. Visiting specialists, including senior officers from the CIB squads, would pop in to give a lecture on their areas of responsibility. Secondary training was also the time when young constables started to give some serious and informed thought to the future direction of their careers. For Roger Rogerson, the choice was obvious. He was headed for the Criminal Investigation Branch.

3

A LAD TO WATCH

Roger was confirmed as a constable after his twentieth birthday in 1961. However, beginning criminal investigation training usually required a minimum of three years' uniform service, though this was flexible if applicants were in short supply.

At the helm of the NSW Police at this time was Commissioner Norman Allan. Allan had spent most of his career as a prosecutor and paper shuffler at headquarters. He was a man of little police ability, but with a certain political skill.

In typical fashion of the police force of the time, progress through the ranks had little to do with merit and more to do with seniority and the passing of exams. Promotion on merit wouldn't become commonplace until well into the 1980s. The studbook – or seniority list – facilitated this very dated management system. Old hands who had passed their exams and were awaiting promotion took pains to ensure that blokes senior to them who had either died, resigned, been sacked or failed promotional exams had a line drawn through their names. It was a period where you could map your career almost to the day. Constable first class after five years, senior constable after ten, sergeant at sixteen – a very neat, if somewhat unrewarding, career path.

Rogerson cooled his heels until he could apply for criminal investigation duty. The NSW Police had usually been short on talented people wanting to be detectives – bright, resolute, intuitive, thorough and with good people skills. Big thugs were easy to find, and though they had their uses, those uses were very limited. Rogerson, who had begun to resemble what journalist Evan Whitton would later describe as a 'youthful Don Bradman', had been noted as a young man to watch. His superiors thought that with the right training, he had the potential to be a great detective. In the NSW Police, 'the right training' meant being schooled in the culture that prevailed in the force at that time.

Roger's application for criminal investigation training was successful, and in early 1962 he slipped out of his suit of blue and into a suit or the Harris Tweed sports coat and slacks that were much loved by the sleuths of the period. On his head was a hat, as regulations demanded. It was either a snap brim number or the pork pie version, often with a few feathers poking upwards, that was favoured by cops in Hector Crawford's television productions, such as *Homicide*. This initial phase of training was called 'A list'.

After a few months, Roger took part in the CIB's rite of passage, the 'bull ring'. It was a gathering of some of the state's most senior detectives at CIB headquarters, then a converted hat factory on the corner of Smith and Campbell streets in Surry Hills. Often the head of the CIB would be among the gathering of heavies. The idea was to grill the aspiring detective on law and procedures they'd been studying and observing over their time on 'A list'. More importantly, it was a chance to size them up for entry into the brotherhood of criminal investigation. The police culture when looking at the public was a fairly insular 'us' and 'them'. Criminal investigation was a tightly knit group within that 'us' culture.

Roger found himself fronting a group of hard men who were keen to see if he was made of the right stuff. On more informal matters, they wanted to know if he was the sort of bloke who wouldn't baulk at giving a crook a hand with his alleged confession (known as verballing), or giving him a firearm, some other type of weapon, or drugs (known as loading). Knowing that a young man wouldn't ascend the high moral ground when offered, or seeing a mate offered, a 'quid' or 'drink' (both police slang for a bribe) was also on their agenda. Within the brotherhood of 'the job' it was best to 'toe the line'. 'Don't ask, don't tell' was the mantra of the time.

Ray Kelly, one of the most corrupt police in the history of New South Wales, was often on the bull-ring panel. One of his favourite questions was: 'Would you load a criminal?' The right answer was 'yes'; a 'no' answer would mean a career spent in uniform. When Rogerson's time came, he passed the ordeal with flying colours.

The young sleuth then went back to Bankstown to await his call to transfer to No. 21 Division, the next step up the criminal investigation ladder. The call came in September 1962.

No. 21 Division had been formed in August 1946 as a mobile squad of plainclothes police specifically targeted to counteract violent crime. This was the Sydney immediately after the war. Rationing was still in place and the black market thrived, bringing with it opportunists for whom a bit of violence didn't present a dilemma. Razor-wielding gangs still terrorised residents of East Sydney and Darlinghurst. The laneways around Crown Street near Hyde Park jumped with sailors, drunks, and prostitutes and their clients. Grog was being sold after hours.

It was all too much for the city's civic leaders, who clutched their collective pearls and demanded that something be done. The government reacted as governments still do. A special squad with wide-ranging powers was formed: 21 Division. Any crime – from simple street matters, gaming and betting up to crimes of violence – was in its remit. If there was a 'problem' area around the city, 21 Division would be quietly tasked to resolve matters. When necessary, more hands were made available to help the specialist squads.

Early in 1947, 21 Division was moved from its original base in the George Street North Police Station to a more discreet location at the Redfern Academy. It was still there when Rogerson arrived in early 1962. It was the perfect place to 'blood' young detectives; Rogerson would have new experiences, hone his past experiences, and form bonds with other men on the force. It would be his first glimpse of what made the CIB tick.

The young detective attached to 21 Division was given some early lessons in the art of loading. Depending on what the mission was, some senior squad members would hand the aspiring sleuth some 'exhibits' to be used to implicate offenders. These 'exhibits' might include a knife, housebreaking tools such as screwdrivers and so on, drugs, or a gun. (A standing joke that would go the rounds of the Academy in the 1970s was of a magistrate castigating a detective for overuse of an exhibit. 'I don't want to see that gun again, Sergeant,' he chided the detective, before finding the defendant guilty.)

At that time, the CIB had been running efficiently, effectively and rather corruptly for years. The gloriously bent

Bob Askin was about to become premier. 'If it ain't broke, why fix it?' It was the era when the word of a police officer held great weight in the courts. The media was behind the police, with the old-style police reporters working their close relationships with sources in both uniform and plainclothes. 'Pissing in each other's pockets' was the eloquent term frequently used by the sleuthing fraternity. Crims were considered to be a low form of life and certainly not to be believed. When arrested, they could expect to lose some cash and get a quick belting from the police, just to let them know who was most definitely in charge. Complain? Never. Vicious and bent thugs with warrant cards, such as Ray Kelly and Freddie Krahe, were the CIB pin-up boys. A former detective and former assistant commissioner would later say of Rogerson and his peers, 'What hope did those young blokes have with arseholes like that in charge?'

When not picking up their daily quota of drunks (an offence until the demise of the *Summary Offences Act*) to keep up the numbers of arrests (as with traffic tickets, there was never an official quota, but you'd be in strife if you didn't lock up a few during the shift), or practising loading, verballing, and legitimate investigations, young Rogerson and his mates at 21 Division would keep themselves amused by drinking. On Saturday nights and race days, they would also fit in a little gaming and betting work.

Gaming and betting was focused on making sure that SP bookmakers, casinos and card games played for money didn't undermine the morals of ordinary citizens. Exceptions were made, of course, for those operators who kept sufficient cash flowing into the wallets of key police officers.

'Thommo's' two-up school, the Forbes Club in Darlinghurst, and establishments run by Perc 'The Prince' Galea or George Walker were raided, but usually by appointment. Easier targets were the old SP bookmakers who could be found lurking in the back of dingy pubs, writing out betting slips while taking sips from a schooner of Reschs and a drag on a Craven A filter tip. Also popular were the card games played in the so-called ethnic clubs. The Chinese, Italians, Greeks and former Yugoslavs were often visited during card games by callers from 21 Division. Money (well, some of it) and cards would be confiscated and the bemused card players bundled into the back of a wagon, taken to the nearest police station, charged, fingerprinted and bailed. It kept the numbers up and the church leaders quiet. Justice was seen to have been done. Even though it wasn't.

It didn't take long for even the more honest, or naïve (or both), young detectives to sort out how the system worked. After a few raids where all that was found were a couple of blokes sipping coffee or playing cards for the prize of a matchstick, it was obvious they had been tipped off.

In 1979, an incident would seal the fate of 21 Division. Illegal gaming was the hot political topic of the day. Displaying his usual finely tuned political acumen, the New South Wales premier, Neville Wran, announced a crackdown. The NSW Police collectively groaned, 'Not another one.' No. 21 Division was to be cleaned out, beefed up and the legendary Merv Beck put in charge. The powers that be made one mistake. They didn't do their research and assumed that Beck would do as he was told. But Beck had a habit of doing what *he* thought was right, and he wasn't happy merely to be window dressing. He attacked the gambling community with vigour. Favouritism and influence were ignored. Gambling soon became hazardous. In a telling photograph that appeared in the press at the time, Merv Beck, immaculately turned out in a sombre single-breasted suit and pork pie hat, is shown standing outside the CIB holding a sledgehammer in his hand.

Beck had a problem at 21: he couldn't get rid of a couple of the old 'hard heads'. They had been left there for a reason, and that was to offer a modicum of protection to a few operators who had some sort of arrangement with certain senior police. One of these 'hard heads' was the late Sergeant Carl Hermes, who could be relied on to make a few phone calls when the targets had been decided on. Hermes was also in charge of handing out the 'exhibits' to the young sleuths.

I joined the NSW Police a generation after Rogerson. In 1977, bored by my university law studies for which I had some talent but no passion, and abandoning the music studies for which I had the passion but not the talent, I decided to follow both my father and great-grandfather into the force. The NSW Police Force at that time was little changed from the one Rogerson – and my father – had joined in the 1950s. (At my final selection committee appearance, the only question I was asked by the collective of learned old cops, their shoulders covered in braid, who were charged with determining my suitability for the job, was: 'How's your father?')

Our training class of around 50 included just three women. They could expect to spend most of their time interviewing women and kids and lecturing in schools. The old school, and very male, view was that females 'couldn't handle themselves in a blue' and thus were a liability in front-line police work.

Hands-on police work in the suburbs or the squads was still a few years away for women officers.

The face of the police force was overwhelmingly Anglo-Saxon. There were mutterings over power plays between the Catholics and Anglicans. The Masons were allegedly the power brokers. In the back of the notebook issued to detectives was a photograph of a man wearing a snap-brimmed hat and a double-breasted suit, intended to help detectives identify suspicious-looking characters. Policing in the late 1970s still had the face of the 1940s.

I had some fine colleagues in the force, the work was challenging, the pay reasonable. I was also lucky when I was on A list at Manly to work with a bloke who was a scrupulously honest, insightful and hardworking detective. He was a bit of an outsider in the prevailing culture, but his skills made him a useful bloke to have around. A much better mentor than the likes of Ray Kelly.

The bull ring I faced was a lot more civilised than in Roger's day. Verballing and loading, though widely practised, were not on the menu. Lawyers were waking up to the game. Discretion, at least until you'd been accepted into the brotherhood, was handy. I passed, and turned my back on a life of motor accidents, domestics and the other fodder of a uniformed cop.

By the time I reached 21 Division, Merv Beck was in charge. He was a tough, old-fashioned and incorruptible cop who'd recently put the cleaners through the place. Despite Merv's efforts, some of the old 'hard heads' were having trouble changing their ways. The culture of corruption (or 'cash', 'bash' and 'gash' as it was popularly known in the CIB) was well entrenched and Roger was one of its shining lights. Some would choose to keep quiet and try to steer a path away from the bent activities of their peers. Often these were men who had the responsibilities that come with a family. For some, like me, refusal to be part of that culture would ultimately lead to departure for a culture outside that of the police.

When Rogerson found himself at the same crossroads early in his career, he sealed his fate by choosing to go over to the 'dark side'.

4

THE SECRET ARTS

After almost two years at 21 Division, Rogerson was posted to full-time criminal investigation duties back in the divisions, eventually ending up at Central in the middle of the city. Plainclothes Constable (PC) Rogerson settled back into the routine of the detectives' office. The work varied, dealing with everything from small stealing matters to murder.

The life of a divisional detective brought with it a large chunk of routine. The stock in trade was patrolling the particular area by car, turning up at run-of-the-mill crimes such as break, enter and steals (what are now popularly called 'home invasions') where rudimentary particulars were taken, and a bit of 'hmmming' and 'ahhhing' was thrown in for PR purposes. Then it was back to the office to fill out the report of crime forms. Turning up at events like these was known as being a 'burglar's clerk', as the primary function of the report was to provide information for the insurance claim that would follow.

Spice was added to the mundane and the routine by serious assaults, usually domestically based and alcohol-fuelled, and safe robberies, which were very much in vogue. Tank men (as safe breakers were called) plied their trade late into the night. These were the gentlemen criminals. No drugs, no violence – just the subtle application of skills to achieve a healthy financial reward. Safes were low-tech models in those days, and they responded to the deft touch of the tank men.

For a young detective the real thrills began when VKG, which permeated everywhere in the station (including the toilets), reported an armed robbery. It would be out to the cars, on with the siren, and then peeling away at high speed, desperately trying to remember the skills acquired at the St Ives Driver Training School. 'Urgent Duty' was fun and brought out the hoodlum, or inner child, in every young police officer.

The other great thrill, particularly for a very smart young detective such as Rogerson, was when the uniform cops discreetly called for assistance. Usually this was done by phone, or popping into the detectives' office for a quick chat to say a body had been found and the circumstances were a little suspicious. If you broadcast the find over police radio, there was a fair chance the media, with their cars equipped with police band scanners, would be at the scene before the detectives. There was no need to hurry – as Rogerson once quipped – as the body 'won't be going anywhere'. Though the uniform blokes would often do a good job of securing the scene, a swift arrival by detectives would minimise police boot prints and the fingerprints of curious and inexperienced young cops appearing over what could end up as vital evidence. Best to get everything battened down and wait for the arrival of the forensic police and the pathologist from the Coroner's Office.

Murder was popular with police because it brought with it a legitimate salary boost, as overtime concerns were pushed aside. You hit a murder investigation hard and fast. The longer it took, the less chance there was of solving the crime.

In the divisions, Rogerson, now in his mid-twenties, was learning the secret arts of police work from men well skilled in their application. He learned the knack of developing inform- ants from the ranks of the local criminal fraternity – what these days we'd call networking. Get to know who they were, a bit about their family, and their associates. If you knew the person you were locking up or someone in their orbit, you could easily squeeze them for a bit of 'drum' on other crooks operating locally. In return there would be a lesser charge or a good word to the magistrate. Discretion came with experience. The detective would learn to turn a blind eye to an offence, as an investment in future intelligence or a favour for the ledger. It was the days of old-fashioned policing, when a kick in the trousers or a clip behind the ears might deter a lad from fur- ther dalliance in crime.

Promotion was by seniority, and there was little rivalry. You bonded with your workmates, drank with them after your shift was over, caught up with them on days off for a bit of fishing or a barbecue with their wives and families. The wives and kids became friends, finding some comfort in each other's company while their men were out fighting crime . . . or drinking at the pub.

For the detectives, schooled in ways to achieve results even if by dubious means, the bonds were even closer. Drinks at the local pub or club were optional on most days and mandatory on paydays. A sensible hotelier or secretary manager would cash the NSW Police pay cheques, comfort- able in the knowledge that a large chunk of them would flow back over the bar. A few complimentary bar snacks – some pieces of battered fish, a sausage roll or two, some cheese cubes and cabanossi in the smarter establishments –

would guarantee a loyal clientele. The way to a detective's heart was through his stomach . . . via his wallet and liver.

Rogerson was immersed in the culture. Life was good; he had a supportive family at home in Stacey Street who kept his clothes laundered and provided him with a comfortable bed, good food and loving company. His luck got even better when his eye caught that of local girl Joy. They had first met years before as youngsters at the local Sunday school. Joy was handsome-looking and, like Rogerson's mother, an avid churchgoer. She and Roger were both smitten.

On 25 April 1964, Joy Mary and Roger Caleb were married. Over the next few years, they would produce two daughters, Melinda and Gillian, both of whom would become teachers.

In August 1965, the young couple bought the house they would share until notoriety would destroy their marriage almost 25 years later. The house at 32 Gleeson Avenue, Condell Park, a five-minute drive from Stacey Street, was typical of the suburban sprawl in Sydney's southwest in the 1950s and 1960s. It was a peaceful slice of working-class suburban Australia, with street names such as Jellicoe (the British admiral dubbed the hero of the Battle of Jutland in the First World War) and Gallipoli commemorating war heroes of the Empire. The houses were secluded from the light industrial area closer to Canterbury and Milperra roads, the well-travelled alternate route to the last gasp of Sydney, Liverpool. Military aircraft that had used the nearby Bankstown aerodrome were long gone, replaced by more mundane Cessnas.

Like most houses in Gleeson Avenue, the Rogerson home was built mainly of fibro. It was easy to maintain with a coat of paint every couple of years, and easy for a handyman to extend as his family grew. The block of land was large, with the house positioned close to the road. Behind was the classic Australian quarter-acre backyard, with room for a garage and for a bloke's shed. He could store his tools there, keep an old but reliable beer fridge well stocked for when his mates came around to visit, and use it as a refuge from the family if necessary. In the yard was the Hills hoist for drying clothes, and which the family could sit under with a tarp thrown over the top on hot or damp days and fire up the barbecue. Rogerson would eventually build a fence across from the house to the garage, which, with the standard six-foot (two-metre) paling fences on the perimeter, made the yard perfect for discreet entertaining.

The house was kept spotless both inside and out. Gleeson Avenue was a street of similarly neat properties, the pride of their Anglo-Saxon owners. The local kids played together, and wives gossiped over the fence and shared morning coffee. Husbands would share a cold beer and pitch in for the handyman tasks that needed an extra set of hands. Rogerson was renowned among his neighbours for always being willing to give them a hand. He and his neighbours were considered to be solid, decent working people. It was a good place to bring up the next generation.

The squads of the CIB – the Special Crime Squad (the forerunner of the Homicide Squad), the Motor Squad and Armed Hold-up, among others – had long considered themselves to be the elite force of policing. They were divorced from the day-to-day work of general duties undertaken by uniform police, usually coming into contact with them only when charging someone at a local police station.

The task was usually performed at Central Police Station, or, at a pinch, Darlinghurst. After a couple of bad experiences

I found some of the 'Darlo' lads to be rather uninterested, to the point of surly, when asked to do a bit of work. Too busy enjoying a beer in one of the cells they had decked out as a bar, or trying their luck with a lady of the night.

In the divisions around the state there was a smattering of ex-squad men working as 'general duty' detectives. Back doing whatever came along, from petty theft to murder. Some had elected to leave the Branch to enjoy a less demanding life, and some had moved back to freshen up their experiences in order to give them a better chance in the promotion stakes. Others had 'hit a hurdle', and the hurdle usually involved bribes or an excess of violence. They were 'too hot', so the divisions were a perfect place for them to keep a low profile. These latter blokes would eventually find their way back to the squads.

When squads were on the search for new blood, they relied on their network of reliable mates to spot talent. Every aspiring detective spent time in the divisions, so former squad members were perfectly placed as scouts. The talented and culturally acceptable, after they'd achieved the coveted designation of 'detective', either put the word out or were approached to move into CIB headquarters and into a squad. In Roger's day, designation required a minimum of five years served with at least three years in criminal investigation duties. Things changed in 1968, after which aspiring detectives had the added requirement of completing a twelve-week, full-time Detectives Course.

The former squad men would recommend any bright young men to their mates still in the squads. Negotiations would commence, references would be checked and endorsements of suitability given, and then, when a vacancy occurred, orders would be cut.

Squads have always had a core element of hard men.

When, later in his career, Rogerson was with the Armed Hold-up Squad, there was a 'definite Rogerson clique that dictated the office', says one of his peers of that time, Robert John McHugh. Rogerson's activities weren't common knowledge outside that clique, he says. 'In retrospect, I just believed they had a tremendous informant relationship . . . where they were able to charge or be able to find sufficient evidence to charge people. I was often left wondering [about] their ability to locate people.'

The core group of a squad kept its workings very much to itself. In major operations, all would play their part; however, in general working, information was shared only when necessary. If the job at hand looked tough, they would turn to their mates in the core rather than seek support from outside. There were guarded conversations in the office or in the pub. Conversations with senior officers were often behind closed doors or conducted in whispers in corridors or the lift. While they drank with everyone in the squad on the fortnightly Wednesday payday (when the 'eagle' shits, named after the Police emblem), on other nights the coterie that was the inner circle would sidle off to their own watering holes.

A Victorian detective who met Rogerson and his then workmate and mentor Noel 'Big Red' Morey (who would later spend years heading up the Armed Hold-up Squad) commented: 'My first impression was that he [Rogerson] was too fast and too dangerous for me. They were way out of my league. They were very aloof because of their "team spirit", as they called it.'

The rest of the squad would get the mushroom treatment: 'Keep 'em in the dark and feed 'em on bullshit.' A young detective might find the conversation would freeze as he entered a lift bearing members of the inner circle. He would be met with poker faces and polite greetings, then silence. These guys considered themselves to be the crème de la crème, the toughest and hardest the force had to offer. They were blokes who usually got the big arrests, and the blokes the heads of the CIB would call on to sort out matters. They were always at the pointy end, and made sure they were there on *their* terms. Roger Rogerson, before his fall, would be at the pinnacle of these insiders. The detective's detective.

5

STRANGE BEDFELLOWS

When Rogerson arrived at the CIB in the mid-1960s, its culture was typified by soon-to-be-infamous detectives such as Fred Krahe, Don Fergusson and his predecessor Ray Kelly.

When Kelly retired in February 1966, around 800 people turned up for his send-off at the very chic Chevron Hotel in Macleay Street, Kings Cross. It was almost a crime not to be there. The Chevron was billed as Australia's first international hotel and was the epitome of sixties' style. It tried to emulate the grand hotels of that other paragon of style, Las Vegas. Its Silver Spade Room was home to visiting celebrity entertainers that included the 'King of Las Vegas', Wayne Newton. Elegantly dressed women sporting beehive hairstyles and cigarettes in dainty holders accompanied men in dinner suits.

Being held in the Cross, Kelly's send-off attracted a slightly more raffish crowd than might be found in the conservative hallways of the other great Sydney hotels of the time, the Wentworth and the Menzies. The crowd of men and women in their evening finery that filled the ballroom to overflowing on that February night included politicians, socialites, judges, magistrates, lawyers, gambling magnates such as the baccarat king Perc Galea, prominent SP book-makers, and hardened criminals such as long-time Kelly informant, Lennie McPherson, later to achieve a career highlight as the reputed 'Mr Big' of Australian crime . . . Oh, and plenty of coppers were there, too.

Premier Bob Askin, never one to miss a drink and a chance to grab a bit of limelight, was centre stage that night. He told the attentive crowd that Kelly was 'a close personal friend that no fictional detective could hold a candle to'. In the New Year's honours list of 1975, Kelly, on Askin's rec-ommendation, was awarded an MBE. As Andrew Keenan of the *Sydney Morning Herald* noted some years later, 'It was not until after Kelly's death that a different view of him emerged as one of the most corrupt detectives of his era. He caught lots of crooks. But half of them worked for him too.'

When Fred Krahe left the police force, it was without a glamorous send-off. He skulked out medically unfit and with a pension for life. 'Medically unfit' was a term that often raised eyebrows in the force. Coppers with a genuine illness or some other debilitating problem could retire with a decent pension that would keep them and their families reasonably comfortable. But the system was also abused, and was often used as a means to parachute out favoured sons who had got themselves into strife. 'Illnesses' or 'con-ditions' would suddenly manifest themselves, and in those days this meant that any investigations or proceedings against them would be put on hold until they 'recovered'. If they were then deemed medically unfit to serve, they would pick up their pension and the investigation would effectively cease.

Krahe's sudden illness was timely. Brian Doyle, a relentless investigator and a tough and honest detective, was on Fred's case. Fred, it seems, was out of control. It was no mean feat, considering the rather bent nature of the Branch at that time. Doyle had recommended a slew of charges against Krahe, most relating to his brutal behaviour and rampant 'snipping quids', slang for taking bribes. He was also the chief suspect in the death of prostitute and madam Shirley Brifman. Her alleged suicide by an overdose of sleeping tablets in March 1972 was timely, occurring just as she was about to squeal on police corruption, and on Fred in particular. Krahe became unwell quickly as fingers started pointing in his direction. Fred Hanson, the then commissioner, gave Krahe the benefit of the doubt and let him retire.

Krahe obviously didn't learn from his near arrest experience, and found gainful employment as a 'security adviser' to developer Frank Theeman, who was in the midst of the redevelopment of Victoria Street in Kings Cross. Fred's speciality was evicting the squatters. It was a licence to indulge in his more violent habits. Lennie McPherson, in what might well have been a purely malicious comment but one that added some spice to his growing reputation as a hard man, noted that Theeman had originally offered him the contract to murder anti-development campaigner Juanita Nielsen. McPherson declined the offer, but put Krahe right in the frame as the bloke who eventually did the deed. However, McPherson wasn't known for being truthful. Nielsen's disappearance endures as one of Australia's great mysteries. Krahe died of cancer in December 1981.

The last of the triumvirate, Don Fergusson, rose to the lofty rank of detective superintendent. All three had made a chunk of money from protecting the abortion rackets that flourished in the 1950s and 1960s before abortions became legal. Bad laws have a habit of creating business opportunities for those not on the high moral ground, and illegal abortions flourished throughout the city, from the dirty backrooms of inner-city terrace houses to the genteel consulting rooms of Macquarie Street's 'golden mile of medicine'. The quality of care varied, of course, from unqualified amateurs to Fellows of the Royal College of Surgeons. A mate of Kelly's, and abortionist to the stars, Dr Reginald Stuart-Jones, was one of the better-known practitioners about town.

Fergusson died in 1970 of two gunshot wounds to the head. His body was found in the toilets of the CIB, in its premises at the former hat factory in Surry Hills. In his book *Mr Big*, journalist Tony Reeves, himself a veteran of the campaign to save Victoria Street (on the side of the good guys, not Theeman and his thugs), wrote: 'A morgue worker told me that the first autopsy report of Fergusson showed two bullet wounds to his head, shot at a range of ten feet, definitely not an act of suicide. "He must have had very long arms and very quick reflexes" the person said. A second report was quickly prepared and adopted as the official version.' The second report, for public consumption, said that Fergusson had been deeply depressed and did himself in with a single shot to the head from his service revolver. Rumours quickly spread of a falling out with Krahe over their business enterprises. Even years later, the smart money had it that Krahe had murdered Fergusson. The ensuing cover-up was necessary to ensure that the status quo was maintained. Business went on, and Don Fergusson was buried with full honours. The old CIB motto comes to mind, 'You can't help bad luck.'

These days, senior police who are found to have encouraged, controlled or even demanded corrupt practice would be in strife fairly quickly. But when Rogerson first arrived at the CIB in 1965, to use a phrase that would later be attached to him, the crook detectives had the 'green light'. David Hickie, in his book *The Prince and the Premier*, nailed the problem when he said that the bent cops 'grabbed the main chance' with the arrival of the Askin government on 13 May 1965. They and the generation that followed would hang on to that 'main chance' until the mid-1980s, when the community finally realised what had been going on under their noses. One of the key motivators for that sudden awareness was, rather ironically, Roger Caleb Rogerson.

The media of the time didn't do their craft or the community any favours either. Police roundsmen kept us enthralled with accounts of the feats of the NSW Police without offering much in the way of objective criticism. These old-style reporters counted police, and particularly the CIB detectives, as drinking partners and mates. The roundsman would frequently find himself out on patrol, getting a first-hand taste of the action. Suck up to your copper mates and you were guaranteed the right 'drum' – provided, of course, you didn't offer anything in the way of criticism.

Gerald Stone, when a young journalist at the afternoon tabloid the *Daily Mirror* and before his *60 Minutes* fame, said of the legendary police roundsman Bill Jenkings: 'One of the things that struck me was that Bill was a hard man but loyal to his contacts. He knew the cops and protected them. Sometimes that brought conflict. Some of the all-round reporters like myself would write a story stitching up one of the cops. You could always count on Bill to give you a lecture about it, saying how he had to work with them and he'd been placed in a bad position because of the story.'

The end result was the papers got their headlines; police became heroes, 'legends' were created, the government was happy, and the public were also happy, if ignorant. Two decades later the media, finally objective, would be key players in the demise of Rogerson's career and the clean-up of the police force.

Rogerson arrived at the CIB on 1 February 1965. Inside, it looked like a set from a Crawford Productions television cop show. Rickety partitions, scuffed lino floors, desks and chairs that had seen better days, manual typewriters on most of the desks. Paper was foolscap size, and copies were made using carbon paper rather than a photocopier. Fax? Try telex. Police offices have never been at what you might call the cutting edge of technology.

Every desk was shared by two detectives. Drawers held ballpoints and the detective's duty book, the document in which he recorded details of his daily tasks and activities. Theoretically, anyway. The book had to tally with the brown cloth-bound notebook detectives kept in their jacket pocket and with the car diary. So, if a cop had been up to a bit of mischief, all his records, and those of his partner, had to dovetail. If they were found wanting by a supervisor, it could be tricky. Matters would get *very* tricky if a defence barrister, during cross-examination, found them wanting. An examination of the detective's actions, or lack of them, would ensue.

In those early years, Rogerson moved about the squads, putting in appearances at the Special Crime Squad and the Motor Squad. The latter was one of the CIB's original specialist squads, established in 1930 to deal with the increasing thefts of motor vehicles. Their lot was to keep an eye on dealers, and try to quell the irritating yet relatively minor crime of car theft. Crooks were organising car thefts, then changing the cars' appearance and identification.

Shonky dealers would buy them at favourable prices and then resell them at a tidy profit. A nice little earner for all. In fact, when some of the lads from the squad noticed what a nice little business it was, they moved into it themselves. Aided by car thieves, panelbeaters and car-yard proprietors, of course.

Rogerson's talents were soon noticed by Messrs Kelly, Krahe and Fergusson, and he was earmarked as one of their heirs. The tap on the shoulder came when he was at the Motor Squad and about to head off to a trial at Tamworth. Instead of taking the train to New England, he found himself on a plane with some of the CIB worthies en route to Adelaide. His partner for the trial, a young and very capable detective named Geoff Hoggett, had to run the Tamworth trial on his own.

No one could have predicted that within twenty years Rogerson would go from golden boy to pariah. He would become too busy, and perhaps too arrogant and inexperienced with the world outside the police culture, to notice that that culture was no longer sustainable. Geoff Hoggett would later spearhead the taskforce that would secure Rogerson's first conviction.

But as the plane carried him towards the South Australian capital, Roger Rogerson made the choice that would set his course. He would opt for the life that would come to a bright, ambitious, ruthless detective, the golden boy who had been earmarked for a dazzling career in the squads. He might even have ended up as an assistant commissioner or detective chief superintendent. The other option – choosing the straight life – held little appeal for him. He *could* just do his job, not take quids, not load or verbal, tell the truth, and head home to his family after a shift rather than spend his free time on the piss with the lads. But he would be viewed with suspicion. He wouldn't be considered a team player. He would probably have to transfer back to the suburbs, or if he wanted to be really squeaky clean, back to a suit of blue. For Rogerson, there wasn't even a moment's hesitation. He knew he was made of the right stuff, and was considered by his peers as being a better detective than even the legendary Ray Kelly. Rogerson felt quite at home in Kelly's shoes.

In 1967, Rogerson was appointed as a member of SWOS (Special Weapons and Operations Squad). We wryly referred to them as 'the trained killers'. SWOS members were drawn from the squads and came together to train or when there was some serious strife. These tough operators would carve a niche in the public's mind with their very open displays of force. On 29 June 1976, during Rogerson's time with the unit, the notorious bank robber and prison escapee Phillip Western was tracked to a fibro house near Avoca Beach, on the Central Coast north of Sydney. SWOS, armed to the teeth with high-powered rifles and Remington pump-action shotguns, known to Americans as 'alley cleaners' because of the volume of lead that flew out of the business end, demolished the house with gunfire. Western ended his career as Swiss cheese.

A couple of years later, a heroin addict named Gordon Thomas locked himself in the tower of a house in Newcastle Street, Rose Bay, a suburb known more for its socialites, opulent houses and the Royal Sydney Golf Club than for sieges. Gordon took potshots at passers-by. SWOS arrived and rushed the house. In the melee, Detective Sergeant Bill Bull was wounded. Thomas was killed. As they used to say, 'A P79A [Report of Death to the Coroner] is a lot easier than a long trial.' Rogerson was also a player at this later incident, though not responsible for the fatal shot.

Police are inveterate gossips, and it quickly did the rounds that Bull had been shot by a stray round from an overexcited colleague, rather than by Gordon Thomas. It remained a rumour. No one who had been there would confirm or deny it. The 'brothers' of the CIB stood shoulder to shoulder.

Part of Rogerson's inheritance from Kelly and his mates was Lennie McPherson. McPherson had been Kelly's 'gig' for years, happily giving up fellow criminals in order to further his own schemes. In return for cash payments to the cops, he would get a helping hand whenever he was close to having his collar felt. Statements would go missing, often into the hands of the underworld's lawyer of choice, Phil Roach. While Roach flew close to the wind, he enjoyed a degree of protection from his fellow practitioners, coppers, and a member or two of the judiciary and magistracy. He died of old age. The same can't be said of his sometime law clerk, Brian Alexander, an unattractive and duplicitous streak of misery who disappeared just before Christmas 1981. His body has never been recovered, and his death wasn't mourned. The popular view is that he was tied to an 'Early Kooka' stove, an iconic piece of Australiana, and dropped off the back of a boat into a deep part of Sydney Harbour. Arthur 'Neddy' Stanley Smith, one of Australia's most vicious criminals, was thought to have done the dumping while a few detectives stood by, sipping their beers. It's both a compelling and chilling image.

Witnesses would also occasionally not make it to court, or if they did, they might have an epiphany and completely change their testimony. Everyone knew that a monkey deal had just gone down, but many of the players were in on the 'giggle', so it was pretty safe. Lennie McPherson was the beneficiary of many of these quirks of our judicial system.

Inheriting McPherson was a boon to a career-minded detective like Rogerson. Still only in his late twenties and a detective constable first class, he was tapped into one of the key players in Sydney's criminal world – Len had cemented his reputation as one of Sydney's hard men when he shot underworld figure Ducky O'Connor to death in the Latin Quarter nightclub in Pitt Street in the small hours of 28 May 1967 in a room filled with punters and coppers. No one saw a thing.

The relationship with McPherson also laid the groundwork for Rogerson's disastrous relationship with Neddy Smith that would blossom a decade later.

Confirmation of his role as the anointed one came in July 1969 when Rogerson accompanied Don Fergusson and Noel Morey to the boardroom of radio station 2GB in Sydney where Dr Bertram Wainer, the Victorian campaigner for abortion law reform, was planning to hand over the names of people running the Sydney abortion rackets. Wainer was unaware that Fergusson was a former bagman and protector of the rackets.

A few minutes into the meeting, Rogerson drew Fergusson's attention to a tape recorder that was discreetly recording the discussion. Wainer, after some bad experiences with the Victorian Police, wasn't too keen on being interviewed by three coppers without any proof of what was said. Fergusson wasn't keen on any evidence of the discussion other than the evidence of his trusted cronies. The discovery led to an impasse. Though Fergusson was prepared to 'tough out' any allegations made by Wainer, partner in crime Fred Krahe wasn't, and made his disapproval known; hence the subsequent allegation that Fred was responsible for Fergusson's demise a few months later. Rogerson wisely kept his nose out of the blue between his superiors.

Sanity entered the abortion debate in New South Wales in 1971 following a decision by Justice Levine that had the effect of putting the mockers on the prosecution of doctors who performed abortions. These were the doctors who had either declined to slip a few quid (or were guilty of an even worse sin in the CIB's view – offering an insufficient bribe) to the police, or who had been named by fellow practitioners who didn't like the competition. Levine's decision took the heat off the government, which was reluctant to amend a law that was very politically sensitive. Not much has changed since then.

The decision was supported by a private member's bill put forward by George Petersen, the state member for Labor's heartland, the Illawarra. Petersen, a former communist, took the view that abortion should be decriminalised, thus shoving the matter back towards the political arena. Neither Labor nor the Liberals wanted to hold this very hot potato. Petersen would evoke a similar response in 1984 when his private member's bill calling for the decriminalisation of homosexual acts between consenting adults propelled the debate on to the front pages of the nation's newspapers.

In an effort to remove Petersen's abortion bill from the debate, some very strange bedfellows gathered. Petersen, key police, a few politicians, and representatives of the Clerk of the Peace (the ancestor of the Director of Public Prosecutions) put their heads together and came up with a compromise. The bill would go away, Levine's decision would be left as an untouchable precedent, there would be no further prosecutions, and the Abortion Squad would be abolished. By 1974, Medibank was paying benefits for the procedure.

The end of illegal terminations of pregnancies put a dent in the cash flows of the bent coppers. But not for long. The entrepreneurial lads soon found other avenues to explore. There were always the traditional sources such as robbers, thieves and their often equally bent legal advisers. The influx of American servicemen on R&R from the war in Vietnam gave local suppliers of alcohol, girls and a good time a big boost. Cash was flowing in torrents from the fleshpots of Kings Cross. But even those coppers with an eye for a chance failed to notice that the Americans were introducing Australian youth to marijuana and heroin. Previously, these had been the tipple of the area's bohemians and artists, and had been enjoyed discreetly. As with many things American, the tipple would grow fast and soon become very obvious and police would finally take notice.

Given the goings-on in the police force from the start of the second half of the twentieth century, it is perhaps surprising that the term 'police corruption' wasn't in common use until the mid-1980s. But not every cop was bent. Many were blissfully ignorant of the activities of their less honest colleagues or simply didn't want to know. Athol Moffitt's royal commission in the early 1970s into the spread of organised crime in New South Wales clubs unearthed a couple of cops whom he found deeply suspect. However, as is the case with many royal commissions, not much happened in the aftermath. After some sensational headlines, a bit of shock-horror, and some sabre rattling, it was business as usual.

It wasn't until 1994 when Ian Temby released the Independent Commission Against Corruption's report, 'Investigation into the Relationship between Police and Criminals', that the breadth of corruption was ever considered.

Temby noted that detectives comprised about 12 per cent of the force. He went on to say that if every police officer mentioned in his report was 'in some way corrupt or crooked', it would involve less than 1 per cent of the entire force. However, he didn't define 'corrupt or crooked'. Did corruption start with a half-priced hamburger or a discounted combination omelette with fried rice at the local Chinese, with the expectation of favourable treatment at a later date? Was calling a tow truck operator or a funeral director for a spotter's fee corrupt?

What the CIB did have was a core of opportunists who wouldn't bat an eyelid in turning that opportunity into a dollar, or personal power. The honest blokes that made up the bulk of the force had one flaw. They kept quiet. 'Go with the flow' and 'don't rock the boat' were two of the unwritten laws of the NSW Police.

By the late 1960s and early 1970s, Rogerson's career was proceeding very nicely. He added to his squad history a stint with Homicide, formerly known as the Special Crime Squad. Australians, for the most part, aren't a murderous lot. And when murders do occur, they are usually straightforward to investigate. It isn't unusual to arrive at the scene and find a family member, lover or friend standing over the body and still holding the murder weapon. Murder is often only an assault gone seriously wrong in the heat of the moment. Where it gets complicated is when passion as a motive is replaced by avarice, opportunism or plain bastardry. Detectives assigned to such a case have to hit the ground running, and keep on running for as long as it takes to solve the case or until the leads run out. It can be a long, hard slog.

It's not unusual in a murder investigation to work non-stop for the first few days, surviving on hastily grabbed naps and food eaten on the go. Days can end at 2 am and kick off again at dawn. These are the hours detectives are expected to put in when working major crimes. The overtime is nice, but it's a hell of an imposition on one's private life.

These sorts of hours were the staple of men like Roger Rogerson. On deck at between 7 and 8 am unless called out earlier. Read the reports of crimes from overnight. Have coffee and a 'mag' with workmates, and then it would be out and about on the streets. The day would end around 5 pm, unless there were raids planned for that night, or an arrest was still being processed, or enquiries needed to be made at night. They had to keep going until the work was done. If they had a day off or were on holiday, they might be called back in for a court hearing. The brutal hours, and the cops' reliance on each other to watch each other's backs, did much to foster the closed-shop culture that pervaded the tougher squads.

On the upside, of course, were the quiet times, when the blokes would come to work and play together. Long 'smart' lunches were common. The usual practice was to start with a few beers, segue into wine or stay on the beer, and then finish with the obligatory port. And then maybe kick on for a 'cleansing ale' or ten before hopping into the police car and driving home, which was much easier than navigating the tricky car park at CIB Headquarters. CIB wives had a bit to deal with, with drunk and amorous husbands arriving home in the early hours.

Home life was always a balancing act. As Rogerson's star began to shine, he found he had made a fortunate choice in Joy. She was the perfect policeman's wife, a strong, stoic, practical and tolerant woman who respected the appalling demands her husband's career placed on him, and who forgave him when he drank to take the edge off a hard week.

Joy took her responsibility to provide a stable and comfortable home for Roger and their girls very seriously. To supplement her husband's wage, she worked with her parents in their engineering business. One detective described her as 'the straight one in the comedy team'. 'She wasn't prim and proper, but very devoted to him, a regular church-goer and a good mother and supported him right through,' he added. Joy and the couple's two daughters, of whom Rogerson was extremely proud, were frequent attendees at the Church of Christ in nearby Greenacre. Joy was a very similar woman to Roger's mother, it would seem.

Despite the hefty responsibilities that went with his work, the young detective managed to keep his family in good order, help his ageing parents with maintenance of their nearby home, and keep his new place spic-and-span. Lawns were regularly mowed and trimmed, the garden was kept free of weeds, and the house was nicely painted. Roger Rogerson was the bloke the neighbours would call on if their kids got into a bit of a scrape. He was also good with his hands and would never knock back someone who required some help about the house. Bill Riddell, a neighbour who was a bit past standing on a ladder wielding a paintbrush, found young Roger hard at work one day painting the fibro exterior of Riddell's house, which had been in need of a good paint job.

At work, Rogerson found himself paired up with one of the notable detectives of the time, Noel Morey. Morey lived nearby, so it was common for the partners to take the police car home, just in case they were called out to a murder or other serious crime during the night.

Morey was an interesting character, who, despite his

dominance in the police world, maintained a remarkably low public profile. A big, tough, gruff man who kept his own counsel, he was markedly different from the charming Rogerson of the easy smile and twinkling blue eyes. He wasn't a bloke of whom many stories were told or reported. One of the few was about his investigation of an arson incident in Kings Cross. Morey was at the Special Breaking Squad at the time. In their ambit was the investigation of larger burglaries and the popular Sydney sport of arson. The incident occurred in the early hours of 26 November 1973, while Sydney was in the grip of a strike by the strippers who performed at clubs around the Cross.

The Staccato Club, located in the basement of 101 Darlinghurst Road, Kings Cross, and smack bang in the middle of 'The Dirty Half Mile', was owned by Peter 'The Black Prince' Farrugia, who wanted to get out of that particular strip club, which was losing him money. At around 3.30 am, James McCartney Anderson, known without affection as the 'Iago of the Cross', was motoring past the entrance to the Staccato when, he would later tell investigators, he saw two men 'acting suspiciously'. (In the Kings Cross of 1973, anyone seen acting normally could have been considered suspicious.) Anderson, a mate of Farrugia's, stopped to investigate and found the front door open. He pushed the door open wider and, with a cigarette clamped resolutely between his lips, entered the club. In doing so, he managed to trip. He fell, and his cigarette, he reckoned, ignited the petrol that had been liberally doused around the place.

Anderson was badly burned. But he was made of stern stuff and managed to take himself to the nearby emergency room at St Vincent's Hospital. It was all just a little too implausible, the cops thought, especially when Anderson

52

was found to have petrol on the uppers and soles of his shoes. Despite the liberal sprinkling of what cops refer to as 'accelerant', Anderson swore that he hadn't smelled any petrol.

Jim Anderson's story was backed up by Farrugia and the case fizzled. The investigating detective was Noel Morey. Anderson went on to have a fine career as an informant to cops from a few of the squads. One of those cops was Roger Rogerson.

The Morey–Rogerson team stood out among the big names at the CIB, and the two detectives were occasionally despatched interstate to assist and advise other forces if there was a common interest in a case. In March 1973 they were sent to display their talents to their colleagues in Brisbane. The Queensland police had a real problem on their hands. On 8 March a fire had gutted the Whiskey Au Go Go nightclub on the corner of Amelia Street and St Paul's Terrace in the inner-city suburb of Fortitude Valley. Fifteen young revellers – ten men and five women – were killed. The Valley, as the locals called it, was Brisbane's answer, albeit a somewhat feeble one, to Sydney's Kings Cross. It would feature about a decade later in the Fitzgerald Inquiry into all manner of corrupt goings-on in the state of Queensland. It was the hub for sly grog, late-night drinking dens, illegal casinos (there were no legal ones in Queensland, at that stage) and prostitution. It was also the hub for corrupt coppers and politicians to mingle with those who kept their pockets well lined and the rails of Queensland, under Sir Joh Bjelke-Petersen, well greased. They didn't want the nation focused on the workings of the Valley.

The fire wasn't an accident. The devastation was caused by a heady mix of nine two-litre cans of petrol, matches, oxygen and the confined space of a stairwell. The petrol cans went up in a fireball.

Thanks to some excellent police work, the list of suspects was soon narrowed down to two very likely lads, James Richard Finch and John Andrew Stuart. Both men had interesting criminal pasts. Finch had done time for taking a potshot at a notorious Sydney gunman, the late (not because of Finch) and quite mad, John Regan. Both Finch and Stuart had been guests of Her Majesty in the notorious Grafton Gaol in regional New South Wales. The prison housed the state's 'intractables'. It was a perfect example of the brutal realities of prison life under the reign of Queen Victoria, and little had been done to soften the place by the time Finch and Stuart arrived there in the 1960s. Their fellow inmates were the worst of the worst. This was a prison dedicated to keeping violent and amoral offenders away from the community for as long as possible.

Another of the august alumni of Grafton Gaol was Neddy Smith, who was inside from around 1970 to 1973 for rape and other crimes. Smith and Rogerson would soon become an 'item'. It wasn't the first time Smith had shared the exercise yard with Finch. They had originally met while teenagers getting their matriculation in crime at the Gosford Boys Home. Finch and Stuart had also been in Long Bay at the time of Smith's first stretch as an adult back in 1963.

Finch had been in Grafton over the death of a Sydney hitman, and had served half of a fourteen-year sentence. He was earmarked as a gentleman of some interest to the Sydney detectives; the sort of crim you kept a close watch on after his release from gaol. The chances of him going straight were minimal. The same could be said of Stuart, who had terrorised prisoners in Long Bay with an iron bar in an attempt to make himself 'head man'. But when the two men crossed over the border into Queensland, NSW Police lost touch. Communication between the states was never a strong point in the days of typewriters, carbon paper, telexes and Bakelite phones.

Criminals making their way through the justice system from arrest to committal in the lower courts, and then to trial before a jury, often have a rather lengthy wait. The fact that Finch and Stuart were in custody didn't really expedite the process. However, the national focus on the bombing made it crucial for the government to be seen to act swiftly. By October 1973, a little over six months after the fire, both Finch and Stuart were on trial for murder in the Supreme Court of Queensland.

Both men loudly protested their innocence. The court heard that Finch had come to Queensland at the suggestion of Stuart. Both had decided to become the 'Mr Big' of protection and standover rackets in Brisbane. The fire-bombing was a calling card to get attention.

These guys may have been vicious, but criminal master-minds they weren't. Stuart's brother, Daniel, and another witness gave statements to police in which they claimed Stuart and Finch had tried to rope them into the scheme. In their defence, the men claimed they had been put up to the fire by a corrupt Queensland Police officer.

A splash of Sydney colour was mixed into the trial with the evidence of Lennie 'Mr Big' McPherson, the sometime Rogerson informant. McPherson began his evidence by deny-ing that he was known as 'Mr Big' or had any involvement in protection rackets in nightclubs. Though the evidence was given under oath, McPherson avoided being hit by a random lightning strike. However, he did admit to discussing the fire, after the event, with Noel Morey. Oddly enough, when

Finch's counsel asked Morey if McPherson had a working relationship with Sydney Police, Morey refused to answer 'on the grounds of public policy'. The court didn't disagree.

The jury thought the prosecution case was overwhelming and found both men guilty as charged. They were sentenced to imprisonment for life. One of the key pieces of evidence, and one readily accepted by both the jury and the judge, was an unsigned record of interview with Finch. Present during the interview were four Queensland detectives, plus Noel Morey and Roger Rogerson. The unkind might suggest that the New South Wales lads were up there to offer a little expertise in the production of records of interview. The defence, of course, cried foul, suggesting the interview was a dud and nothing more than an attempt at verballing. They may have been right. Records of interview in New South Wales had been the backbone of successful prosecutions for years but by the mid to late 1970s had started to develop a whiff that was none too pleasant. When a person agreed to participate, one detective would slide the paper and carbon for copies into the typewriter. He'd type his mate's questions and the responses word for word. At the end, the person would be asked to read through the interview and sign it if he wanted to. Some would sign; others would decline but acknowledge the interview was correct. Often they'd decline, citing the old Hollywood notion of 'my lawyer told me never to sign anything'. OK so far. When the cop giving evidence introduced the interview and was examined about it, the courts tended to accept what they'd heard.

It dawned on some enterprising police that this might be a handy trick to use as a slightly more upmarket version of the verbal. Interviews would be typed up while the person was somewhere else at the station. When the interview arrived in court, it would come as a surprise to the hapless crook. The detective would solemnly intone that while the crook had agreed to the interview he had declined to sign up. Variations on this theme were only confined by the detective's creativity. Lawyers shouted loudly, but didn't do themselves any favours by challenging genuine interviews as being nothing more than verbals. By the late 1980s the record of interview was utterly discredited, intelligence finally prevailed, and tape- and video-recorded interviews replaced tapping at the keyboard.

However, in the Finch trial the judge and jury sided with the stalwart police officers. And so it was back inside for Finch and Stuart; this time in Brisbane's rather unpleasantly named Boggo Road Gaol.

Australia has had its fair share of interesting crooks, and Finch and Stuart rate high on that list. Throughout their trial they protested their innocence and accused the police of all manner of vile tactics. Their cries fell on deaf ears. The public were happy they were behind bars, and the press were busy complimenting the cops on a job well done. The squeals of 'foul' by two career felons were of no interest to anyone. Well, almost no one.

As is often the case when prisoners resolutely protest their innocence, some supporters eventually answer the call. (One supporter, the wheelchair-bound Cheryl Cole, married Finch in 1986 at a ceremony behind bars.) The case became a cause célèbre. To add spice to their pleas and garner a little more of a profile, both men took up self-mutilation. One favoured ploy was to remove some wire from their bed springs, sharpen it a little, fold it into a shape that could be swallowed, wrap the wire with sticky tape to make sure it didn't unfold on the way down, and then swallow it. The stomach acids would break down the tape, the wire would

57

unfold and unpleasantness requiring emergency surgery would ensue. It was a tough but effective way to get a headline, but it didn't go far enough for Finch.

Next he removed a finger. This required, as he related in an interview, about four hours of hacking at the skin with the only sharpish objects he had access to. When he got to the bone, he chewed at what was left. Insisting on his innocence, he attributed his actions to feeling 'hopeless and frustrated'. It also gave the public a glimpse of the resolute nature of some of the people police have to deal with. Stuart took a less dramatic route and in 1979 began a six-day hunger strike that resulted in his death in prison.

The suicide was rather badly timed. If he had waited until the mid-1980s, he would have found himself a free man. One of the key pieces of evidence which the supporters of the two men mustered in 1984 was expert testimony they believed would prove that the unsigned record of interview was in fact a verbal. The Reverend Andrew Morton, a linguist and internationally renowned expert in the scientific examination of speech patterns, analysed the document and formed the opinion that there was only one chance in 236,472 that it was genuine. The analysis was based on speech patterns and noted that the alleged responses by the prisoner were similar to the patterns of three Queensland Police officers and not the prisoner. (In an investigation, this is called an 'oops'.) The reverend commented, 'If that is all the evidence they have against him, I think it is dreadful they have convicted him.'

Finch was by this time eleven years into his sentence. An appeal to the governor and ten earlier appeals hadn't managed to spring him. Morton's evidence wasn't going to rock the boat of law and order in Queensland. That would happen three years later.

Thanks to the nosy nature of a couple of journalists on Brisbane's *Courier-Mail*, the activities of the Queensland Police and mates in the Bjelke-Petersen government were raising some questions. Queensland didn't really want to know, so the journalists contacted Australia's flagship current affairs program, the ABC's venerable *Four Corners*. The 'Moonlight State' program rocked the nation, and Queensland had no choice but to act.

Former Federal Court judge and then Brisbane QC Gerald Edward Fitzgerald was appointed, with royal commission powers, to look into 'possible illegal activities and associated misconduct' by members of the Queensland Police. Fitzgerald was known, somewhat surprisingly, as Tony. This is usually attributed to his first day at a convent school as a child, when a nun suggested that being called 'Gerald Fitzgerald' wasn't a good idea. 'We'll call you Tony,' she decided and the name stuck. If only Roger Rogerson had enjoyed the benefits of a Catholic education.

Unlike many official inquiries, the results of the Fitzgerald inquiry weren't a foregone political conclusion simply awaiting a rubber stamp. Fitzgerald had a mind of his own and the obfuscations of the government weren't going to get in his way.

It soon became clear to all that the Queensland Police Force was a basket case led and dominated by crooks, opportunists and political toadies. Dodgy records of interview, dubious convictions and police shenanigans were probed and publicised. This climate of distrust in the police and the criminal justice system proved fertile ground for Finch. He was granted parole in 1988 on the condition that he be deported to England, where, as a child, he had been in the care of the Dr Barnardo organisation before being sent to Australia. He readily accepted the offer of a ticket back to the Old Dart. He and his wife swapped the high walls and sunshine for grey skies and freedom.

Before departing, Finch took the opportunity to tell his story to Neil Mercer of *Four Corners*. He protested his innocence, railed against the police and their tactics, and told, in gory detail, of his miserable life in prison. It was a most persuasive performance. When safely back in England, he dropped the mask. In an interview with Channel Nine's *A Current Affair*, Finch decided to tell the truth. After all, he was now a free man and well out of the jurisdiction.

In the interview, he confessed that he and Stuart had been the culprits and he relished having duped the media. He described how he and Stuart had gone to the club dressed 'like the Black September terrorists' who had terrorised Europe in the 1970s. After lighting the taper and standing well clear, 'there was a sudden whoosh; it just started to burn'. The fact that fifteen people died didn't seem to worry him unduly. Cheryl, however, promptly divorced her duplicitous husband and came back to Australia. She died in 1991.

6

'THE BARBECUE SET'

The first bank robbery committed using firearms in Australia took place in Carcoar, in the central west of New South Wales, in 1863. These days, Carcoar is a very quiet 'boutique' village, bypassed by the highway and filled with all manner of stores flogging 'country cute' to the well-heeled. Back in 1863 it was a wealthy grazing town and close to the goldfields. The Commercial Bank provided rich and easy pickings for Ben Hall and his gang of bushrangers. These sorts of robberies didn't become a major problem again until almost a century later.

Australia doesn't have a long history of crimes involving firearms. Like the British, we have shied away from the use of guns. When a crime occurred that featured guns, such as armed robbery, people took notice. In the early to mid-1960s there was a spate of robberies involving guns. It was becoming a trend that neither the public nor politicians would wear. These criminals were the hard men of crime, and they weren't carrying guns for decoration. Professional crooks, rather than opportunists desperate to feed a drug habit, as is often the case today, they planned ahead and went into a robbery quite prepared to use a firearm if necessary. To catch these hardened and skilled criminals required detectives who were harder, more skilled and equally as ruthless. The public would settle for nothing less than success.

Roger Rogerson joined the Armed Hold-up Squad on 1 May 1974. (Established in 1966, within a decade it would be one of the larger squads in the CIB, with around 30 detectives.) The 33-year-old had a reputation for being someone who didn't make idle threats. One colleague said of him later, 'He had physical strength. If he said he'd carry something out, you could be sure he'd do it.' He was then a detective senior constable and on the cusp of getting his third stripe. Detective Sergeant Roger Rogerson.

Detective Inspector Dave Leach, a long-time boss of the squad, said of Rogerson, 'In my mind he was one of the best detectives I've ever worked with. He was thoroughly reliable. He knew his law. He was a hard worker, all the time a goer. He wanted to take on some of the hardest and toughest criminals. The men would look to him for advice and leadership. Some people just stood out.'

Backing Rogerson at the squad was his old mate Noel Morey, who would become officer in charge. Rogerson soon found himself the dominant male in a room of dominant males. The CIB was still based at the old hat factory in Surry Hills, and on pay nights the faithful would gather at the 'jam tin', the Royal Albert Hotel, just around the corner from Campbell Street in Commonwealth Street, to cash their cheques and drink a chunk of the proceeds. As with most squads, particularly those tasked with high-stakes investigations, an elite within the elite formed. The bond was forged by the tough decisions made on the street and the need for solidarity in court, and was lubricated with lots and lots of booze.

An unusual trait of the elite of the Armed Hold-up Squad

was that their professional and private lives overlapped. Up to this point in his career, Rogerson, as did many of his peers, kept his family life separate from his private life. Like many police, his home and family were an escape from one of the toughest jobs in the country. Though police and their families gathered for events such as Christmas parties for the children and maybe an occasional outing during the year, they were usually not close to their colleagues. The elite of the Armed Hold-up Squad were. As he ascended through the ranks of the squad, Rogerson included his family in social gatherings with the families of other members of the elite. Wendy Bacon, writing in the *National Times* in the mid-1980s, dubbed these gatherings 'The Barbecue Set'. It was a cute title that stuck. The detectives and their families would gather at weekends if the lads weren't out on a job. Snags, chops and steaks on the barbecue in someone's backyard. The lads would cook, the girls would do the salads. Plenty of cold beer for the blokes, and white wine or a shandy for the girls. Number 32 Gleeson Avenue, with its fenced backyard offering some privacy from the passing traffic, was a frequent venue. Former Assistant Commissioner Ross Nixon, father of the current Victorian commissioner, Christine Nixon, when asked if Rogerson was a man of striking personality, said: 'Let there be no doubt about that. He is the life of the party.' John Burke, a mate of Rogerson's during their time with the Armed Hold-up Squad and a man who had often held a pair of barbecue tongs at these social gatherings, has described Rogerson as 'a very charismatic person, a close friend, and I must say, a brilliant detective'.

While 'The Barbecue Set' was later viewed with suspicion by some, it was a chance for Rogerson and his colleagues to kick back and relax. Bonds were formed in this social context that both supported and alleviated the demands of their challenging professional lives. For the wives and families, it was a chance to share some of their tough experiences, such as waiting at home when their men were out on tough assignments, dreading the arrival of sombre-faced uniformed police at the front door in the middle of the night.

Rogerson, the 'brilliant detective', had made the choice to embrace the prevailing culture of the NSW Police Force at a time when the line between right and wrong was very blurred, and when there were few morally upright authority figures within the force for a bright, able and arrogant man to model himself on. His path in life from this time on would be determined by his having made that decision – and by his association with the vicious thug Neddy Smith.

Smith was born in Sydney on 27 November 1944. A 'war baby', he was the product of a quick fling between his mother and a serviceman. He was raised in Redfern by his maternal grandmother, his mother not wanting to have anything to do with her illegitimate offspring. He was a man pretty much doomed from the start. According to Smith, his grandmother used to 'flog me all the time', as did his half-brother, Edwin, also illegitimate. At around eleven years of age, Neddy stabbed Edwin through the hand with a carving knife. The Children's Court described him as 'uncontrollable' and ordered that he be sent to the Mittagong Boys Home. After a year at the home, he returned to live with his grandmother.

School at Cleveland Street Boys High had little appeal for Neddy, who soon took up a life of petty crime. But he was a busy crim, not a good one. After making a few appearances at the rather Dickensian-looking Albion Street Children's

Court, conveniently located near what was then the harsh slum of Surry Hills and only a stone's throw from Redfern, Neddy Smith was again a guest of the government. This time he wasn't sent to the bucolic retreat of Mittagong, but to the aspiring criminal's finishing school, the Gosford Boys Home.

By age sixteen, at the start of the sixties, Smith was back living in Sydney, this time in what was still the bohemian heart of the city, Kings Cross. It was a place where the cream of society mingled with artists, entertainers, writers and the ladies of the night. Abe Saffron had just introduced Sydney to the art of striptease at his Staccato Club in Orwell Street; overseas artists were wowing Sydneysiders at Chequers and the Latin Quarter. Frank Sinatra had knocked our bobby socks off at the Stadium in nearby Rushcutters Bay. Rock 'n' roll was the new music fad. Old hands muttered that it wouldn't last.

Neddy took up residence with a 26-year-old prostitute in one of the less salubrious blocks of flats in the Cross. He lived reasonably well on her hard-earned cash, spending his time 'fucking, fighting and stealing', as he would later put it. The arrangement lasted twelve months before he was arrested for 'living off the earnings of a prostitute' and returned to Gosford. He finished his juvenile career in the infamous and brutal Tamworth Boys Home in the New England region of New South Wales.

Smith returned to Sydney at age eighteen and began in earnest the life of crime he had trained for. Stealing, breaking and entering houses, and assaults were his stock in trade. Planning and subtlety weren't the hallmarks of his early career. In May 1963, at just nineteen years old, he was sentenced to six-and-a-half years' hard labour on three charges of break, enter and steal. His new address was care of PO Box 1, Matraville NSW – Long Bay Gaol. High sandstone walls, guard towers, huge iron gates, and swaying palm trees. The only luck that came Smith's way was courtesy of the Court of Appeal, which viewed his sentence as a little extreme and reduced it to two years on each count, all to be served concurrently.

His 'good fortune' was short lived. On 22 September 1967, Smith was back in Long Bay, this time for rape and a stealing matter. The sentence was twelve years' hard labour, with a non-parole period of seven years and nine months. During his sentence, Smith got to see a bit of New South Wales, being shuffled around Long Bay, Grafton, Parramatta and Maitland gaols. He also managed to meet some interesting people, including Raymond John Denning who ended up doing life for the murder of a prison guard, and the barking mad John Stuart Regan, who was reputed to have murdered most of his friends, and anyone else who got in his way. When Regan was eventually gunned down in a Marrickville laneway in Sydney's inner west, the rumour that went quickly around the traps was that he had been murdered either by one of his remaining 'mates' or by a member of the police force doing the public a service. Everyone reckoned that whoever had done it deserved a medal.

On 5 March 1975, Neddy Smith walked out of Parramatta Gaol. He had behaved himself, and three months were clipped off his minimum sentence.

While Roger Rogerson had been consolidating his move up the career ladder within the NSW Police Force, Smith's career as a criminal had seen him progress through the criminal justice system. For the time being, they were on opposite sides of the law. It wouldn't be for long.

*

Smith didn't have much chance of going straight. Barely a few months after he got out of gaol he was nabbed for stealing. It was a relatively minor offence, but for a bloke on parole it could have meant heading back inside. The police didn't know at the time that Smith had also graduated to a spot of armed robbery with an old mate from gaol who was on parole too.

This arrest gave Smith his first taste of how some members of the NSW Police did business. In the privacy of the interview room, a deal was put to Smith by the arresting police: effectively, 'Hand over $2000 and you'll get bail.' The deal would require the cops to split the sum with the prosecutor to ensure that certain things were suppressed . . . such as Smith's lengthy criminal record and the fact that he was presently on parole.

For Smith it was the only game in town. Going back inside wasn't an option. He quickly agreed to the deal. Quiet conversations were had, records were adjusted, and Neddy Smith walked out of court on bail instead of being taken to the cells to await the prison van that would have driven him back to the Metropolitan Remand Centre at Long Bay.

Enter Brian Alexander, law clerk, bagman and, as I mentioned earlier, now a missing person. Alexander was the man appointed by the arresting police to be the middleman between them and Neddy Smith. His job was to collect the cash for the bail bribe, scrape a percentage off the top for his trouble, and then negotiate a further fee for the charge to go away. Smith stumped up the cash again, and the prosecution faltered then keeled over in the lower court due to 'lack of evidence'. It was the first of many such deals for Neddy

Smith, and just another deal in the busy life of the pasty-faced Alexander.

Smith obtained funding for his bribes from his lucrative sideline in armed robbery. While crime got him into strife, it was also his means of getting out of it. That problem out of the way, Smith resumed stealing and robbery. He also at this time met and eventually married Debra Bell, with whom he had three children.

On 26 October 1976, two detectives arrived at the door of the home in Rockdale where Smith was living with his wife and son. The cops wanted to chat with him about a mate of his, Robert William McKinnon, who had gone missing. He had last been heard of a few weeks before, around the time of an armed robbery in which police thought he might have been involved.

Smith wasn't a very hot suspect, so the police arranged for him to meet them at Kogarah Police Station the next morning. It was a sleepless night for a bloke who had been rather busy in the armed hold-up business himself. Smith arrived at the police station with his then solicitor, Leon Goldberg, in tow. It was a better bet to arrive with counsel rather than a toothbrush lest an arrest follow. Goldberg, along with Bruce Miles and sometime employer of Brian Alexander, Phil Roach, was one of the few 'characters' working in the criminal law in Sydney at that time. (Alexander was far too vile to be considered a 'character'.) Goldberg, small, stoop-shouldered and large-featured, kept his office in the back of an ageing Volkswagen. He favoured somewhat stained and worn three-piece suits and large, heavy-framed black glasses. He was also irritating, socially inept, tardy and frustrating. His brother and fellow criminal lawyer, Charlie Goldberg, was his antithesis. What the brothers did share, however, were fine minds and finely honed skills in the courtroom. Both had also 'been around the traps' and knew exactly how the game was played.

Leon Goldberg's presence by Smith's side unsettled the police, and the game was played fairly. Smith completed a record of interview and the matters passed into history. However, the spectre of McKinnon would soon return.

The worlds of Roger Rogerson and Neddy Smith intersected on 20 October 1976. The events of that day would lead to a meeting and to the start of a relationship that would see Smith put behind bars for the rest of his life on a murder charge, and see Rogerson go from 'golden boy' to 'Australia's most notorious detective' and, finally, to 'the prisoner'.

7

'A GOOD FRIEND AND
A BAD ENEMY'

Neddy Smith was in the armed robbery business with his old pal from gaol, Bobby Chapman. The robberies had been fairly unambitious, but profitable. Neddy's share had been sufficient to bribe the police and to care for his wife and child. He also liked to drive a flash car and to have a drink with his mates, and he wasn't going without. Both men thought that, as small fish, they wouldn't attract the serious heat of the Armed Hold-up Squad. In fact, the squad was very interested in small armed hold-ups, particularly those where they could detect a pattern emerging – similar-looking crims described by witnesses, similar methods of operation. Smith later estimated that each robbery pulled between ten and fifteen thousand dollars, a not insignificant sum for a few hours' work.

Their target on the morning of 20 October 1976 was the Fielders Bakery payroll. Every Thursday at about 9 am, two young male employees of the bakery went to a bank in Granville, in Sydney's west, to collect the payroll. On this particular morning, they arrived on schedule, though in a souped-up GT Ford Falcon instead of the usual bread van. Chapman, who had been doing surveillance on the place, recognised them, and he and Neddy Smith – the Keystone Kops of armed robbery – swung into action. Almost.

Both Chapman and Smith were armed, and Neddy was the wheelman in their stolen brown Holden. The plan was for Chapman to intercept the men between the bank and their vehicle, and seize the bag containing the money. Chapman was a bit slow off the mark, and by the time he was close enough to be a threat to the bakery boys, they had reached the GT and were about to drive off. When they saw an armed man with a hood covering his face chasing after them, the driver put his foot down on the accelerator, only to stall the car. Smith then swung his vehicle in front of the car to block the boys' escape.

Chapman fired off two shots as he lunged towards the stalled car, shattering the rear window. As the driver managed to restart the car, Chapman fired again, this time hitting the pillar just behind the driver's head. After this second shot, the boys from the bakery didn't hang about. The GT Falcon, now under control, powered over the median strip and around the vehicle that had blocked its path, and sped away. Chapman fired some shots at and through the back window of the fleeing car, but its occupants escaped unscathed.

Smith and Chapman hastily fled the scene. Sensibly, they had stashed a second getaway car in nearby Harris Park. In an armed robbery, the police response is very quick. Uniformed and plainclothes police, with sirens blaring and lights flashing, appear at the scene within minutes from every direction. Armed robbery is serious business, and it's imperative that at least one team gets to the scene as soon as possible and obtains a clear description of the offenders, their vehicle and their direction of travel. The other cars circle the area, looking for the getaway car or anyone appearing a little suspicious. Police also know that it's common practice to have a second car stashed nearby, so locating the dumped first vehicle can provide clues about the second.

Smith and Chapman were in luck, finally, and managed to make their way back into the city in the second car without being stopped. The vehicle they were using was a fairly new blue-coloured Ford Falcon sedan registered and belonging to Gail Nancy Chapman (nee Handley), Bobby Chapman's wife of just six days. The pair had concealed themselves in the back seat and boot of the car, which to any observer appeared to contain only a pretty woman at the wheel.

On 26 October, when the cops came knocking on Smith's door to chat about his missing mate Robert William McKinnon, Neddy, understandably, would have been feeling nervous.

On 13 November, officers from the Special Breaking Squad (the 'Breakers') paid Chapman and his wife a visit. (The Breakers investigated robberies and major thefts. The Armed Hold-up Squad handled robberies where firearms were used.) Conducting the interview was the very capable Detective Senior Constable H. J. Lowe. Gail's car, the Falcon, had been spotted at the scene of a robbery involving Robert McKinnon on the night of 12–13 October, Lowe told her. McKinnon and his accomplices had broken into a factory and made off with a large quantity of cookware. The police wanted to know what Gail had to say about it. At the time, they were unaware of the attempted armed robbery at Granville.

As the owner of a car spotted at the scene, Gail Chapman was a good suspect and would need a good excuse. Lowe began the interview by cautioning her in the usual way: 'I want you to understand you need not say anything unless you wish, as anything you do say may later be used in evidence. Do you understand that?' Thinking on her feet, Gail decided that McKinnon had had custody of the car from about 9 October. She was temporarily off the hook.

Concerned, however, that someone may have noticed the shenanigans during the changeover of getaway cars at Harris Park on 20 October, Gail then panicked and decided to report her car as having been stolen. She walked into the Rose Bay Police Station four days after being questioned by Lowe and told police she was unmarried and had lent her car to one Robert McKinnon on 9 October. He had promised to bring it back the following Monday, she told police, but she hadn't seen him since. In her statement to police, she said she was 'seeking compensation in the sum of $5300 from McKinnon if the vehicle is not recovered intact'.

Instead of throwing suspicion for the bungled robbery on to McKinnon, Gail's statement opened the door for the Rose Bay Police to look into the matter more closely. On learning that McKinnon was missing, they decided that Gail's version of events didn't quite smell right.

Soon the Armed Hold-up Squad got involved, along with the Observation Squad (the 'Dogs'). The 'Dogs' followed Gail and learned that, not only was she not unmarried, as she had claimed, she was, in fact, married to the notable crook Bobby Chapman. Chapman, they knew, was a mate of the equally notable Neddy Smith. Both men fitted the description of the crooks responsible for the bungled Fielders Bakery payroll robbery. It was time to get serious.

Police finally connected all the dots, and on 20 November 1976, Gail Chapman found herself sitting across the table from two very testy members of the Armed Hold-up Squad. Their interest was the botched payroll robbery. At the same time, in another interview room at the CIB, Bobby Chapman was also being interviewed. Chapman had drawn the short straw. The man on the other side of the desk was Detective Sergeant

Roger Rogerson. At the typewriter was his good mate Detective Senior Constable Brian Harding, who would feature in many of the significant events in Rogerson's future career. In later years, after getting into strife and then being exonerated, Harding was for a time head of security for Ansett Airlines.

Though Gail had signed her record of interview with Lowe of the Breaking Squad, she declined to do the same after being interviewed by the men from the Armed Hold-up Squad. She would later accuse them of having verballed her. Bobby Chapman claimed before the ICAC to have had the same experience at the hands of Rogerson and Harding. According to her alleged interview, Gail nominated Neddy Smith as the wheelman in the payroll job.

A week later, on Saturday, 27 November, Neddy Smith was arrested when he reported to the Rockdale Police Station as part of his bail conditions. Waiting for him when he arrived at the station were around ten detectives. Smith told later of being thrown to the floor, from where he looked up and saw an affable-looking, sandy-haired bloke with twinkling blue eyes and a broad smile. In his face was the business end of a shotgun. 'Got you, Neddy,' said Roger Rogerson. It was to be their first date.

Smith later said of that first meeting with Rogerson, 'I must admit at the time I was frightened by him, not so much the man but by the power he seemed to have over the other police around him. When he spoke they jumped – all of them.' Rogerson was 'a good friend and a bad enemy', he would say on longer acquaintance.

Detectives Brian Harding and John Burke attempted to interview Smith at the CIB for around six hours before charging him. Handcuffed to a chair, he had maintained his silence and wouldn't be goaded, despite being harangued by the detectives.

While he was in the interview room, other detectives had visited his home at 130 Botany Road, in Alexandria. His wife, Debra, was at home. They searched the house and found a pistol. Or at least they *said* they had found a pistol. Debra Smith had a different view. 'I was up and down the stairs trying to sort of look at what they were doing and things like that while they were searching the house ... I can remember [Detective] Aarne Tees and Detective Ryan, it was mainly Ryan that was present, went into a linen cupboard.' In the cupboard under the stairs, Ryan found the pistol. Debra said, 'Well, I seen him pull something from his jacket and he no sooner pulled it from his jacket and put it up to the top part of the cupboard.' She reckoned Ryan didn't have time for the gun to leave his hands before he said, 'Hello, hello, hello. What have we found here?' When she accused him of planting the gun, Ryan replied: 'It's your word against mine.' If the gun *was* planted, it was to provide some leverage to get Smith talking. It was also a handy charge to level against a convicted felon if the armed robbery charges became hard to prove.

Years later, Tees and Ryan would give evidence to the ICAC and strenuously deny planting the gun. Tees eventually left the police force and became a barrister, specialising in representing crooks and police. When he died, some of those who attended the funeral did so, they said, 'to make sure the bastard was dead'.

Rogerson was aware that a gun had been 'found', and threatened to charge a member of Smith's family with possession. This old trick was usually effective with crims who had a shred of decency. Smith, of course, didn't. 'You'll just have to charge Debra,' he said. 'You weak cunt of a man, letting your wife cop the blue for you,' replied Rogerson, the staunch family man.

Smith steadfastly denied any involvement in an armed robbery. It was common practice, if the accused admitted to a couple of hold-ups, to have a few more added to the list. In return for helping the arresting police to clear some unsolved cases, they would put in a good word for him in their antecedent report (a sort of potted biography) at his sentencing. The usual wording was something like 'He played football and was good to his mother', if police liked the bloke or he'd been cooperative.

Smith's denials didn't get him far and he was charged with 'assault with intent to rob' and two charges of 'shoot with intent to murder' (one charge per bullet fired by his co-accused Chapman), and for possession of the pistol. Bail was refused. Smith had correctly called Rogerson's bluff, and Debra wasn't charged.

Smith alleges that before he was moved to Long Bay, he was taken aside by Brian Harding and told that someone would contact him 'to do a bit of business'. By 'business' he meant payment of a bribe to help Smith's problem go away. And that 'someone' was Brian Alexander, the law clerk. A figure of $20,000 was allegedly mentioned when he visited Smith in prison. When Smith complained that he didn't have that sort of money, Alexander replied: 'Well, something could be done about that.'

At his first court appearance on 14 December, Smith alleged that he had been approached by John Burke and Brian Harding in the holding cells. They told him that bail would be arranged, and that someone would contact him about 'earning' the $20,000. As Chapman later noted, 'I know Smith had no money. No one knew that better than me. I don't care what anyone says. Smith had four bob, so if Smith paid money it must have been time payment, $50 per week because he never had any money to give to anyone.'

Things went smoothly that day, and to Smith's surprise an unsigned record of his interview was tendered to the court. In it, Smith denied any involvement in the robbery. It was implied to the court that the only evidence against him was the rather dodgy word of Gail Chapman, who in fact ended up as a co-accused. The evidence given by a co-accused always lacked weight, in the eyes of the court. The firearm charge was relatively minor by comparison.

In the interest of fairness, John Burke told the ICAC, when they reviewed this affair a decade and a half later, that he had requested the prosecutor to oppose bail. He denied seeing Smith in the cells, and recalled that the prosecutor, magistrate and counsel for Smith had gone out together for a long lunch. On their return at about 3 pm, all presumably a bit worse for wear, the prosecutor didn't oppose bail. Unfortunately, both the magistrate and counsel were long dead by the time of the inquiry.

8

OPPORTUNITY KNOCKS

The flat-broke Smiths moved in with Neddy's formerly estranged mother. Smith then went straight for a brief period, working at the very rough Governor Burke Hotel in Parramatta Road, not far from the Glebe Coroner's Court. The pub was a bloodhouse. It was here that Smith was reunited with a gaol mate, the unlovely Graham 'Abo' Henry, nicknamed for his swarthy complexion rather than possible indigenous roots.

A few weeks passed until Smith was contacted by a mate and told it was time to earn the $20,000. As was a habit with Smith, the contact was made in a pub and involved a large amount of beer. The next morning, Smith went as ordered to the Rose Bay Marina. His new 'employer' was the infamous Kenny Derley, an old acquaintance from Maitland Gaol and former South Sydney Rugby League player. Derley had a long history as a drug dealer and hit the headlines when he was caught aboard the *Anoa*, a large yacht packed to the gunwales with a record amount of marijuana. Arrested with him was Murray Stewart Riley, a former detective sergeant and rowing partner at the 1956 Melbourne Olympics of Merv Wood, the New South Wales police commissioner from 1976 to 1979.

Riley's foresight and entrepreneurial skills in the drug and illegal gambling markets shortened his police career. That, and trying to bribe an honest police inspector in New Zealand in 1966. After numerous scrapes with the law over drug and fraud matters, Riley moved to England, where he was arrested and sent to gaol for a $100 million fraud. In 1993, while in Aldington Prison, the affable rogue went to a dentist's appointment and simply kept going. He has never been seen since and, unlike the hunt for escaped train robber Ronald Biggs, the police weren't exactly diligent in chasing him. The smart money reckons Murray has retired to that haven of rogues, the Queensland Gold Coast.

Kenny Derley's drug-importing enterprises were highly profitable. From his poor start in life in the inner west of Sydney, he moved on to buying houses in Dover Heights, overlooking the ocean, or harbour waterfronts in Watsons Bay. He also acquired a taste for speedboats and slinky Aston Martins. What brought him unstuck were his brazen schemes and lavish lifestyle. He was as flash as a rat with a gold tooth. To give himself a safety net, he kept certain members of the NSW Police happy with cash and information on his competitors. Derley is currently serving a very lengthy prison sentence, after being caught on his way back to Sydney from Melbourne in a car filled with amphetamines.

It was Kenny Derley, at the bidding of his mates in the police force, who steered Neddy Smith into heroin trafficking, a business at which he would prove himself to be exceptionally talented. The proceeds from his early collaborations with Derley quickly paid off his alleged 'debt' and kept him and his family in some comfort.

When Smith was finally before the lower courts on the

armed robbery and shoot with intent charges, the prosecution failed to make the charges stick. The evidence of his co-accused, Gail Chapman, of course wasn't going to get them anywhere near 'beyond reasonable doubt'. The other co-accused, Bobby Chapman, kept silent about Smith's involvement.

The arresting police copped some flak later for charging Neddy Smith and pursuing the prosecution based only on Gail Chapman's evidence. However, if he hadn't been charged, they would have found themselves in hot water. If a copper feels they 'have reasonable cause to suspect' that a person committed a crime, then that's enough to arrest them. Once arrested, proceeding with the prosecution is out of their hands and in the hands of the court. If the matter is 'kicked upstairs' to the District Court or Supreme Court, then the decision to prosecute rests with the Clerk of the Peace. Gail Chapman's evidence had amounted to reasonable cause to suspect. The detectives in this instance would have been damned if they did charge Smith and damned if they didn't.

The firearm charge was a decidedly quirky matter. Smith, still protesting his innocence and alleging the gun was a 'load', was committed for trial in August 1977. His barrister, Frank Lawrence, had been present at the long lunch with the magistrate during the bail hearing the previous December. In cross-examining Detective Ryan, Lawrence asked whether Debra Smith had said, 'You rotten mongrel, fancy saying that [the pistol] was under there. I seen you take it from your shirt, you cannot say it was there. I will tell my solicitor and the Magistrate.' Ryan denied Debra's assertion, but the seed of doubt had been sown.

The murky story got even murkier when it played out two years later at Neddy's District Court trial, which began on 5 February 1979. Justice isn't always quick. By that time a relationship had developed between Roger Rogerson and Neddy Smith, to the point where Smith felt comfortable popping into the CIB to see Roger. A very unusual practice, as crooks tended to keep well clear of police premises unless they found themselves there unwillingly. The upshot of that relationship was that Debra Smith completely changed her story. Her evidence, and a brand-new story, was that the gun belonged to her father, Robert James Bell, who at the time of the trial was dying a slow and painful death from cancer. She was just minding the pistol for him, she told the court. Why he had a pistol in the first place remains a mystery.

The trial judge and jury then repaired to Bell's bedside at the Royal Prince Alfred Hospital. He answered questions usually with just a nod or shake of the head. Maureen Madden, Debra's sister, also corroborated the story. The prosecution was looking almost as unwell as Mr Bell by the time the final defence witness was called. This witness was a showstopper: Detective Sergeant Roger Rogerson.

It is extremely unusual for a police officer directly involved in a case to be called to give evidence for the defence. What is even more unusual is for the evidence to be so strongly supportive of the defence case. His mates Brian Harding, John Burke and former Detective Chief Inspector Ross 'Rocky' Morrison all denied knowing that Rogerson would be giving evidence for the other side.

Morrison, who had almost 40 years' service under his belt, was questioned about this very odd occurrence at a later hearing into some of Rogerson's hijinks:

> *Q:* Did it subsequently come to your attention that
>   Rogerson had given evidence on behalf of the accused?

A: Yes.

Q: You looked surprised?

A: Yes.

Q: Why is that so?

A: Well, it's not usually the case for police to give
    evidence for people accused – defence evidence.

It was a masterful understatement. Rogerson's response – that he had been asked, or subpoenaed to give evidence, he couldn't recall which, and had just fronted up without his colleagues knowing – didn't hold water. Getting a police officer to court in circumstances like this was a formal matter. The squad would have known if he had been formally subpoenaed or summonsed.

When Rogerson finally got into the witness box, he testified that Neddy Smith had come to see him at the CIB on 17 August 1978, almost two years after the offence. By this time, the armed robbery and shooting charges had been chucked out by the magistrate in the Court of Petty Sessions (these days called the Local Court). Smith had brought a document with him, Rogerson said. Under oath, he continued:

> He came to me about something else and told me that
> he wanted to speak to me about the charge of pistol in
> possession. He said that there was a reason why the
> pistol was found at the home at 130 Botany Road,
> Alexandria and he handed me that piece of paper with
> the names of his de facto wife, her sister, his wife's
> father and also the names of two doctors, and he told
> me – I didn't record the conversation, I can't give it in
> the first person. He told me the real story was that the
> pistol was owned, had been owned by his father and
> that unbeknownst to him, his wife, with her sister, had

83

arranged to place this pistol at his residence and that he wanted me to interview the three people concerned and also the two doctors just to verify or justify his story.

Rogerson gave his account of events with a straight face.

However, juries can be full of surprises. They didn't swallow the defence story, and on 5 February 1979 Neddy Smith was convicted on the possession charge. Rogerson and the lads from the squad went off for a beer as Smith headed, yet again, to Long Bay. On 25 May, the Court of Criminal Appeal raised a middle finger at the jury, quashed the conviction and declined to order a new trial. Smith was a free man at last.

Years later, Smith would allege that the story was concocted 'like a stew' using the combined culinary talents of John Burke and Roger Rogerson. 'It started off as my idea,' he said, 'and we [Smith, Burke and Rogerson] developed it together.' Burke had been in and out of the room as the plotting proceeded, he said. Smith later alleged that the price for the stew was $10,000 paid to Rogerson. In cash, of course.

The Chapmans didn't do quite as well as Neddy Smith, but Rogerson and his pals weren't exactly unhelpful. After his arrest, Bobby Chapman was interviewed by Rogerson and Harding, and in yet another unsigned record of interview, he admitted his involvement in the robbery and claimed that the shots fired at the fleeing vehicle had been 'accidental'.

The Chapmans were both granted bail, thus avoiding a Christmas turkey dinner behind high walls. However, Bobby Chapman obviously didn't learn much from his arrest. On 19 February 1977, he was arrested for an armed robbery that had taken place on 4 February that year at the National Bank at Mascot.

Chapman had applied for bail to the Supreme Court a couple of times, but he was unsuccessful until 6 October 1977, when the very credible Rogerson handed the judge hearing his application a document which stated that Chapman had been very helpful to police. There was less fear now of Chapman running or re-offending, the document implied, and bail was finally allowed.

On 9 February 1978, Chapman pleaded guilty to possession of an unlicensed pistol and to both the Fielders and National Bank armed robberies. He was given thirteen-and-a-half years' hard labour. His remaining charges, and the charges against Gail Chapman, were listed for trial. The police, who tend to prefer indictments that push the most serious offences, such as the shoot with intent to murder charge that Chapman faced, went a little limp and were satisfied for him to 'nod the head' to the lesser charge of shoot with intent to commit grievous bodily harm. That charge came with a lower maximum penalty. The Crown didn't go along with this plan and decided to steam on. But Rogerson was about to lob a spanner into the works.

On 15 February 1979, the Chapman trial for the shooting during the Fielders robbery got under way in the dusty old courtroom in Darlinghurst. It was a miserable place in the winter, but nice and cool on this hot summer's day. Judge Hicks of the District Court was on the Bench. At the bar table were Alan Saunders for the Crown and Ian Strathdee for Chapman.

It is the usual practice in criminal trials, after the jury is selected and empanelled, for the prosecution to present its witnesses first. The typical running order is civilians, followed by police. The trial hit a very large speed hump the next day, when Detective Senior Constable Brian Howard entered the witness box, took the Bible in his right hand, faced the judge and swore to 'tell the truth, the whole truth and nothing but the truth, so help me God'. Howard then gave his evidence in chief, led by the Crown prosecutor Alan 'Slipper' Saunders QC. A tough prosecutor, Saunders took on some of the state's hardest cases, including some years later the trial of Andrew Kalajzich for the murder of his wife Megan in January 1986. When the time came for cross-examination, Chapman's counsel had a surprise for Saunders. He asked Howard, 'And you are aware, are you not, that Detective Sergeant Rogerson has been given information that the man Robert Chapman was not responsible for firing the shots?'

Saunders was taken completely by surprise. This allegation cut straight to the heart of the prosecution's case. Though a man of some substance, Saunders was on his feet in the twinkling of an eye, blood pressure spiking and objections flowing. After a decent argument, the question was withdrawn but with the defence reserving the right to recall Howard at a later stage. The set-up was complete. Saunders knew that the Crown case had been knobbled, but he had no choice other than to bat on. What had looked like a walk-up start wasn't.

Later that day, Saunders's problem got much worse. Detective Sergeant Roger Rogerson's name was called three times outside the courtroom. (Witnesses who haven't yet given evidence are required to wait outside the court until called, to avoid having their testimony influenced by evidence given by earlier witnesses.) Rogerson entered the witness box, gave his oath on the Bible and turned his attention to the Crown prosecutor, who immediately got down to the business of evidence in chief. Saunders led Rogerson through his statement. It was in cross-examination that

Saunders was again sandbagged. Rogerson agreed with Chapman's counsel that without the verbal admissions made by Chapman, there was insufficient evidence to put him on trial. On its own, this wasn't too much of a problem, as the police had asserted the integrity of the interview. However, when Rogerson resumed giving his evidence the following Monday, he agreed with the defence counsel that 'up until the present stage' he had continued making enquiries into the matter. This was somewhat problematic, considering that he was giving evidence at the alleged culprit's trial some two-and-a-half years after the robbery attempt.

Saunders may well have slumped at the bar table by this time. But it got worse. Rogerson told the court that he had 'been given other information' and 'certain inquiries' had been made. The defence then asked if Rogerson was hunting another person. Saunders again leapt to his feet and objected. The lunch recess came at just the right moment. No doubt the jury were becoming a little perplexed.

If the morning had been lousy for the learned prosecutor, lunch would be even more unpalatable. Saunders, quite reasonably, smelled a very large rat. In the middle of what had seemed a run-of-the-mill trial, the police – and particularly Rogerson – had deftly derailed things. Chapman no longer looked like the bloke they could pin 'beyond reasonable doubt', and the doubt had entered the trial courtesy of the police. Even more infuriating was that the defence counsel seemed far better briefed than the prosecutor. Saunders' instructing solicitor, Gary Cleghorn (instructing officer from the Clerk of the Peace), took detailed notes at a discussion that took place between Saunders and the police.

> Sgt Rogerson said that he had information from an informant which satisfied him that Robert McKinnon

was the man who fired the shots not the accused Robert Chapman. [This was curious considering that police had been looking into McKinnon's disappearance following the robbery on 12–13 October 1976 and it was a fair bet that he was dead.] He also claimed that he had told Mr Saunders of this some months before (he first said 6 or 7 but later said it could have been 8 or 9). He said he had told Mr Saunders this in Mr Saunders's Chambers in the building at 200 Goulburn Street, he being at the Clerk of the Peace office for some other reason for which he was not sure, possibly to deliver antecedents. He at first thought at the time he told Mr Saunders that he (Mr Saunders) had been drinking but when Mr Saunders said he had not had a drink for the whole of last year, Sgt Rogerson then qualified this by saying that Mr Saunders in any event did not appear interested or words to that effect.

Cleghorn also noted:

On a previous occasion when this matter was before the Court, the exact date is not known but possibly on the 11th August 1978, Det Sgt Rogerson spoke to me outside No. 3 Court at Darlinghurst and told me 'Don't be surprised at some of the answers I might give in cross examination' or words to that effect. I told Mr Saunders of this conversation.

Rogerson had done a consummate job. Cleghorn really should have pursued Rogerson's comments, which put Saunders in a rotten spot, having been suckered and then placed in a position where his own professional prowess might be dragged into the argument. Rogerson had detected a weakness and had deftly taken advantage. Game, set and match to Rogerson.

After lunch, Saunders stood to address the judge and requested that in the light of recent information, the jury be discharged without giving a verdict. The jury went home, and Chapman went back to Long Bay to resume his sentence. Gail Chapman walked free.

Later that week, at 2.25 pm on 19 February, Saunders began an interview with Rogerson, Brian Harding and Cleghorn. Rogerson maintained his line that the incriminating interview wasn't fabricated, yet he was certain that the informant, who wasn't at the scene, was highly credible. The tension in the room was palpable.

Saunders didn't believe there was an informer, Rogerson wouldn't disclose the informer's name, and Harding reckoned he didn't have a clue who the person might have been. Stalemate.

The matter caused a bit of a stir. The Clerk of the Peace reported to the Undersecretary of Justice. In that report, he noted:

> I am very disturbed by the conduct of Detective
> Sergeant Rogerson. I am curious too that the defence
> was obviously aware of the information and the Crown
> was not. I completely accept that Mr Saunders was not
> informed of the information. I find it puzzling in the
> extreme that the Detective, having taken the record of
> interview with the accused in which he said that he
> himself had fired the shots, that the Detective should
> not consider the information (which he said he gained
> from the informant to the contrary) important enough

to be made available in a formal way to the Crown over the period of 8 or 9 months that he was in possession of it prior to the trial. It would be interesting to inquire whether he informed his superiors of it.

Despite all these concerns the Clerk of the Peace went on to say, 'I do not believe an enquiry would be very helpful in the circumstances, since it would degenerate into a question of credibility between the Crown Prosecutor and the police officer involved. I nevertheless want to register my concern over the incident and place my views on record.' In other words: 'Let's avoid a blue in which mud would be flung by Rogerson.'

The New South Wales government didn't want the spectre of a senior Crown prosecutor being publicly accused of having a problem with alcohol that may have affected his ability to prosecute serious criminal matters. Saunders did later admit to a drinking problem prior to giving up alcohol in December 1976. As well, he admitted turning up to prosecute a fraud trial while well under the influence. It is also a fair bet that the Undersecretary of Justice was none too keen on rocking the political boat. New South Wales was politically stable; the recently elected Wran government was kicking goals; the bad guys – at least, so the public thought – were being put away. The public had gotten over the fact that the Moffitt Royal Commission of 1973–74 had been justifiably worried about organised crime in clubland. Having some very serious questions raised about the cream of the state's detectives and the pointy end of the state's prosecutorial arm would never do. Better to cover one's arse, and then sweep the whole dirty story under the mat.

The whole episode didn't reflect well on the state's senior police either. They did what most of the force did when confronted with something smelly 'in the job'. They looked the other way. At that time, Internal Affairs was a very small group known, without even a scintilla of affection, as 'the toecutters' (not to be confused with the criminal gangs that go by the same name). They weren't experienced detectives; rather, they were a dedicated group of blokes who had spent most of their careers in administrative functions in head-quarters. It wouldn't have been a fair match. Internal Affairs could only act on a complaint; it couldn't action something itself. It was an interesting little loophole. Significant changes were still a few years down the track. Had senior police, politicians and bureaucrats got off their collective backsides, the train wreck that was Roger Rogerson may have been avoided.

Rogerson had done his research and used it superbly. He would tell a later inquiry, when questioned about his sources for the Chapman story and the McKinnon fiction:

> I didn't just work on my own informants . . . we all
> worked on each other's. We were working together . . .
> we had different lines of information and that
> information was pooled and my recollection is that it
> came from some other detective – either another
> detective or other detectives.

Had the other detectives in the squad been working with Rogerson on this dramatic turn of events, they might also have considered mentioning it to the Crown. They didn't. Infor-mation of such significance should also have been mentioned in Rogerson's duty book, along the lines of: '1 pm, met Joe Blow at the Bourbon & Beefsteak in Kings Cross. He told me that Robert McKinnon was the gun man in the Fielders hold-up.' Or he should have noted it in his official police notebook, the slim brown volume detectives kept in their jacket pockets, or in an information report to the Criminal Intelligence Unit (later the Bureau of Crime Intelligence, or BCI). But no, it was all in Rogerson's head. Although he did recall that 'that information would have been spot on. I would have accepted it was good information.' Corroboration or investigation, it would seem, were unnecessary.

To his credit, Chapman responded truthfully when questioned about McKinnon's alleged involvement at an inquiry into police conduct held some fifteen years later:

> *Q:* Certainly it wasn't the truth that someone else fired the shots. You'd fired them?
> *A:* That's so.

Chapman also stated that he had never given any information to Roger Rogerson. This contradicted documents dated 12 July 1977, 9 February 1978 and 6 February 1979 where Rogerson made notes of information he reckoned was given to him by his informant, Bobby Chapman.

When pressured, Chapman also admitted that, prior to going to prison for a very long time, he and Rogerson had a 'few drinks together' and became quite friendly. So friendly, that years later, in 1986, Rogerson put to use the ironworking skills he had inherited from his father and made some security grilles for an elderly relative of Gail Chapman's. He had also given Gail a hand in getting her car repaired at a panel-beating shop Rogerson was involved with at the time. In Rogerson's later relationships with other notable criminals, he would occasionally exhibit this compassionate, domestic aspect of his character that was out of keeping with the hard-nosed, crim-hating professional detectives of the time.

Following the debacle at the Darlinghurst District Court, Bobby Chapman's case was re-listed for hearing, this time with a different team of prosecutors. He offered to plead guilty to the lesser charge of shoot with intent to commit grievous bodily harm, and this time the Crown acquiesced. The police finally got the result they had been after. Ian Temby QC, when ICAC commissioner, nailed it right on the head when he said of the Smith/Rogerson/Chapman escapade, 'The law became a game, manipulated by Rogerson to help Chapman.' And Neddy Smith.

Within just three years, the relationship between Rogerson and Smith had progressed from detective versus criminal, to Rogerson for the defence. Smith would later say, 'My success depended entirely on the connections that I met through The Dodger.' (Rogerson always denied that his nickname was 'The Dodger', and it was certainly never uttered around the corridors at the CIB.)

By now, Rogerson had consolidated his position as the ascendant detective in New South Wales. The only other possible contender was the beaming and clean-cut Nelson Rowatt Chad, surf club captain, qualified lawyer and, by the late 1980s, another disgraced and sacked former detective.

Neddy Smith had also done well, thanks to his introduction to Kenny Derley. He had gone from being 'down to the bones of his arse' to driving a Mercedes, buying his first home with Debra in Sydenham, and dining regularly at the very fashionable Eliza's in the equally fashionable eastern suburb of Double Bay. Not bad for a rough kid from the wrong side of the tracks. By 1978, Smith was one of the biggest dealers in the country, buying around fifteen kilograms of the drug from the importers every six weeks. The heroin was cut, and then sold through Smith's dealer net-work in Sydney's east.

Smith and Rogerson were often in contact by phone. Neither of them knew that their burgeoning relationship had attracted some interest from the Australian Federal Police (AFP), and that Smith's phone had been tapped ('knocked off'). Rogerson called himself 'Inspector Frank', but his measured tones and rather old-fashioned Australian accent, were quite distinctive. But when 'Inspector Frank' told Neddy Smith to back off on his business relationship with a noted drug dealer, the Trinity College-educated David John Kelleher, as he was 'too hot', the AFP did nothing. The tapes languished until the Stewart Royal Commission started poking about some five years later.

February 1978 proved to be a busy period for Rogerson and his inner circle. That month, Australia, with Prime Minister Malcolm Fraser at the helm, played host to the dwindling membership of CHOGM (the Commonwealth Heads of Government Meeting). The various heads were whisked to the Southern Highlands, staying at what was then the decid-edly chic Berida Manor just out of Bowral and, when in Sydney, at the city's finest hotel at the time, the Sydney Hilton.

Just before 1 am on 13 February, a garbage can on the George Street frontage of the Hilton exploded. Killed were the garbage collectors trying to pick it up and a young con-stable standing guard outside the hotel. Others were injured. The attack was thought to have been the work of 'terrorists'.

The NSW Police Special Branch, a stand-alone entity that operated out of Police Headquarters in College Street, headed the investigation. The Special Branch was focused on gathering intelligence against what might be called 'enemies of the state'. In the 1970s and early 1980s these included neo-Nazi or Soviet sympathisers, warring Croatian and Serb nationalists, the Spartacus League, the Communist Party, gay rights activists, vocal university students and anyone on the left of politics. Readers of the *Nation Review*, a feisty, intelligent and very entertaining weekly of the time, could expect to have a file opened on them. Other states had similar organisations, all formed out of the uncertain political alliances appearing immediately after the Second World War. Unfortunately, the Special Branch had broadened its remit over the years to cover those fond of freedom of speech and thought.

At the time of the Hilton bombing, things were a little tough for the Special Branches around the country. In South Australia, the commissioner, Harold Salisbury, was in deep strife after the Dunstan Labor government was tipped off that some of its key supporters were subjects of the Branch's interest. A judicial inquiry headed by Justice White had decided that the Special Branch in South Australia were pretty much a law unto themselves. Pressure was building for the Special Branches in other states to come clean about their activities as well.

This very tense political climate gave birth to an early rumour that the bomb had been placed in the bin by either the NSW Special Branch or the Australian Security Intelligence Organisation (ASIO), and that they had intended to 'find' the bomb before it detonated. This would have been a public relations coup and a compelling reason for their own existence. The trouble was, the garbos arrived a little early that night. The rumour spread like wildfire around the state's police stations.

The Special Branch, despite their intelligence-gathering skills, weren't noted for their front-line investigative work.

They were, however, noted for playing their cards close to their chest. 'Need to know' was the usual chant. While the CIB shared intelligence, the Special Branch would do so only under sufferance or when absolutely necessary. In this case, they had no choice but to hand over responsibility for the investigation to CIB.

The call went out for the cream of the crop. Roger Rogerson and his mates John Burke, Aarne Tees and Brian Harding, and others, soon found themselves at the sharp end of the investigation. They were the police who were demanded when the going got tough.

The investigation, with the aid of an informant, the fringe-dwelling Richard Seary, soon came to focus on the Ananda Marga. The Ananda Marga, or 'Path of Bliss', was a religious sect of Indian origin. Lots of meditation and yoga. However, some members were reputed to be a little on the radical side, which tweaked the interest of the conservatively thinking types of the Special Branch. On 16 June 1978, Tim Anderson and three of his fellow Ananda Marga members were arrested by Rogerson and his men on charges of conspiracy to murder.

Rogerson led the interviews, and produced an unsigned record of interview. Anderson would later claim that he had been bashed and verballed by Rogerson. 'I had never heard of him until that time,' he later said. 'Why, when it was the Special Branch who had been investigating our case, was Rogerson brought in? He knew nothing about us. The only answer is that he was well known as an interrogator, an expert in getting a confession. That confession, which I never made, [which] was 100 per cent fabricated, was central to the evidence against us. I believe we were convicted because of those verbals. The juries should have been warned it was not safe to convict on a verbal, but all along the way every judge indicated it was outrageous to suggest police would lie. They gave verbals a character reference.'

Justice Maxwell found the police evidence most impressive and sent Anderson and his co-accused away for seven years with hard labour. Throughout the trial, because of a perceived threat by the remaining members of Ananda Marga, Maxwell's house in Rose Bay had a police car permanently stationed on the grounds, and both he and his wife were accompanied everywhere by a policeman.

Anderson's views on the acceptance of police evidence were on the money. The force would be very quiet on the subject some years later when Rogerson, by then no longer a detective, said: 'Verbals are part of police culture . . . Police would think you're weak if you didn't do it. The hardest part for police was thinking up excuses to explain why people didn't sign up . . . They're still doing it.'

Some lawyers, however, had got the message, and particularly about the skills of Roger Rogerson in the witness box. One said, 'You have to watch him continually. You must never give him an inch. If I was to ask him: "Why did you handcuff my client?" He would answer, "Well, sir, I knew he was wanted interstate on three armed hold-ups and I was concerned for the public's safety."'

Such a question was known as a 'free kick', or an invitation for a 'bombing mission'. By the time the barrister had finished objecting, the 'bomb' would already have gone off. One Sydney QC quipped of Rogerson, 'If Roger Rogerson was directing traffic, I wouldn't leave the kerb.' Barristers don't take well to being bested by a humble copper.

The Ananda Marga saga would drag on for years; Anderson would be arrested again, and released again. On 6 June 1991, New South Wales Chief Justice Murray Gleeson, sitting in the Court of Appeal on an Anderson matter, commented: 'I do not consider the Crown should be given a further opportunity to patch up its case against the Appellant. It has made one attempt too many to do so.' The courts were waking up.

9

DEATH IN THE AFTERNOON

The swiftly developing relationship between Roger Rogerson and Neddy Smith should have set alarm bells ringing in the Armed Hold-up Squad and in the hierarchy of the CIB. Rogerson would later comment, 'It's difficult to describe exactly what a police/informer relationship is. I've seen it – I've seen it where they try to describe it in police television shows and the like where, you know, a detective gets a phone call and sees a man in the back lane and something is whispered and he's the informer but it doesn't work that way. So it's difficult to describe in short terms exactly what a police/informer relationship is.'

Informants are an important part of a criminal investigator's life, but, like forensics, they are only tools. Informants have their own agenda, which means that any information they share with the police needs to be taken with a grain, or sometimes a handful, of salt. Nothing can replace an experienced, intelligent and insightful detective who is able to bring all the elements together and find the truth. A good detective is very nosey, a little devious, and has a sixth sense that is well honed. Rogerson had all these qualities, but his

99

judgment would become clouded by his lust for power. He knew that he could get away with 'blue murder' and he set out to prove it.

The burgeoning relationship between Smith and Rogerson experienced a brief hiccup following the Hayward and Fellowes arrests. Warren Fellowes, a former hairdresser, was Smith's heroin supplier. He and his business partner, one-time Rugby League star Paul Hayward, had been arrested on drug charges in Bangkok on 12 October 1978. The repercussions were swift. Smith's home was raided, and large amounts of cash were found there and in a safety deposit box. He was charged with 'goods in custody' (having something believed to be stolen or otherwise unlawfully obtained). Debra was also charged. Rogerson was an early visitor to Smith in his dingy cell in the dank old complex beneath Central Police Station. Smith took stoically the 'goods in custody charge' for the large amounts of cash found in his possession. He said later, 'The money was confiscated but that didn't worry me too much as there was a lot more where that came from.' Smith had a bit more bad luck when his old parole of 1967 was called up, requiring a bit more gaol time. He was also charged, along with David Kelleher, with conspiring to import heroin. Brian Alexander visited Smith in prison and suggested that a payment of $50,000 would see his wife Debra avoid being charged with the conspiracy as well. Smith agreed to pay the amount. Rogerson wasn't the beneficiary of that particular alleged bribe, which in any case failed to have the desired effect. When Debra was charged, Smith demanded his money back from Alexander. He was eventually reimbursed half the amount.

*

The Woodward Royal Commission, which would unmask the drug lord 'Mr Asia' (the New Zealander Terry Clark), was bringing the drug trade to the attention of the public. Up to that time, they'd associated heroin and other hard drugs only with the sordid back streets of the Cross. Ordinary Australians were discovering that drug trafficking and drug use were rampant in the suburbs, in their own backyards.

The royal commission, which sat between 1977 and 1980, would also lead indirectly to Brian Alexander departing the scene. During that time, Alexander's role as bagman to three CIB squads (most likely the Armed Hold-up Squad, the Drug Squad, which had grown to 35 detectives by 1979, and the Special Breaking Squad) had brought him to the notice of the commission's investigators. They put the squeeze on him and he squawked at the first hint of pain. News of Alexander's cooperation with the commission in exchange for immunity soon leaked back to the cops he had been doing 'business' with. He was last seen on 22 December 1981. His car was found abandoned at the Gap at Watsons Bay, a spot favoured by suicides, but – unusually for a suicide victim – no trace of his body was ever found.

As Neddy Smith tells it, Alexander met his early demise attached to the Early Kooka stove that was thrown into Sydney Harbour, watched by three detectives (not including Rogerson) who had got him very drunk at the Kings Head Tavern, on the corner of Park Street and Elizabeth Street in the city, before driving him to the Darling Street wharf in Balmain, from where the four men took a boat ride. Only three returned. The sharks welcomed one of their own.

Neddy Smith denied any involvement in the disposal of Brian Alexander, despite seeming to have an intimate knowledge of the events surrounding it.

Debra Smith's charges were dismissed at the committal

hearing, but Neddy and David Kelleher were committed for trial. Luck came Neddy's way after a sizeable bribe saw the heroin in question disappear from the police exhibit room at Central Police Station. In its place was a heavily diluted package, and not the stuff he'd been charged over. The jury acquitted the two men.

Although he had spent about two years behind bars on remand and finishing his parole and goods in custody sentences, Smith had kept his finger on the pulse. Rogerson hadn't been twiddling his thumbs either. His reputation as the hard man of the CIB had been consolidated when he used a Smith & Wesson to solve an armed robbery case. The robbery took place one Sunday morning in 1977 at South Sydney Juniors Leagues Club, in the suburb of Kingsford. The armed robbers, who included a Neddy Smith acquaintance named Butchy Burns, fled the scene after grabbing $60,000 from a courier taking the money to a nearby bank but were cornered by Detective Sergeant Third Class Roger Rogerson and the lads from the Armed Hold-up Squad. Waving a gun at the detectives proved fatal for Burns, who died later that day in hospital from gunshot wounds inflicted by Rogerson. The coroner was satisfied that Rogerson 'held grave fears for his life and the life of others' and had fired in self-defence. In 1980, for his work in this and a number of other investigations, Rogerson would collect the coveted Peter Mitchell Award, an annual award given to 'exceptional' police.

A year after winning the Peter Mitchell Award, Rogerson would add a second notch to the grip of his short-barrel .38-calibre Smith & Wesson six-shot revolver.

*

While lingering in Long Bay, Neddy Smith had befriended a good-looking, fit and extremely wild young man named Warren Lanfranchi. He was the very black sheep of his family. When both men were back on the street in late 1980, Lanfranchi approached Smith for a bit of work. Smith, who had slipped back into his role of big-time heroin dealer, welcomed the aspiring star.

Lanfranchi took to the business like a duck to water and was soon earning around $10,000 a week. Unfortunately for Lanfranchi, his looks and enthusiasm weren't matched by common sense. Sticking to heroin dealing and keeping a low profile would have seen him wealthy and free. It wasn't an easy matter to lock up heroin dealers, particularly those who worked for men like Neddy Smith. Even when a culprit was caught red-handed with the evidence, prosecutors weren't guaranteed a conviction. Corruption or incompetence could see the case thrown out or charges dropped. The brief could go missing or be 'sold' to the other side, exhibits and witnesses could be knobbled or made to disappear, and sometimes the arresting police were the last to know.

Warren Lanfranchi decided to expand his empire by adding armed robbery to his portfolio. However, he omitted to tell Neddy Smith of his plans. One day, when he was running out of a bank from which he had just made a large and illegal withdrawal, he ran straight into a motorcycle cop who had arrived first on the scene. The cop's Smith & Wesson .38 was no match for Lanfranchi's pump-action shotgun. Lanfranchi immediately took a shot at him, then made his escape in the ensuing turmoil. In the policing business, being involved in dodgy dealings was one thing; shooting at a copper was quite another. Lanfranchi now had a serious enemy in the NSW Police Force.

According to Neddy Smith, although Rogerson would

always deny it, Lanfranchi was already in Rogerson's bad books after ripping off a drug dealer who had 'been doing business' with Rogerson. The attempted murder of a cop iced the cake.

Rogerson was aware that Smith was supplying Lanfranchi. In a classic police move, Rogerson now put the onus on Smith to deliver up Lanfranchi. It was a move not dissimilar to his earlier threat to charge Smith's wife Debra with possession of a firearm. Once again, Smith put his own interests first. His whole business would come crashing down if he tried to thwart Rogerson. Having the patronage of the most feared copper in New South Wales was a boon. So, when Rogerson told Smith he wanted to 'chat' with Lanfranchi, Smith made the arrangements.

According to Lanfranchi's girlfriend, Sallie-Anne Huckstepp, Rogerson wanted money. Specifically, he wanted $30,000 to make the armed robbery and the cop shooting go away. Ten thousand down. Huckstepp also alleged that police had told Lanfranchi he could be guided into a few armed robberies to get the remaining $20,000. The police would soon launch an all-out attack on Huckstepp's credibility, making public the fact that she was a heroin addict and a prostitute. However, they hadn't counted on her also being very bright, articulate and vocal.

The first meeting place suggested by Rogerson was in a council car park in Redfern. Lanfranchi wasn't keen on the idea. A car park in Redfern in 1981 was dangerous enough without the police being there, he knew – let alone most of the Armed Hold-up Squad.

Plan B was to meet in Dangar Lane, in a wedge between the main thoroughfares of Abercrombie and Cleveland streets, in

Chippendale. Chippendale is somewhat on the chic side these days, but on 27 June 1981, in place of the modern apartments whose garages now open on to Dangar Place were grimy old industrial buildings run as sweatshops and light engineering works. They were surrounded by the last gasp of inner-Sydney slums. Nearby pubs included the Lansdowne, a favoured Smith watering hole, and the Broadway, where Lanfranchi and Smith had wreaked havoc during a vicious bar-room brawl that saw Lanfranchi ride through the bar on a motorbike.

Dangar Place was an ideal spot for the meeting, Rogerson decided. Traffic in and out was minimal at the best of times, and with a couple of burly coppers standing beside their 351-cubic-inch V8 Falcons, the preferred vehicle of the CIB's very serious squads, at the exit and entrance to the lane, the place was well and truly under control. The locals tended to keep a low profile and weren't the sort to go rushing off to the police or the media. Besides, on a winter Saturday afternoon, most of them would be inside, watching the rugby league on TV or listening to the races.

Detective Inspector Doug Knight was the duty officer rostered on that afternoon at the CIB's new headquarters in the Remington Centre, a late 1960s-era concrete pile in Liverpool Street, in the city. It commanded exquisite views of Hyde Park and Sydney Harbour to the north and of the rooftops of Surry Hills to the south. Normally assigned to D District, in Chatswood, he had been brought in especially to work the afternoon shift in the Duty Office on the second floor of the Remington Centre. He had paid his dues in the force and was considered to be rock solid. 'If things went pear-shaped, you could rely on Doug,' was the general consensus. Taking care of business in D District was his reliable assistant, Lloyd 'The Hook' Noonan.

Knight's career had blossomed under the Askin reign. He

had been a trusted mate of the premier, and a long-time resident in Askin's electorate. When his integrity had been given a hiding by Athol Moffitt's royal commission in 1974, his career hadn't been affected adversely. He had hopped up a rank and ended up with a nice, comfortable job close to home. He would achieve higher rank before he retired.

In the Armed Hold-up Squad a few floors above where Knight was warming the chair, matters had been meticulously planned. The 'inner circle' – Graham 'Fritzy' Frazer, Brian Harding and Rod Moore – would guard Rogerson's back. The other detectives – there were nineteen in total – would seal off the ends of the lane, precluding members of the public from entering the area.

What happened in Dangar Place that afternoon has never been successfully resolved. Did Rogerson simply murder Lanfranchi in cold blood? Was he shot by Rogerson in self-defence? Huckstepp would swear that Lanfranchi was unarmed. Smith would back up Rogerson. The great problem with sorting out the truth was that there were no witnesses aside from the police and Neddy Smith. Lanfranchi may have been unarmed when last seen by Huckstepp (who would later say he was wearing pants that were so tight-fitting he wouldn't have been able to conceal a weapon), but there is no way of knowing whether he was still unarmed when he arrived at the scene. Lanfranchi had a reputation for violence, access to guns and a devil-may-care attitude towards the police. Rogerson may have concocted his story about shooting Lanfranchi in self-defence, but then again he may not have. Rogerson's version, no matter what it was, would be supported word for word by his brother detectives. Any chance of finding out the truth died around the same time as Lanfranchi.

What we do know is that Neddy Smith had been directed

to drive Lanfranchi to the meeting. Smith picked him up in his silver Toyota Celica. They arrived at the entrance to Dangar Place just before 3 pm. Rogerson and Lanfranchi approached each other. Shots were fired. By Rogerson's account, Lanfranchi had pulled a silver Harrington & Richardson pistol (a bit of a museum piece) from the front of his pants, and Rogerson, believing his life was in danger, opened fire in accordance with police regulations. Lanfranchi fell to the bitumen with one shot to the neck, which wasn't fatal, and one shot to the heart, which was.

Two girls in a nearby house who told investigators they heard the shots estimated they were eleven or twelve seconds apart, thus fuelling speculation of a shot followed by a coup de grâce. (Standard police practice is to fire two shots in close succession.) However, nothing came of this speculation.

Usually when police are involved in a shooting, things happen fast. The call goes out and cops from miles around rush to the scene to give 'back-up'. In Dangar Place, the Armed Hold-up Squad had everything nicely under control and no call for assistance was made.

In the twinkling of an eye, the scientific police (forensics) were called to photograph and examine the scene. They also took possession of all the exhibits, including the guns, which were later handed over to the ballistics police. Doug Knight, in the Duty Office at the CIB, arranged the call-out of Internal Affairs police to investigate the shooting, fielded all the media enquiries and made sure that everything ran smoothly.

Rogerson breached regulations when, later in the afternoon, he spoke directly to the media without getting the nod from senior officers. Such tasks are usually handed over to Police Public Relations, to avoid giving the public confused or con-flicting accounts of matters involving the police. Journalists from the *Sunday Telegraph* and *Sun-Herald* who rang through to the Armed Hold-up Squad office were surprised, therefore, when Rogerson chatted with them, on the record, about the afternoon's events. The media portrayed it as a battle between good and bad, with good triumphing. The *Sunday Telegraph* headlined the front page the next morning with 'Police kill gunman – High Noon shootout in lonely city lane'. The press photographers had made it to the scene even before the body of Warren Lanfranchi was cold. Their cameras captured his crumpled form on the roadway and Rogerson and his fellow detectives in a huddle nearby.

Quotes flowed from Rogerson. 'I think he caught sight of Graham Frazer and panicked.' 'I think he wanted to talk about something and thought I would be alone.' In a sentimental moment, Rogerson said that his family 'gets a bit worried' about his job. The journalist asked, 'Was it like *High Noon*?' Rogerson replied, 'Well, unfortunately it is a bit like that with these sort of people with guns going around the place.'

One of Rogerson's colleagues was quoted as saying of him, 'He knew how to handle a gun, knew how to handle himself in a life or death situation.' Rogerson told the journalist that Lanfranchi was wanted in connection with an attempted armed robbery at Drummoyne on 14 May that year. He had shot at a Highway Patrol policeman who had tried to stop him for a motoring offence. The shotgun jammed. 'An informant contacted us and said he was prepared to give himself up.' That informant was Neddy Smith. All in all, it was a good afternoon for the NSW Police in general and for the reputation of Roger Rogerson in particular.

The only jarring note came from the *Sunday Telegraph* journalist who, with the presses almost ready to roll, contacted Warren Lanfranchi's father, Keith, who lived almost within hearing of the gunshots, in Camperdown. The journalist quoted him as saying, 'A girlfriend warned me that two police officers were going to shoot him on sight. I told my solicitor that I believed my son was in danger. There is no way he would have carried a gun. He would not have carried one if he was going to give himself up.'

Hours of paperwork followed Rogerson's media debut. When he went home that night he found that the place was under round-the-clock police guard. His daughters would be driven to and from school every day – just in case Lanfranchi's mates tried to get even, or so went the PR.

The Internal Affairs investigation into the shooting was headed by former Bureau of Crime Intelligence luminary, the then Detective Inspector Ron Ralph. Ralph was famed at the CIB for his dazzling memory for crooks, and for a later more personal brush with the law that killed his career. On 15 July 1981, investigators interviewed Sallie-Anne Huckstepp, who told them of the circumstances leading up to the shoot-out at Dangar Place. When asked if she had anything further to say before the record of interview was concluded, she replied: 'Only that I believe Warren was murdered in cold blood by Detective Sergeant Roger Rogerson, and was not carrying a gun.' She then signed the record of interview.

Rogerson was never interviewed about the allegations in the Huckstepp interview. On 25 October 1981, Internal Affairs curtailed their investigation pending the outcome of the coronial inquiry. This was common practice at that time if legal proceedings that impacted on an investigation were under way. If the court chucked out much of the evidence against police officers, then the Internal Affairs inquiry would fizzle very quickly.

The PR machine kicked into action when Tony Lauer, then head of the NSW Police Association and later commissioner, offered the following thinly veiled criticism of Huckstepp and her supporters. Rogerson, he said, had been 'the subject of a continuing attack, well-financed with clear indications that it is supported by radical, and even anarchistic beliefs'. In other words, the cops were really pissed off that someone was accusing them of involvement in a serious crime. Rogerson commented rather dryly, 'I don't think Miss Huckstepp'ed be satisfied short of me getting twenty years.'

To the police, Warren Lanfranchi was nothing more than a vicious, drug-dealing hoodlum. Whatever the circumstances of his death, the general view in the force was that it was good riddance to bad rubbish.

Roger Rogerson always denied being involved in drug trafficking. He said, 'I am not now and never have been involved in the drug trade. That suggestion is as ludicrous as it is vile.' The denial, however, didn't quite explain his relationship with Neddy Smith.

In late 1981, the state's coroner, Norm Walsh SM, with the aid of a jury, found that Lanfranchi was killed by Rogerson 'while endeavouring to effect an arrest'. However, the jury declined Walsh's offer to find that Rogerson acted in self-defence or in the unfortunately termed 'execution of his duty'. Although there were complaints from Huckstepp, the Lanfranchi family and Liberal politician John (later Justice) Dowd, the attorney general (and later judge) Frank Walker declined to do anything further. An inquiry by the ombudsman, George Masterman QC, also didn't get very far.

The inquest was something of an oddity. Warren

Lanfranchi was from a respectable family who weren't going to stand by and accept what they reckoned was the 'summary jurisdiction' of Roger Rogerson. Nor did their lawyers take the same 'sit back and see' approach as Internal Affairs. They began their own investigation. While peering under a few rocks they happened upon two guests of Her Majesty, John Klimenty and Peter Haggart, who alleged that in 1977, after their arrest on charges relating to an armed robbery, they had divvied up the proceeds of the robbery with Rogerson, John Burke and another detective nicknamed 'The Doctor'. There were a few 'doctors' in the police, usually nicknamed for their ability to network their way to a solution to a problem. For their kind contribution to the police pension plan, the two robbers were offered a hand to have their sentences lightened in exchange for 'being helpful to the police'. It was a recommendation always viewed favourably by judges. Additionally, the police would ensure they had a steady supply of heroin both while in the police cells and in prison. Both alleged that, while they were in prison, Rogerson personally delivered the drugs during visits where he purported to 'interview' them.

These allegations weren't fresh, and Klimenty had written to the then premier Neville Wran back in 1977. When he didn't get a reply, he gave a copy of the allegations to the visiting justice, usually a magistrate, who regularly visited the gaol to hear internal matters. The visiting justice passed the letter on, and Internal Affairs popped by shortly afterwards for a chat. The matter fizzled when Klimenty heard on the prison grapevine that he would be knocked off if he continued.

Klimenty and Haggart now volunteered to give evidence at the inquest, but the coroner declined their offer. He also ruled that much of the 'evidence' gathered by the Lanfranchi legal team was 'inadmissible'. The real oddity came when he declined to admit evidence offered by Sallie-Anne Huckstepp.

What was inadmissible for some seemed to be admissible for others, however. Walsh allowed Paul Ostara, a sometime Lanfranchi mate, to give evidence about some of Lanfranchi's exploits. It wasn't much of a character reference and raised doubts about Lanfranchi's integrity. As well, the coroner decided to protect Neddy Smith – against *whom?*, one might have wondered – by suppressing his identity and referring to him as 'witness G'.

The case also had a whiff of political expediency about it when, in 1982, counsel acting for the Lanfranchi family, Ian Barker QC, who had led the prosecution in the Lindy Chamberlain trial, wrote a submission arguing for a royal commission into the shooting and subsequent inquest. When the silence on that score became deafening, the family's solicitor, Gerald McCarthy, wrote to the attorney general, Frank Walker, stating that he had heard that Crown advocate Roger Court QC had agreed with Barker but noted that 'the Premier [Neville Wran] did not want another "Allen affair"'. (Wran was referring to visits by Sydney's 'usual suspect', Abe Saffron, to Deputy Police Commissioner Bill Allen at Police Headquarters. Allen's meteoric rise through the police ranks had been with the active support of Wran. Allen had also offered bribes to licensing police sergeant Warren Molloy, who was busy cleaning up the acts of hoteliers and restaurateurs around Kings Cross.)

Matters got a little murkier when evidence emerged that Ostara had bragged to a fellow prison inmate that the police would give him a helping hand with his current armed robbery problem in return for favourable evidence given at the inquest. Ostara, who didn't know he was being taped by his fellow lag, said: 'Detective Rogerson said to me, "If we make a deal and you do the right thing, you will have no doubts or worries whatsoever regarding these charges. I'm a man of my word and I won't go back on my word.'" Ostara appeared before Judge Foord (who would soon swap the Bench for the dock, and later be acquitted on charges of attempting to pervert the course of justice by allegedly having a word in the ear of then Chief Stipendiary Magistrate Clarrie Briese about the imbroglio involving Sydney solicitor Morgan Ryan and Justice Lionel Murphy). Ostara got a bond. The allegations about the inquest went nowhere.

The last gasp went to Opposition Leader John Dowd. On Friday, 26 November 1982, Dowd moved an urgent motion in the Legislative Assembly, calling for the attorney general to establish a judicial inquiry into the Lanfranchi shooting. He also wanted them to look into allegations of police involvement with a mate of Smith's and fellow crook, Neville Biber, and his company Harry S Baggs, a discount store chain. The motion was defeated.

The next morning, while enjoying a peaceful start to the day in leafy Lane Cove, Dowd got a phone call. It was Rogerson. Police tend to be very wary of politicians, so Rogerson's call might be thought odd if one didn't suspect that Rogerson saw himself as at least the other man's equal in status and power terms. Rogerson said, 'It is easy to make allegations in Parliament.' Dowd, with his back up, gave things a push. 'It is easy to make threats outside Parliament.' Dowd was chilled by Rogerson's reply: 'It is very easy. I have read about your background because you have spoken about your family and how important it is to you. I am worried about my own family.'

Dowd went back to Parliament and told the House he was 'intimidated' by Rogerson's actions. Given Rogerson's reputation and recent past, intimidated was precisely how he should have felt.

Although there would be no further investigation, people upstairs at CIB Headquarters were starting to talk.

The shooting of Warren Lanfranchi was the third error in the career of Roger Rogerson. The first had been deciding to go with the flow at the CIB; the second, getting too cosy with Neddy Smith. While the full consequences of the third error would take a few years to manifest, an immediate effect was to make his star shine even brighter among his peers. Over the years, Rogerson had become extremely confident in his abilities. He sought and enjoyed power. Money, in itself, was of little interest to him. In despatching Lanfranchi, Rogerson had found that he could literally get away with murder – or a very aggressive form of self-defence. The inner circle now had a very clear idea of what Rogerson was capable of. He was fearless, and willing to operate with impunity outside the constraints that bind most people. In his annual performance reviews, his rating went from 'excellent' in 1976 and 1977, to the rarely encountered 'outstanding' from 1978 to 1981.

While his peers and superiors thought he was dazzling, one colleague, not from the inner circle or one of Rogerson's acolytes, would later say of him: 'As a young detective he was a good worker, but a smartie. The sergeant said, "Watch him, he's too flash." When he reached the rank of Detective Sergeant Third Class, his head just got bigger and bigger.' With the killing of Lanfranchi, his head swelled even more.

Neddy Smith, despite his appalling past, reckoned he was stunned by the events that took place in that Chippendale laneway on that winter Saturday afternoon. Rogerson and his cronies had dragged Smith close to their bosom when

114

they had him arrange the meeting and bring Lanfranchi to Dangar Place. When he gave evidence to Internal Affairs and to the coroner's inquest in support of Rogerson and the police version of events, he in effect stepped over the line. For a career criminal, it was a major step.

Smith would say in the early 1990s, 'I was ashamed of what had happened to Warren, ashamed because I had gotten up in the witness box for a cop. And not just any cop, but the most hated cop in Australia, Roger Rogerson.' Smith alleged that two of the Armed Hold-up Squad inner circle spoke to him just after the inquest was over. They thanked him for 'doing the right thing by Roger'. Rogerson, they said, was feeling all warm and friendly towards Neddy Smith. The comment should have given him chills, but the already rattled Smith was about to get a bigger shock.

Smith's early 'business' with Rogerson and the lads had got them thinking, and his recent performance as a witness had concentrated their hearts and minds. One of the detectives allegedly said to Smith, 'You are not a fool; we have spoken amongst ourselves about your future. It's clear to us that you are always going to be involved in crime in some way or other, so we decided for helping Roger we are going to give you a Green Light. Do you have any idea what we are saying?' Neddy certainly did. He reckoned he underwent a 'transformation'. Suddenly one of Sydney's most vicious career criminals was joining Rogerson and his friends at their frequent luncheons.

The long lunch had been an integral part of business in the corporate world in the 1980s, but the CIB made 'smart lunching' an art form. Rogerson's circle favoured spots like Eliza's in Double Bay, the restaurant of choice for the well-heeled and major drug dealers, or Dimitri's Five Doors in Surry Hills, where Dimitri Karageorge would make sure that lunch was both discreet and lavish. Friday was a popular day to lunch at the Malaya, on George Street in the city, affectionately known as 'The Blazing Arsehole', or 'The Blazers' for short. Tests of manliness would be waged over the prawn sambal, with extra chilli. Chinatown was another frequent haunt of the Hold-up Squad boys, usually preceded by a beer in the Covent Garden Hotel, an establishment frequented by both cops and crooks. Stanley Wong's Old Tai Yuen, up a staircase above the pub, was discreet, and a bit of a favourite with the ALP boys and union officials from Sussex Street too. The food was reliable, unchallenging Cantonese; the waiters were old, efficient and pleasantly surly, and you could get a decent drink. (Wong would later be murdered during a robbery at his Maroubra home.)

Neddy Smith got the 'green light', and started to receive luncheon invitations, not because of his fine work as a witness; it was because Rogerson and some of the lads from the Squad knew it was in their power to grant Smith immunity. Interestingly, when the 'green light' allegation later became public knowledge, none of the players sought legal redress. A defamation action can open a can of worms, and do so under privilege. Sometimes sleeping dogs are best left to lie.

Neddy Smith's career took off from that point. The bloke who had managed to get himself arrested with monotonous regularity now managed to avoid getting locked up for the next six years. His dream run ended on 31 October 1987, when he was arrested for the murder of tow-truck driver Ronald Flavell.

The day before, Smith had started drinking at lunchtime at the Lord Wolseley Hotel in Ultimo and had moved on to meet Rogerson, who by then had been dismissed from the force, at the Covent Garden for more drinks and a spot of lunch. They spent the afternoon back at the Covent Garden, where Rogerson kept up a steady stream of jokes and patter. At around sunset, they headed to the Australian Youth Hotel in Glebe before driving to the eastern suburbs at about 8 pm for something to eat. Smith was drunk at the wheel of his car when he ran into the back of Flavell's vehicle, which had stopped suddenly in Coogee Bay Road. It was only a minor bump, but a fight broke out and Smith fatally stabbed Flavell. Smith left his car, which was registered to Debra, at the scene. The green light changed to red. Neddy Smith was convicted of murder on 20 June 1988 and will spend the rest of his life behind bars.

The likelihood is that Smith was telling the truth when he dobbed on Rogerson. The relationship between the two men was common knowledge shortly after Lanfranchi's death. For some detectives around the CIB it was something of which to be envious, one of the best conduits for information into Sydney crime they could imagine. No one outside that inner circle could have guessed the true nature of the relationship. It was inconceivable that someone like Smith would be given carte blanche – and even active support – to commit robberies and supply drugs without fear of prosecution. It was this power that Rogerson relished. Rogerson had achieved the unthinkable and in doing so had surpassed the achievements of his mentors.

Until this time, Rogerson had always kept his family very much out of the limelight. Apart from firing up the barbecue for the occasional Sunday gathering with the lads, his two worlds of home and work rarely overlapped. But now he did something inconceivable: he took Neddy Smith, one of Sydney's most violent and dangerous men, home to meet Joy. It surprised Smith, too. 'One day I was meeting Roger at a hotel when he said, "Hop in, mate. I've got to make a pit stop at home on the way for a few seconds. Come with me, I want you to meet my wife, Joy."' Smith was even more surprised when Rogerson introduced him to Joy as a friend.

Smith was a habitué of the Lord Nelson Hotel in The Rocks, these days a nicely renovated old sandstone hotel. Some 25 years ago, it was a little less genteel, catering to seamen from the nearby docks, dockworkers, and the often rough-and-tumble local residents. One day in the early 80s, Rogerson was passing by with his family when he spied Smith. He introduced his by now teenaged daughters to Neddy. Soon both men's families were socialising together regularly. Debra never liked Rogerson, Smith would say later, but she was very fond of Joy. Joy, a polite and loyal woman, kept her thoughts about the Smiths to herself.

10

THE PAPER TRAIL STARTS

Police work provides a magnificent insight into human nature, but many in the force are utterly naïve about money matters. In the eighties, putting a Fraud Squad detective up against a smartly dressed corporate crook was a bit like chasing a Ferrari in a Hyundai. The only way you could catch them was if they made a mistake. Cops then knew very little about the nuts and bolts of handling money (even their own house and car loan repayments, which were deducted from their pay cheques by the credit union), so there was little chance of them outwitting smart white-collar criminals.

There was a problem, then, if you came into money that wasn't salary, and particularly if it came in large wads of used notes. Managing that sort of cash was a bit out of the typical cop's league. You could hardly stroll into a bank with a bag full of money and expect not to attract attention.

Roger Rogerson was as ignorant as the average cop when it came to money, as a few of his future transactions would show. However, in April 1982, he did something that on face value was half clever. The half that wasn't clever was that he started a paper trail.

Rogerson and Gail Chapman, the wife and sometimes co-accused of Neddy Smith's mate Bobby Chapman, went together into the National Australia Bank on the corner of Castlereagh and Campbell streets in the city, and only a few blocks from CIB headquarters. They were there to open an account for Gail. She says she was never a fan of Rogerson, despite the fact he had given the family a hand when Chapman was in gaol. She described her acquaintanceship with Rogerson as 'slight' and denied that she had ever had an affair with him. (Rogerson also denied that they were ever lovers.) She said that she had initially found him 'repugnant', though she would later say that 'he seemed to have a little bit of compassion'.

Their 'slight' acquaintanceship notwithstanding, Rogerson introduced Gail to the manager, whom he knew. At that time it wasn't necessary to produce 100 points of identification to open an account. 'Identified/Introduced by Det Sgt Rogerson', as the official records noted, was sufficient validation for Gail to open an account using her maiden name of Cooper. She gave her address as that of her grandmother.

Over the next twelve months, Gail deposited in total around $119,000 into the account. When questioned later about the cash, she said she had been hiding it in a safe for 'taxation purposes', which raises the question of why she then put it in the bank. Her husband had given her the cash, she said. When the unlikelihood of this was pointed out to her – Chapman was then part-way through a gaol sentence – she changed tack and said the money had come from armed robberies and a bit of SP bookmaking prior to his incarceration.

Rogerson, when later questioned, had a failure of memory and was unable to recollect taking Gail Chapman to the bank and wrongly identifying her to the bank manager as 'Gail Cooper'.

*

At the CIB, the mutterings of Rogerson's superiors had finally become audible. Rogerson's relationship with Neddy Smith, the killing of Warren Lanfranchi, the indications that Rogerson was on the take, and his intimidation of John Dowd were all becoming something of a political problem.

These weren't the first allegations they had heard about Rogerson's shenanigans. They came hot on the heels of complaints by a prison escapee, John Powch, that in August 1980 he had been shot at by a bloke in an unmarked police car. Powch was subsequently arrested. Though he reckoned he had never heard of Roger Rogerson, he spotted the detective about a year later when he was on a routine visit to Long Bay Gaol and identified him as the shooter. Rogerson denied Powch's allegation of attempted murder – he was at a family barbecue at the time, he said – and the allegation didn't go anywhere. The fact that the shooting occurred at Revesby, a few minutes' drive from Rogerson's home, was obviously just a coincidence.

The allegation was later re-investigated by the ombudsman, George Masterman, who exonerated Rogerson and his cronies. Rogerson, who was on sick leave when Masterman released his report, contacted radio station 2GB and said the ombudsman's inquiry had cost him both money and worry. 'I have had to have all my friends who were here at my home [at the time of the alleged shooting] go to the trouble of giving evidence at the ombudsman's inquiry at their own expense.'

Powch wasn't the only prison escapee to come into Rogerson's orbit in that month of August 1980. Gary Purdey, an armed robber, had escaped from Goulburn Gaol, purportedly a maximum-security prison. Purdey was at the wheel of a car travelling near the Holsworthy Army Camp in Sydney's southwest when the car in front stalled. Purdey slowed to avoid running into the back of the car, and an occupant of the back seat of the stalled car then opened fire at the very surprised escapee, who did a U-turn and fled. The occupants of five other vehicles on the road at the time had also fired shots at him, Purdey reckoned.

Rogerson, who was in charge of the Purdey investigation, said he was elsewhere at the time – whether at home firing up the barbecue, he didn't say.

Purdey concluded the cops wanted him, and preferably dead rather than alive. He contacted radio station Triple J. 'They've already told my ex-wife they intend to fill me full of holes,' he said. 'I won't carry weapons if I am not to be shot, but if I am going to be shot, yes of course I will carry weapons.' Shades, yet again, of *High Noon*.

Purdey didn't give himself up. Instead, he committed another armed robbery with a mate, Patrick Harland, who died during the botched hold-up. Rogerson hadn't fired the shot; he was chasing Purdey, whom he finally cornered in a garage. Purdey would later tell the court that he yelled out to Rogerson, 'Don't shoot! I'm unarmed.' He had wiped his gun clean and placed it near the garage door, he said. Rogerson's version of events differed. He told the court that Purdey had said, 'Don't shoot me, this is jammed,' indicating his gun. Rogerson then said, 'Drop it,' which Purdey did. At the inquest into Harland's death, a police expert testified that he couldn't find Purdey's fingerprints on the allegedly jammed gun. The discrepancy in the two men's testimony wasn't investigated.

At Purdey's trial, he alleged that he had been assaulted by Rogerson. When the allegation was put to Rogerson in the witness box, he replied: 'I then said to him: "Do you require any medical attention?" Purdey replied, "No. Can I have another cup of coffee?"' Rogerson said that he replied, 'Yes.

And we'll have a cup of coffee ourselves.' They all then supposedly had a cup of International Roast, the standard-issue coffee in police stations around New South Wales. Rogerson's version of events didn't stack up after a doctor who examined Purdey found abrasions to the top of his scalp, bruising of the right eyelid, tenderness of both ears and the right cheekbone, abrasions of the cheek and nose, scratch marks on the right cheek, tenderness on the ninth rib and bruising to the right thigh. He was 'missing a bit of bark', in popular police parlance.

To get to the top in the NSW Police Force, you need to have an ear reasonably well tuned to politics. Rogerson was becoming a little bit of a handful. The government, while standing firm in the House, was asking questions quietly in the backrooms of power. It was time to lower the heat.

In typical police style, Rogerson was simply transferred back to divisional work. This was a common practice for long-term CIB detectives, and usually it was only for short periods. Rogerson had the same expectations. A year or so of penance, the heat would diminish, and then he would quietly return.

But his bosses didn't have somewhere nice and close and quiet, like Bankstown, in mind; instead, they told him he was heading out to No. 3 Division, Darlinghurst. It was a case of just changing one frying pan for another. Rogerson's descent 'from the penthouse to the shithouse' had begun.

Even before Rogerson and his fellow detectives got news of his departure, many of his colleagues, sensing that he was becoming a bit too hot, had begun to distance themselves from him.

The CIB had a variety of watering holes near the Remington Centre. The 'heavy' squads, such as the Armed Hold-up and the Breaking Squads, would often pop down to the Macquarie on the corner of Wentworth Avenue and Goulburn Street. This was a no-frills old pub that delivered good beer and discretion. Some of the old-timers would visit the Hollywood or the Jam Tin in Surry Hills if they needed to stretch their legs a bit. Others would pop into establishments owned by Keith Kelley, an ex-detective, very successful hotelier and mate of Rogers. The rest of us would head to the Elizabeth, a lovely old art deco pub, overlooking Hyde Park in Elizabeth Street. On paydays, however, all would converge on the Elizabeth. The reason for this fortnightly popularity was the publican would cash all police pay cheques. Earlier in the day, and accompanied by two armed detectives, the publican would slip up to the bank and come back with bags of cash, much of which he would recycle back into his tills by the end of the night.

Rogerson could usually be found holding court at the centre of a throng of detectives mainly from the 'heavy' squads. Acquaintances would sidle past, acknowledge Roger and the lads, maybe with a quick handshake, some smiles and banter. Roger knew almost everyone there, and they certainly knew him. But around the time the rumours started that he was getting too 'hot' and a transfer out of the squads was on the cards, no one apart from a few close mates wanted to know him. He was no longer the blue-eyed boy of the CIB. A few weeks later he was in Darlinghurst.

If Central, Regent Street and Phillip Street were quietly referred to as 'punishment' stations, Darlinghurst might be considered to be a cross between Devil's Island and an asylum where the lunatics were in charge. The station was in an old brick building just off Taylor Square in the midst of inner-city Darlinghurst, and just across the road from the District Courts and Central Criminal Court, where Sydney's most serious crimes were tried. Access to the courts was either across Forbes Street, or through the labyrinth of tunnels that connected the cell complexes.

Darlinghurst had got off to a genteel start as Sydney grew. There are still remnants of the grand homes that once populated the hill that overlooks what is today Sydney's CBD. The domestic staff and other lesser mortals occupied the gully that separated Darlinghurst from the city. However, when the government erected the court and gaol complex in the middle of the nicest part of the suburb in the 1840s, the swells muttered 'Not in my backyard' and promptly moved out to Elizabeth Bay and Darling Point.

Darlinghurst soon suffered from an image crisis and, like its neighbouring suburb of Surry Hills, became a slum. The gaol closed in 1914 and its inmates were sent to the new Long Bay prison near the beach at Malabar. The site then became an internment camp during the First World War, then later a technical college; today it houses the National Art School.

The demise of Darlinghurst as a desirable address saw the grand houses turned into boarding houses and cheap flats. Prostitution and sly grog became boom industries, particularly in the laneways around Crown Street. The beacon of civility was Kings Cross, with its bohemian ways and upmarket residences. However, that didn't last either. The beginning of the decline of the Cross can be dated to the arrival of the American soldiers on R&R leave from the Vietnam War. They arrived in waves between October 1967 and 1972, bringing with them rock 'n' roll music, wads of cash, insatiable appetites for food, sex and booze, and newly acquired addictions to heroin. (Vietnam was ideally positioned for easy access to the opium poppy fields of the Golden Triangle and US servicemen provided a willing new market.) The bars, strip clubs, restaurants and brothels of the area flourished. Fortunes were made. And those with an eye on the main chance saw the possibilities inherent in importing their own supplies of heroin into Australia.

Heroin soon took over as the addictive drug of choice. By the mid- to late 1970s, Darlinghurst was at the heart of the heroin trade in Australia. The drug was reasonably easy to get hold of, reasonably safe to handle, the profits were astronomical, and the demand was high. It was the perfect cash cow for someone wishing to progress up a notch from the unpleasantness of armed robbery. Someone like Neddy Smith.

Heroin also presented an opportunity for dishonest police to make a bit of money on the side. They could take a slice from the drug dealers in return for keeping them out of strife, or, if they got nabbed, they might tamper with the prosecution or get the charges reduced, in exchange for a wad of cash. If they really didn't like the dealer, they could even take his cash and stash and charge him anyway. The dealers might 'bleat', but who would believe them? It was a win–win situation for the cops involved, and it filled the void left by the demise of the abortion rackets. Heroin also had a massive growth potential.

By the early 1980s, the drug trade had taken over in the Cross. No longer was it largely a bohemian haunt of artists, visiting celebrities and showgirls with ample cleavage. The 'Boss of the Cross', Abe Saffron, was vehemently anti-drugs. The Cross he had loved and been a part of since the heyday of his Roosevelt Club in the late 1940s was now stone dead.

The drug dealers, such as Rogerson's mate Louie Bayeh,

were now running many of the clubs. The prostitutes were usually addicts working to earn money for their next fix; kids, outcasts from their homes in the suburbs, littered the streets. The dregs from every city and town in Australia were calling the Cross 'home'.

Jimmy Anderson, the former 'First Officer' to Abe Saffron's 'Captain' (to use his own analogy), was doing his best to assume the mantle of 'Boss of the Cross', even resorting to hiring a man to 'hit' Saffron. Saffron was horrified, but even more so when it was suggested that he himself should have Anderson 'whacked'. Roger Rogerson was highly amused when he heard of Saffron's squeamishness.

The Cross's nickname of 'The Dirty Half Mile' was an understatement. Law and order was provided by the men and women of No. 3 Division, based at Darlinghurst Police Station. There were uniform police in a substation located at the Cross, in view of the young male prostitutes plying their trade in Fitzroy Gardens and the landmark El Alamein Fountain. Darlinghurst Police Station was just around the corner from where the young male prostitutes worked 'The Wall', the old sandstone walls of the gaol and court complex.

Darlinghurst Station was a law unto itself. Stories that have emerged of sexual assaults on prostitutes, a cell being converted into a bar, and gay bashing whenever the mood struck (nearby Oxford Street was just emerging as the gay Mecca), were all pretty much on the money. While there were many good officers, there were more than a few duds – drunks, drug addicts, rapists and crooks. If something nasty happened in Darlinghurst, the suspect list would often include some of the local police. Direct complaints against Darlinghurst police were few, vigorous investigations by Internal Affairs fewer, and prosecutions fewer still.

Working in the first-floor Detectives Office were men like

the second in charge, John Brown, and the policewoman's friend (thanks to his charm), John Openshaw. They would soon be joining Rogerson and Neddy Smith as drinking mates, and it would be business as usual. Like Rogerson and Smith, Openshaw would end up as a guest of Her Majesty. Though Rogerson was now out of the Armed Hold-up Squad, his act didn't change.

Rogerson said of his transfer, 'Barney Ross [the deputy commissioner] said he thought I needed a rest, something about getting out of the limelight. I was disappointed and I think that the blokes on the squad were sorry to see me leave. But I'm still a detective and I've got a job to do at Darlinghurst and there's no point carrying on [about the transfer].'

The Darlinghurst detectives and the squads dominated the Cross – and everyone in it. Many of the senior divisional detectives were ex-squad men themselves. They roamed the Cross, catching up with crooks and coppers alike. They mingled where they chose. The other squads could usually be found on afternoon shift at specific places. The Armed Hold-up Squad favoured the Texas Tavern in Macleay Street, and the Breakers regularly enjoyed Jimmy Anderson's company at the Venus Room. All the squads found common ground at Bernie Houghton's Bourbon & Beefsteak.

Rule number one in the police force is: support your mates. It didn't do to dob in other people in 'the job'. But as a young detective at around the time of Rogerson's departure from the Remington Centre, I was aware that something was awry in the world of criminal investigation in Sydney.

I had started to have niggling doubts about some of my peers at the CIB when I was at the Juvenile Crime Squad, a squad at the other end of the pecking order from Rogerson and the lads of the Armed Hold-up Squad. We had been barred from investigating the shenanigans in a couple of places, including the vile Costello's Club in Kellett Street in the Cross. Fifteen years later, the antics that went on in the club would be revealed in the Wood Royal Commission, but it would be fifteen years too late for some young men. It was Vice Squad turf and we weren't allowed through the door, by order of the men at the top of the CIB.

At Chatswood, we had caught a bloke for a couple of dozen armed robberies. They had all been reasonably profitable, and no one had been hurt. When we caught him, our superiors had been keen to hang on to him, and in particular to be the first to search his house. It finally dawned on me that they were looking for his stash of cash. When they had rampaged through his house, and were contemplating digging up his backyard, he had finally confessed that all the money had been lost on the horses. Our superiors lost interest at that point, although the Armed Hold-Up boys, minus Rogerson on that particular day, did suggest that our friend plead guilty to a few extra hold-ups just to improve the 'clean-up rate', in return for a good word to the court.

However, the penny finally dropped for me when I was at the Fraud Squad in 1983. After a couple of years of scratching my head and thinking, 'No, they can't be *that* bad', I found out they probably *were* that bad. Despite its belief in its own ascendancy at the CIB, Fraud had similar grubby elements to the rest of the place. One case had come to my partner and me as one that should be looked at and 'given the flick', or thrown out. We took a look and decided there was a case for charging someone. It was called having 'reasonable cause to suspect', and fortunately it was our decision, and ours alone. We couldn't be directed *not* to charge someone.

The victim of the crime finally confided that when he first spoke to some of the senior people at the squad, he had been informed that it would cost him $10,000 in cash to get the investigation going. He had declined the offer, thinking that the police should investigate crimes without needing a cash incentive. I later heard one of the senior blokes at the squad had offered the crook a deal: if he were to pay them a larger amount than $10,000, the investigation wouldn't proceed. Things fell apart when my partner and I decided to charge the bloke. We got into a bit of strife, but there was little that our bosses could do.

After poking about a bit more, I discovered that deals with both victim and crook weren't uncommon. Frauds can be complicated to prosecute, and this was a way of resolving matters. I was relieved when I was told I was being offered a transfer to Internal Affairs. Of course, the offer was one I couldn't refuse.

11

FRIENDS IN HIGH PLACES

The culture of the NSW Police Force did a pretty good job of isolating it from the realities of the world. For years, the police had been protected by politics and the media, which hardened the 'us' and 'them' mentality of the force. So, when the first whiffs of the chill breeze of change were in the air, they didn't notice. Rogerson, being at the epicentre of that culture, would be among the last to know. Rogerson was the definitive police dinosaur. He had come into the culture fresh from school and been embraced by the hard men of the CIB. He knew nothing else. But the early 1980s saw the beginnings of a slow shift in the perceptions of the public, the media and those who drive opinions. The writing would soon be on the wall for dinosaurs like Rogerson.

New South Wales at that time was a hotbed of corruption allegations, so it was only a matter of time before our political masters chucked a bone somewhere else to draw focus away from them. When your ship is taking water you bail like buggery, and you don't care where the water goes so long as it's over the side. The NSW Police in general, and the prominent figure of Roger Rogerson in particular, would soon become collateral damage and the focus of the public's interest. Years of police culture would slowly unravel.

John Kenneth Avery, the police commissioner appointed in August 1984, would be offered – and would take – much of the credit for the eradication of dinosaurs such as Rogerson and the flow-on through the police culture. I think that credit was due elsewhere. The change began because of a confluence of things. A very bad smell permeated the corridors of power in New South Wales. Premier Neville Wran's favourite cop, Bill Allen, had been booted out of the force in April 1982 (though it was said he had retired). In early 1983, the ABC's *Four Corners* program suggested that senior members of the Rugby League, magistrate's courts and the government had been up to something nasty. The government was forced into holding a royal commission and Premier Wran stood aside until it was over.

One of the upshots of the commission was that Murray Farquhar, the chief stipendiary magistrate, found himself on the other side of the bar table, and later in Long Bay Gaol. Trains came to a standstill for nineteen days when railway employees went on strike. Corruption allegations were made at the inquiry into the disappearance of Kings Cross heiress and anti-development protester Juanita Nielsen.

Rex Jackson, Wran's minister for corrective services, would soon resign, then be arrested, tried and gaoled for taking money in exchange for having his charges released early. He didn't get an early release. The '*Age* Tapes', tapes allegedly made illegally by NSW Police, would soon be casting doubt on a cache of lawyers, judges, politicians and police. And down in Canberra, National Party identity Ian Sinclair would be accused, but later acquitted, of signing cheques for his dead father. Chris Puplick, the former New South Wales senator, is reputed to have once quipped to a group of schoolchildren he was showing around old Parliament House, 'There goes Ian Sinclair. Why don't you ask him for his father's autograph!'

As a result of all this kerfuffle, the media finally got its act together and began to address the facts, rather than the spin. The public was after answers, and the media shook itself out of years of spoonfeeding and finally got back to being nosey. Their focus would be that symbol of the rapidly dying old-school police culture, Roger Rogerson.

Rogerson, not surprisingly, wasn't a fan of the new police commissioner. He would later say of Avery, 'He was never a detective, has never done anything. Try to find anything about him in the past and you won't. See if he had any good marks or commendations for bravery.' It was a view held by almost every man and woman in the CIB, but then again, Avery was no fan of the CIB.

Despite all the rumours swirling around, for Rogerson and his new mates from Darlinghurst, and those old mates at the CIB who weren't giving him a wide berth, it was business as usual. Rogerson introduced Neddy Smith to Openshaw and Brown. Drinks flowed at the Gaslight, a rather down-at-heel pub in Darlinghurst's Crown Street that was the favoured watering hole of the Darlinghurst mob. Lunches lasted well into the early hours. At home in Condell Park, Joy Rogerson kept to herself any reservations she may have had about her husband's professional life.

As a senior detective, Rogerson wasn't overworked. His role was to lead any major investigations that couldn't be flicked to the specialist squads, to keep an eye on the day-to-day running of the office, and to mentor junior officers. He would often find himself as officer in charge. He maintained a busy social calendar between the demands of regular court appearances and conferences on briefs arising from his time at the Armed Hold-up Squad. Joy and the kids even got to see a little more of him. His transfer back to the divisions hadn't been without some advantages.

Although a little off the pace at Darlinghurst, Rogerson still had plenty to keep him occupied. And being the helpful fellow he was, both socially and professionally, he could always be relied on for a bit of advice. What he didn't know was that the phones at the Darlinghurst Detectives Office were occasionally monitored, and that Neddy Smith's phones were of great interest to the Australian Federal Police.

Detectives at the CIB had always been very careful about what they said on the phone in the office. If they wanted to ensure privacy, they would head to a public phone. The preferred public phone was out the front of the newsagency on the ground floor of the CIB. Lunchtimes would see a small queue of furtive-looking detectives waiting to invest a few coins in a 'discreet' phone call. Nobody had the wit to tap that phone. It would be with the clarity of hindsight that New South Wales would find that 1983 was the year of the phone tap. Even our learned judges weren't spared.

At the Council for Civil Liberties' annual dinner on 6 April 1984, the premier, Neville Wran, had a major dummy spit. The dinner was held at the Menzies Hotel in the city. Master of ceremonies was the late John Marsden, solicitor, notable old queen, Campbelltown resident and soon-to-be-president of the Law Society and later a member of the NSW Police Board. In the audience were the premier-in-waiting Nick Greiner and his wife Katherine, food god Tony Bilson, a mix of Liberal and Labor hacks, David Combe (in the middle of allegations that he was involved with the KGB's Mr Ivanov) and me.

Wran accused the Council's members of being chardonnay-swilling socialists, which was odd because that's what I thought he was, with his house in Woollahra and his electorate in Bass Hill in Sydney's southwest. Wran tried to shift the focus of the taped conversations from the chatterers to those who had, in some cases, 'illegally' taped the calls. His attempt to 'shoot the messengers' was a hoot and failed dismally. It is simply too damned sexy to have on tape evidence of two crooks plotting.

In April 1983, one early 'victim' of police taping was Neddy Smith's solicitor of choice, Val Bellamy. Unluckily for Val, the taping was legal this time and done by the Australian Federal Police. Bellamy would also represent Rogerson in the slew of cases soon to head his way. He was a rather dumpy man with a beard. His daughter was a student at Sydney Girls High School, and Val was its P&C President. On one memorable occasion, he shocked students, teachers and parents by turning up at a school function wearing a girl's tunic.

Bellamy had a problem – apart from making a decidedly unattractive woman. One of his clients had offered him 500 gold coins in lieu of his fees. In Bellamy's words, 'A client approached me, he had some matters on, the nature of which I can't specifically recall. He said that by way of fees he had a number of $200 gold coins, which I think were newly introduced then. I was extremely suspicious. I asked him about their provenance. He gave me assurances they were legitimately obtained. I wasn't satisfied. In conversation with Smith I asked him whether he might be able to make some inquiries. I knew that Smith was a police informer and had contact with the police. He made some inquiries. I think he told me that as far as he was concerned, or as far as he could ascertain, they weren't hot. I decided nonetheless not to take them.'

Bellamy rang Smith at his home on the afternoon of 18 April. At 2.51 pm that same day, Smith rang Rogerson at home. Rogerson was a little cagey on the phone, though not quite cagey enough. He told Smith, 'Be careful what you say anyhow, mate, on this thing.' Smith said, 'Something handy . . . something handy we could earn a dollar on . . . ' They arranged to chat again at 4.15 pm on safer phones. However, the safer phones weren't safe at all. The tapes were rolling.

At 3.18 pm, Bellamy rang Smith at Smith's girlfriend's home. (Neddy wasn't noted for his fidelity.) He admitted to Smith that the coins were on offer from a safecracker client. Smith said to Bellamy, 'Ring him up and tell him you've got some client here interested in a third . . . and it'll be cash straight up.' Smith told Bellamy he would get back to him after his 4.15 pm chat with Rogerson.

Rogerson, though on holiday, called his new best friend John Brown at Darlinghurst. Brown called the Modus Operandi section, where records of crimes were stored. Brown asked if there was any record of '300 to 400' Australian gold coins having gone missing. There wasn't.

At 4.15 pm, Smith rang Rogerson. After agreeing that the phones were 'right', which they definitely weren't, they got down to business.

Smith:	I believe there's five hundred in them two hundred dollar gold coins.
Rogerson:	Right.
Smith:	Can we do anything with them?
Rogerson:	Five hundred two [hundred] dollar coins?
Smith:	Yes. You know them ones they minted?
Rogerson:	Yeah, I know. Yeah, the ones for the – what is it – the anniversary of something, wasn't it?
Smith:	Yeah, one bloke's got five hundred. I don't

know if they're hot or what they are. They'd
have to be hot because he won't put them over
the counter.

After a bit more chat, Smith rang off. Fifteen minutes later,
Rogerson rang him. 'Yeah, mate, well, I've just had a check,
mate. There's nothing on record, mate, of any of them being
stolen. But a bloke I spoke to, he seemed to recollect that there
was a deficiency from the Mint when they printed them.
There were quite a few found to be missing.' That would
explain why the person whose safe was cracked didn't report
the loss.

The deal with Neddy Smith didn't go through. Smith later
alleged that Bellamy had told him he had flogged the coins
elsewhere for $50,000, half their face value. Rogerson didn't
bother to pursue the chain of evidence that would have led an
investigator back to the crime and the criminal. The conversation revealed that the relationship between Rogerson and
Smith wasn't that of a detective and his informer.

Val Bellamy would find himself in some very hot water a
little over a year later. Bellamy had trouble accounting for
about $60,000 he was meant to be holding for a client, a
criminal. The money was to have been securely stashed in
a safe deposit box at the Commonwealth Bank in Martin
Place. As an added precaution, the box was taken in the
name of Bellamy's elderly father. Bellamy was a little concerned that the client wouldn't take the news of the loss too
well and decided that faking a robbery en route to the bank
was the best solution to the problem. He called his most successful client, Neddy Smith.

Smith arranged for another of his mates from the CIB (not
Rogerson or his cronies) to be Bellamy's minder for
the sum of $10,000. On 19 September 1984, Bellamy and his

137

father were in Martin Place walking towards the bank when a 'thief' snatched the vinyl bag containing the money from out of Bellamy's hands. Unfortunately for Bellamy, an off-duty constable saw the snatch and gave chase. Even more unfortunately, a Good Samaritan had been able to snatch the bag from the 'thief'. Bellamy told the constable he didn't want to press charges. They had the money back, he told the copper. Just forget about it. However, the constable continued his search for the thief, during which time Bellamy again had the bag snatched from his grasp, he later alleged. He reported the theft to the Rocks Police. As luck would have it, the coppers who took the statement from Bellamy were in on the giggle to the tune of $10,000. After interviewing the young policeman who had accepted the initial 'crime' at face value and given pursuit, they recorded the loss of the $60,000 as a theft.

At 9.52 am on 18 May 1983, Neddy Smith was back on the phone. This time, he was after Rogerson at the Darlinghurst Detectives Office. He chatted first with Openshaw. It was obvious from the conversation that the two were on very familiar terms. After a social chat, it was down to business:

> *Smith*:   What's doing?
> *Openshaw*: Not a great deal. How did you finish up?
> *Smith*:   Drunk.
> *Openshaw*: Drunk. That's not like you, mate.
> *Smith*:   That's unusual, isn't it? Do you remember, mate?
> *Openshaw*: You were pretty pissed when I seen – when I left you.
> *Smith*:   So was you.
> *Openshaw*: Oh, bullshit. I done you like a dinner, mate.
> *Smith*:   Are we having lunch?

> *Openshaw*: Hang on, I'll find out. Just hang on a second.
> *Smith*:   Righto then.

Roger Rogerson then came on the line. The two chatted about the Lanfranchi inquiry, which had finished a few months before, and then, more importantly, lunch. Rogerson said he had some court commitments and suggested they have a drink later if he couldn't find someone else to go to court for him. Openshaw then came back on the line.

> *Smith*:   Do you want me to bring that thing with me?
> *Openshaw*: Yeah, I think so, mate.
> *Smith*:   How much?
> *Openshaw*: *Laughs.*
> *Smith*:   Come on, you old cunt.
> *Openshaw*: Oh well, what?
> *Smith*:   I've got 10 here. Do you want me to bring the 10?
> *Openshaw*: Yeah.
> *Smith*:   Are we going to whack it up three ways?
> *Openshaw*: Yeah.
> *Smith*:   Well, I'll just bring the fucking 7-Up. Stop putting your hand over the phone.
> *Openshaw*: I can't hear you. I don't want to talk on the phones, see. I'll leave it up to you.
> *Smith*:   We could just split it three ways and I'll just bring yours and his up.

Smith's next call was to the aspiring – and not particularly competent – criminal Harvey Jones. Jones was at the time on bail for conspiring to steal a pile of gold bars, and for harbouring the thief. He was also very anxious 'to do business' with police and see the charges go away. Rogerson was in charge of his case.

Jones was a good Parramatta Road car salesman, and made a few quid on the side running a fairly successful brothel called Aunt Lucy's, in Homebush in Sydney's west, in the midst of Sydney's magic miles of motor car dealers. Both police and criminals attract groupies. Jones was a crim groupie. He liked to drink with the crims, listen to their stories, and buy them drinks and dinner. He could bask in their badness. To get attention, and to give himself what he mistakenly thought of as street cred, he bought himself a gun. Clint Eastwood's final Dirty Harry movie, *Sudden Impact*, had just hit the cinemas and the magnum, 'the most powerful handgun in the world', had titillated both crooks and cops alike. SWOS had acquired a few of the guns to see how they went operationally. In one of their earlier outings, they had opened fire on a bloke who was responsible for an extortion attempt on Coles supermarkets. He was a bit of a copycat, basing his scam on the work of the Woolworths bomber, Larry Burton Danielson, the former owner of a nightclub in Manly frequented by some of the Manly detectives. Burton wasn't too successful and got caught. The Manly detectives flushed briefly and said little. The Coles bomber wasn't so lucky.

He lured the detectives bearing the ransom up to a remote hillside on the Bells Line of Road in the Blue Mountains, and laid a few booby traps as a precaution. When the lads arrived to make the handover, with one detective secreted in the boot of the Valiant they were using, they broke out the Eastwood specials and opened fire. Booby traps and armed crooks don't engender goodwill in a detective, and they shot to kill, which was the usual practice. Trick shots are best left to film cowboys; just point at the biggest target and pull the trigger. The guns were so weighty that instead of the bullets hitting him in the trunk, they hit him lower than intended. The Coles bomber ended up auditioning for castrato roles in the Long Bay men's choir.

In nightclubs, Harvey Jones would whip out his new firearm and fire a few shots into the ceiling. Jones also befriended Neddy Smith, who didn't mind having a mate hanging around who would buy him drinks. When Jones learned that Rogerson was a mate of Smith's, he reckoned they could do some business together.

According to Smith, when he suggested this to Rogerson, Rogerson replied: 'He is a fool, Ned, but a fool and his money are easily parted. A fool's money spends the same as the next guy's. If you want to do the business yourself without bringing anyone else into it, then it's a go.' Harvey Jones was delighted.

A little later, Neddy and his wife, Debra, and a group of friends including Harvey Jones, were at the very fashionable Coachman restaurant in Redfern, a stone's throw from the Police Academy. Just for laughs, Smith called Rogerson, who was working the night shift at Darlinghurst. He turned up at the restaurant with a few young detectives in tow. On seeing them walk in, Jones turned 'the colour of bad shit', Smith said, before realising it was a social call, not a business one. They drank through to 4 am. Jones, now in on the joke, spent about $2000 on Moët & Chandon.

A fee of $70,000 was required to make Harvey Jones's problems go away. When Smith rang him on the morning of 18 May, he was after the down-payment of $10,000. The threat of upsetting Rogerson was sufficient to make Jones pay up. Rogerson managed to get out of his court commitment, and he, Smith and Openshaw split the ten grand over a long 'hair of the dog' lunch at the Sydney dining institution Dimitri's Five Doors. At least it was in the Darlinghurst patrol area.

When Openshaw was later questioned about his regular social get-togethers with Neddy Smith, and was asked, 'Did it ever strike you as being an awkward situation when you were doing this sort of thing?', he replied: 'Not at the time, no, but it was just a way of encouraging people to be more open in your company.' In addition to his duties at Darlinghurst, Openshaw was a negotiator for SWOS.

The deal wouldn't be completed. Harvey Jones and his weapon got into a spot of trouble shortly thereafter. The venue was Sheila's Disco, in North Sydney, on 14 July. The place was busy through to the early hours and was very popular with detectives from North Sydney and with the crew of wireless car D/E which operated on the north side. Wireless cars were part of the detective tradition. Two detectives from each district were supplied with a car and a driver, and tasked to look after serious crime that happened in their district during the night. The wireless car for D/E district kept an eye on things from the harbour to Palm Beach and as far west as Ryde. Jones had gone to Sheila's with a crook known as 'Bob the Basher'. Big-noting himself as usual, Jones opened fire on the chandeliers.

The second in charge of North Sydney detectives was Ron Daly, who wasn't liked or trusted by anyone on the force. Daly was also well acquainted with Smith and wasn't too happy about having a nightclub on his patch shot up by one of Neddy's mates. He told Smith, 'He's off [dead] when I get my hands on him.' Tim Bristow – a former copper, private eye and retired gangster – had 'See you off' painted on the side of his boat. He was the only one who found it funny.

Smith was called to negotiate a truce, but as Neddy would allege, he had found that cash was the best way to appease

Daly. A few days later, Smith arranged to meet Jones at the Star Hotel in Alexandria. Before heading off, Smith alleged that he met with Daly at a coffee shop across the road from the North Sydney Police Station. Jones was offering $30,000, he said, to avoid being charged with possessing and discharging a firearm. The cash payment would see the prosecution evidence become so muddled, a conviction would be impossible.

Daly agreed to the figure. 'Take every fucking penny [he] has and tell him what I said. I never want to see him again,' he told Smith

Harvey Jones wasn't seen again. He didn't even make it to the meeting at the Star. Neddy Smith became a leading suspect on what was a reasonably long list. When hauled in for an interview, Smith allegedly asked the detective, 'Will I need a lawyer for this? It is all shit.' The detective replied, 'There's no problem. Roger has vouched for you. Just pop in when you can and I will get you to sign a formal denial of the allegation. That's all that will come of it.'

12

A DYING DEPOSITION

At the end of 1983, I was asked to volunteer for transfer from the Fraud Squad to Internal Affairs, where I would be working again with Josh Wilson, my former boss at Manly Detectives when I was on A List. This was an offer I couldn't refuse, and which I was happy to accept. I wanted to escape from the Fraud Squad.

After it had dawned on me that the Fraud Squad had a few less than reputable members, it became evident that I wasn't a 'team player'. My occasional partner, whose nickname was 'Inspector Clouseau', once said to me: 'Here at the Fraud Squad the rules of evidence don't apply.' It was a good time to leave.

Internal Affairs had undergone a transformation a few years before I arrived. As usual, it was a political response to a few mutterings by the public and in parliament. As window dressing, the staff levels were boosted to give the place an 'edge'. Unfortunately, many of the new senior staff were former general duties police or from specialist areas such as the Prosecuting Branch. Their knowledge of criminal investigation was pretty rudimentary; however, increasing the staff levels gave the public the perception that police were serious about their housekeeping. The critics were temporarily stifled; the best they could muster was the hoary old argument against police investigating police.

The reality of Internal Affairs was very different. The avalanche of allegations – from minor infractions through to loading, verballing (more formally known as conspiracy to pervert the course of justice, perjury, and so on) and other criminal practices – weren't, on the whole, vigorously investigated. A complaint had to be in writing. If it wasn't, it wouldn't be investigated. The next step was to see the complainant and take a statement. Any reluctance on their part and the matter would be buried by an eloquent report suggesting that the complainant's heart wasn't in it, or they were so dodgy they had minimal credibility. Internal Affairs weren't always subtle in their approach, so if you had already been monstered by the cops, the last thing you wanted was to be monstered by Internal Affairs. Complaints were often withdrawn. This was called 'conciliation'.

If the case had some merit, and the complainant wouldn't go away, then it was investigated. But not with a great degree of energy. The next step, if the subject of the complaint was a detective, or former detective or a 'good bloke', was to call a trusted mate or superior to give the subject a 'heads up'. The 'heads up' was usually a discreet phone call, or a beer somewhere quiet away from the observant eyes of fellow police. The Internal Affairs source would disclose details of the complaint. The subject of it then had time to get his or her story straight before Internal Affairs came calling. A visit for a formal interview would follow. If the subject was on holidays or on sick leave, then you had to wait. If there were criminal charges pending against the complainant, then you would wait until they were finalised. Basically, we did a lot of waiting. It took a real effort to get into strife with Internal Affairs.

Doing something stupid, such as being caught red-handed or pleading guilty, was one of the few ways you could get into trouble.

If things looked really bad for a copper, we would seek legal advice and consent of the commissioner to charge him. But even then, there were ways to escape prosecution. The copper could be retired as medically unfit, as a result of a sudden illness, the flaring up of an old work-related injury, or stress. Once an officer was declared medically unfit, any investigation into his or her conduct would cease. They would disappear into the private sector with a pension for life, without further ado. Squawks from the complainants were largely ignored.

Overseeing the complaint process was the New South Wales ombudsman, who had the power to review and reopen investigations. His staff were all well-educated, politically correct public servants, many with law degrees. They had even less chance of finding their way to the truth than the non-detectives at Internal Affairs. The police considered the ombudsman to be little more than a yappy little terrier that snapped at their heels. The occasional nip around the ankle was annoying, but it wouldn't ruin their day.

I lasted at Internal Affairs until mid-1986, but within my first six or so months it became clear both to myself and my superiors that I had the wrong attitude. I was all in favour of investigating and, if appropriate, having corrupt police appear before the courts.

When I volunteered to be seconded to the ombudsman's office to advise on investigations, my superiors were pleased to see the back of me but also curious as to why I would volunteer to work with a potential enemy of the police force. It was seen as a serious cultural breach.

On completion of my secondment, I was sent back to

147

Internal Affairs, though I was no longer trusted there to 'do the right thing'. After a few months of doing very little, I was sent to Central Detectives, back in temporary premises at the old hat factory in Surry Hills. In October 1986, my resignation was on my boss's, Vince Rynne's, desk and I had a new job waiting in the private sector.

My decision to leave the police force had been building for quite some time, but it was an incident involving Roger Rogerson that was the final catalyst.

This incident, which could be considered Rogerson's fourth major error of judgment during his career as a detective with the NSW Police, led to charges being laid against him, though the jury that heard the case declined to convict him on those charges.

On 6 June 1984, Detective Senior Constable Michael Drury was at his home in the modest North Shore suburb of Chatswood. It was a quiet area, with tree-lined streets, meticulously tended gardens and solid middle-class brick houses dating from the early 1900s. It boasted an excellent regional shopping hub and good schools. The local cops were kept busy dealing with motor accidents, shoplifters caught at Westfield Shopping Centre, and break and enters perpetrated by lads visiting from Sydney's more westerly suburbs.

At about 6.15 pm on that winter evening, Drury was in his kitchen, pottering about. Moments earlier he had finished feeding his three-year-old daughter. With no warning, two gunshots shattered the window, the bullets striking Drury in the chest and abdomen. Always aim for the biggest target, police are taught, and the unknown gunman did just that. Drury was raced to the nearby Royal North Shore Hospital.

His mates from the police were quickly at his side, offering blood for the numerous transfusions he would need.

Drury's condition was still precarious on 9 July when the investigating police, Detective Sergeant Les Knox, Detective Sergeant Barry Smith and Detective Senior Constable Ken Bowditch, paid him a visit. They were an interesting team. Knox was an old friend of Drury's, and Bowditch would later be involved in an investigation into a collection of stolen paintings, one of which, a Dobell, was bought by Murray Farquhar for a tidy sum from a bloke in a pub. An old line, but in this case a true one. Murray, though protesting his innocence, was arrested and subsequently acquitted for having possession of the painting. Murray later told me that while he was being interviewed, Bowditch showed him my old police identity photo and asked if I was the bloke in the pub. I wasn't; however, I was doing a spot of private work on the case. Bowditch's wires were a bit crossed. He also lent his investigative talents to the name of Rugby League in Coffs Harbour when allegations were made in early 2004 about the conduct of visiting Sydney teams the Roosters and the Bulldogs.

In the month between the shooting and the visit, rumours had been flying thick and fast in the NSW Police. The unkind would suggest that arses were being covered; others would argue that the investigation was being both diligent and objective. Les Knox would later end up as a defence witness for Rogerson when he faced charges that came out of the shooting and its prelude. There were precedents, after all, for coppers appearing for the defence.

According to Knox's recollection when appearing for the defence, the conversation with Drury went something like this:

Knox: Have you got any idea who shot you and why you were shot?

Drury: I don't know who shot me but I'm sure it has to do with [Alan] Williams and [Brian] Hansen from Melbourne.

Knox: Have you got any other idea why you were shot?

Drury: No.

Knox: For Christ sake, Mick, if you have copped a quickie or you've been rooting out of school, tell me?

Drury: Honestly, Les, nothing like that has happened. I would tell you if it had.

Knox: A Detective Sergeant Inkster from Newcastle [not Bob 'The Snake' Inskter] has told McDonald [Angus McDonald, then acting chief of the CIB and a mate of Roger's], that he has an informant that has alleged that you accepted a sum of money and have not fulfilled your obligations. Also that you have been rooting out of school.

Drury: That isn't true.

Knox: Have you ever received any offers in relation to the Melbourne job?

Drury: About 18 months ago [detectives] Lewis Roussos and Neville Smith told me that Roger Rogerson wanted to see me. I saw Roger and he told me there was between $25,000 and $35,000 if I would give evidence to assist McLure [Alan David Williams].

Knox: Did you reject the offer?

Drury: Yes.

Knox: Was there anything else?

Drury: About 3 months before the shooting Rogerson saw me again and offered between $15,000 and

> $25,000 if I would give evidence that would
> assist. I again told him no. About a fortnight
> before the shooting Roger was in the Drug Squad
> room and made a similar offer. I told him I was
> not interested.

Knox: Is that the last you heard?

Drury: No, I received at least two phone calls a day from
> Roger. The last was on the Friday before I was
> shot. He asked me for my home phone number.

Drury's recollection of the conversation differed from Knox's.
A devoted family man, he said he would have recalled allegations that he had been involved in any sexual escapades. His
recollection was that he had told the detectives at his bedside
that he wanted to tell them something, but that they were to
promise never to disclose what he had to say. 'I asked them to
go and see Roger Rogerson to ask him to go through his friend
[in Melbourne] to find out, if he could, about Williams and
who Williams got to shoot me and then I revealed the whole
lot to them . . . I really can't remember what prompted me to
say it.'

Apparently, Drury, while working as an undercover detective at the Drug Squad, had found himself in Melbourne,
where he met the heroin dealer Alan David Williams. In
early 1982, Robert Richardson, a Sydney-based heroin
dealer, had introduced a Sydney buyer to some of his mates
in Melbourne, including Drury, and to one Brian Carl
Hansen. A deal was agreed. At around 9 pm on 4 March,
Drury (with $110,000 in his possession) left the Old
Melbourne Inn with Hansen. The money was to make a
heroin buy. Out on the street they met a bloke Drury would

later identify as Williams. Williams also used the name 'McLure'. Williams went to his car and pulled out a package containing around 300 grams of heroin.

Drury then gave a signal and police swooped on the scene. But things didn't go according to plan. Williams jumped back in the car and fled, taking the heroin with him. He was later caught in Adelaide and extradited to Victoria. Richardson was tracked down and arrested in August of the same year. Williams, Richardson and Hansen ended up sharing the dock on charges of conspiring to traffic heroin.

Drury's evidence was central to the prosecution's case. By the time Rogerson allegedly approached him, Drury had given evidence in the lower court and the matter had been kicked upstairs for trial. Not unlike in the case of the Chapmans, the prosecution could easily be persuaded to 'run dead'. All Drury would have to do was bugger up his evidence. Reasonable doubt would be established, and Williams would walk free.

At Rogerson's subsequent trial for attempting to bribe Drury, Drury would give evidence that Rogerson invited him up to the Darlinghurst Police Station, where he told him: 'That bloke Alan Williams you have got charged in Melbourne, I've got a friend who is a friend of his and they are prepared to pay 15 to 25,000 dollars for Williams to get off.' Drury replied, 'I can't do anything. I am the only one who can give evidence against him. Under no circumstances [will I] take any money off anyone. Say no. All I can do is go to Melbourne and give my evidence and he will have to take pot luck.'

The problem for Rogerson, whose influence obviously now extended into Victoria, was that he was being thwarted by an honest man.

Three days after his chat with Knox and his mates, Drury's

condition worsened. He would have to undergo surgery, and feared he wouldn't survive it. John Abernethy, a chamber magistrate and later the state coroner, was summoned to Drury's hospital bedside, from where Drury made a statement. Depositions made in such circumstances, where the person doesn't expect to live to appear in court and has nothing to gain from lying, carry considerable weight when used in evidence.

In his deposition, Drury recalled his conversation with Knox, putting Rogerson right in the firing line for an attempted bribe and, most likely, one would have thought, the shooting. The next morning, the deposition arrived at Internal Affairs, where it would be the final nail in the coffin as far as my faith in the police force was concerned. Drury's shooting had been very much on the mind of every copper in New South Wales. One of our own had been shot, and shot in his home with his wife and kids nearby. It was unheard of. Despicable. God help the shooter when we caught up with him!

Detective Chief Inspector George Shiel, a usually quiet and affable man, was grey-faced and grave as he passed Drury's deposition around the group of us who had gathered in his office, drinking coffee. We read it, and shook our heads. 'Fuck,' we all said. Shiel then shook his head and said, 'It *can't* be Roger, he's too good a bloke.' As I looked across to the Kings Cross skyline to the east, I thought, 'Shit, I've got to get out of here!' Taxi driving would be an improvement on a career with the NSW Police, I felt.

Detective Superintendent 'Black' Angus MacDonald was appointed to head the investigation. He was assisted by Detective Sergeant Dennis West. MacDonald was an interesting choice. Having one of the most senior investigators in the state, and a man with a fine record, head the inquiry looked good. MacDonald was built like a brick outhouse. He was one of those blokes that looked as though bullets would bounce off them. Unsmiling, somewhat lacking in humour, levity and interpersonal skills, he fitted the mould of the tough, relentless detective. He would have been a perfect choice, apart from his long history with Rogerson. They had worked together at Central years before, followed by stints in SWOS and in various squads. Both were hard men of the CIB. It wouldn't exactly be an objective investigation.

MacDonald set up shop in an office beside mine, where he spent quite a bit of time poring over paperwork, talking on the phone, and wandering across Hyde Park to the CIB in the Remington Centre. He was elusive most lunchtimes. Not a lot of shoe leather was worn down in the investigation. Dennis West did a lot of fetching and carrying under MacDonald's direction. He became a dab hand at making the coffee.

In 1986, Angus MacDonald was interviewed by Eric Strong, a slow-talking, easy-going country bloke who was one of the smartest detectives in the force. He had been brought into Internal Affairs to smarten things up and get rid of the 'CIB taint'. MacDonald told Strong that he would 'try until the day I am dead to find out who shot him [Drury] and I hope that [is] the attitude of a lot of other members of the Police Force'. Well, the case is still 'unsolved', and it's my view that MacDonald didn't try too hard.

*

It would be unfair to imply that Rogerson was the man squeezing the trigger outside the kitchen window at the Drury family home. He was elsewhere and with an alibi. But attempting to murder a policeman isn't something that happens by whim or accident. You need a reason and a plan. While Drury had been in some tight spots, the only motivation he could think of for the attempt on his life was the Melbourne incidents, and Rogerson's chats. In my mind that's good enough to consider Rogerson as the chief suspect for 'conspiracy to murder', which carried the same penalty as murder.

In my own career, the Drury/Rogerson affair found me at a moral crossroads. In police parlance, it was time for me to 'shit or get off the pot'. When Mick Drury returned to active duty following his convalescence, he wouldn't find life very easy after pointing a finger at one of the force's own, I knew. It wasn't a fate I fancied sharing.

At a hearing a few years later into the allegation that Rogerson attempted to bribe Drury, Chester Porter QC, the doyenne of the Sydney criminal bar, appeared for Rogerson. Porter relished his nickname 'The Funnel Web'. He was considered to be a brilliantly effective and ruthless cross-examiner. After employing some initial bullying tactics aimed at shaking Drury's composure and damaging his credibility with the jury, Porter made much play of why Drury had kept quiet about his meetings with Rogerson, and the alleged offer of a bribe, up until he gave his deposition from his hospital bed.

'Why would an honest policeman keep that to himself?' he asked the jury. Then he offered them an answer: 'The reason he didn't report Rogerson is because there was nothing to report.' It was smart tactics, but bore no relation to the facts.

Drury had seen what had happened to others in the force who had opened their mouths. He was a detective who had operated on the very edge when working undercover. He knew of Rogerson's power and the esteem in which he was held. More importantly, he knew that the only body he could have taken his case to, Internal Affairs, leaked like a sieve. It would have been simpler to paint a target on his back. He also had the welfare of his wife and family to consider. There was no one he could safely tell.

Two years later, Bob Shepherd, head of the recently established Internal Security Unit (ISU), a body that could investigate on its own motion, rather than by written complaint, commented that New South Wales was the most corrupt police force in the country – if not the world. The Drury inquiry was seemingly stonewalled by MacDonald. There appeared to be no will to investigate the allegations against Rogerson properly. Neither Internal Affairs nor the CIB seemed keen to do anything. Indeed, MacDonald ordered investigators not to interview Rogerson, and discounted him as a suspect in the shooting. He said of this decision, 'I completely disregarded my previous association and/or friendship with Rogerson.'

I went as far as discussing my concerns with a close friend at the CIB, who had his own concerns about other dodgy occurrences there, and we spoke off the record with *National Times* journalist Wendy Bacon. An article that appeared in the *Sydney Morning Herald* some years later said:

In 1984 two detectives told Bacon they were disturbed
that allegations of police bribery against Rogerson were
not being investigated. Without naming names Bacon
wrote a story on November 9 1984 saying that a dying
detective, Michael Drury, had made a statement in
which he alleged another detective had tried to bribe
him.

While most crime and police reporting of the day involved
crime reporters 'pissing in the pockets' of police, and vice
versa, Fairfax's *National Times* was on the front foot.
Journalists such as Brian Toohey, Marian Wilkinson and
Wendy Bacon were doing real investigative journalism and
putting themselves on the line. They were giving the NSW
Police a good, hard shake, and the public was listening.
Their coverage of Rogerson and his mates was instrumental
in changing the way the public and police viewed corruption. Copies of the *National Times* would be snapped up as
soon as they hit the newsstands by coppers eager to see
which of their colleagues were the latest to be in the firing
line.

But despite the scandalous revelations, the message didn't
seem to be sinking in and the culture of the NSW Police
remained largely unchanged.

13

WENDY BACON AND
THE NATIONAL TIMES

Wendy Bacon, born in 1946, was the daughter of a Melbourne doctor. She studied history at Melbourne University. In 1967 she moved to Sydney and took up a teaching position at St Mary's Convent in Liverpool. A year later she swapped colleagues wearing habits for colleagues wearing yarmulkes when she took a post as assistant to the editor of the *Jewish Times*. Around that time she began part-time study in sociology and did a bit of tutoring at the University of New South Wales. The lure of ink on hot metal proved to be strong, and she was soon taking a swing at the conservative side of Australian life with pieces published in the UNSW student newspaper *Tharunka*.

Under Askin, the New South Wales government didn't welcome dissent. When protesters blocked city streets during the visit to Sydney of US President Lyndon Johnson in October 1966, Askin ordered his motorcade to 'run the bastards over'. It was only a matter of time before Wendy Bacon would end up in strife. In 1970 she was arrested for exhibiting an 'obscene' publication. (Dressed in a nun's habit, she had protested outside a court house by carrying a sign that said, 'I was fucked by the finger of God.') She was sent to prison 'on remand' for a week.

The budding journalist spent her brief sojourn in gaol listening to her fellow prisoners' stories of bashings, bribes, verbals and loads. She emerged from prison determined to right a few wrongs. The curious relationship between some police and the developer Frank Theeman at Victoria Street, in Kings Cross, also took her interest even before the disappearance of Juanita Nielsen. In 1975, Bacon began studying law. She graduated in 1979, but the Supreme Court declined to admit her to the ranks of the legal profession because of her previous arrest. She wasn't considered to be a 'fit and proper person'. Years later, in another attempt to be admitted, her adversary at the hearing was Chester Porter QC.

Wendy Bacon struck my colleague and me as the obvious person to talk to about our concerns. I purloined a copy of the Drury deposition prior to our first meeting, which I set up during a phone call made well away from the office and the frequently used public phone at the newsagents downstairs from the CIB. We arranged to meet that evening at the Student Prince Hotel in Parramatta Road, Camperdown, just across the road from Sydney University.

When my mate and I arrived at the pub, dressed casually and hoping not to look like coppers, we made the classic mistake of stopping as we entered the bar and surveying the room from back to front. Unfortunately, instead of being filled with young student types, as we had anticipated, the public bar was favoured by lads who looked like they may have had a few brushes with the law.

One wag yelled, 'Shit, it's the coppers!' Everyone in the room stopped talking. Some rough-looking blokes stopped their pool game and stared at us. So much for our attempt to be discreet. We skulked off into the ladies lounge on the other side of the pub. Wendy Bacon – as was her habit, we would soon learn – was late, leaving my mate and me feeling self-conscious in that unfamiliar part of the pub.

When she finally arrived, a little flustered and very sensibly apprehensive, we got down to business. After talking about our dilemma, she softened. The copy I had made of Michael Drury's deposition sealed the deal. It soon became apparent that Bacon had a couple of other well-connected sources in the NSW Police. Years later, Detective Chief Superintendent Ernest Septimus Shepard (known as 'The Good Shepard') would confide to me that he and Bacon had chatted frequently.

Bacon used our information, along with other bits and pieces, and wrote a few articles, including one published a few weeks later entitled 'Detective Rogerson and the Police Barbecue Set'. Wendy Bacon and the *National Times* had declared war.

With the cat now well and truly out of the bag, those at the top of the NSW Police hierarchy had a very engaging problem on their hands. Mick Drury's deposition would carry great weight at law. He was a decorated and respected young detective; winner of the Peter Mitchell Award for exceptional police work, and a man who had been shot in the line of duty. But his finger was pointing directly at another Peter Mitchell Award winner. A man many considered to be 'the best of the best'. A mate to many. A good neighbour and good family man. It must have given the bosses an ulcer. In the end, the faint smell that had gathered around Roger Rogerson in his last days at the Armed Hold-up Squad may have been what tipped them over the edge.

There were no independent witnesses, yet there was

'reasonable cause to suspect'. Police are also quite fond of the saying 'discretion is the better part of valour' and so, on 28 November 1984, Rogerson was served with a summons asking him to appear at court on 10 December, on charges of attempting to bribe Michael Drury. No mention was made of his alleged involvement in the attempted murder, but it was a start down the right road.

The decision to charge Rogerson had been made rather easier for those at the top after he was involved in a number of incidents that had alienated some of his younger and keener colleagues at Darlinghurst Station. Once he monstered a plainclothes lad named Robert John Williams who had been investigating allegations of drug sales at and around the Tradesmans Arms Hotel, on the corner of Liverpool and Palmer streets in East Sydney, a very dangerous little pub just down the hill from the police station.

Rogerson was unhappy when Williams started arresting some of the crooks who hung around the pub, and ordered the junior policeman to leave the area alone. Williams didn't take any notice. In July 1984, Rogerson came straight to the point: 'I'll load you up and set you up and see you out of the job.' Williams, knowing there would be no point in complaining to his other superiors or to Internal Affairs, said to Rogerson: 'Go ahead and do it. I'll go to *Willesee* [the forerunner of *A Current Affair*]. I'll go to the newspapers.' He had nicely called Rogerson's bluff, but soon found himself transferred off the streets and into duty at the Darlinghurst Court complex. Rogerson still carried plenty of clout.

A month later, on 15 August, Rogerson was involved in another incident, following a very long lunch at the Korea House restaurant in Kings Cross. The lads had gathered to farewell colleagues who were heading off to the Los Angeles Olympics. At around 8 pm – it was a *very* long lunch –

Rogerson and a mate, Laurie Burgess, got involved in a scuffle in the bar. Rogerson was accused of giving the proprietor, Mrs Un Sook Pak, a 'really heavy' slap across the face, with his open palm, according to the night manager, Matthew Chung. Rogerson then ordered Burgess to arrest Mrs Pak, presumably for assaulting *him*. When Chung intervened, he was told he would be arrested as well. Rogerson, whom Chung described as having had 'far too much to drink ... his voice was shaking', then demanded that Chung prove he was living in Australia legally. Some clearer heads intervened and put an end to what was heading towards a very big mess. Rogerson's self-control was clearly slipping.

Police Internal Security investigated the matter in December that year, and Rogerson and Burgess were summonsed for assault in February 1985. Mrs Pak's husband tried to have the charges dropped after someone popped around for a word in his ear.

It was the usual practice for very senior detectives to spend a short time back in uniform to gather some experience at station level. This would stand them in good stead when they were considered for promotion to the commissioned ranks. It was one of the early benefits of merit-based promotion, which was slowly seeping into the old-fashioned structure on to which the NSW Police held with grim determination. It was therefore decided to 'flick' Rogerson to uniform duties at Bankstown, nice and close to home. Joy and the kids would see a lot more of him. At least, that was the theory.

On 18 November 1984, just ten days before a summons would be placed in his hands, Rogerson got the news that his career in criminal investigation had hit a brick wall. The blow came on the cusp of his being appointed as a sergeant first class. He wasn't the only one to feel the chill breeze of change that day. John Brown, his boss at Darlinghurst and sometime lunch and drinks partner, was also heading back to a suit of blue, along with four other senior detectives.

The media's growing interest in the career of Roger Rogerson made his transfer newsworthy. A spokesman for Commissioner Avery explained that the reason for the transfer was an excess of sergeants at the CIB. Rogerson was on holiday when the orders for his transfer were made.

His first day in blue was scheduled as 16 December. However, the service of the summons for a criminal charge meant that Rogerson was suspended from duty, without pay, until the case was finalised. (So much for the presumption of innocence.) Rogerson was called in from holidays to Police Headquarters in College Street, the summons was served, and he handed in his warrant card and appointments (gun and handcuffs). When he left headquarters that day he was, for the first time in 25 years, without the powers of a police officer. For a bloke who was in the game for power, it was a crushing blow.

The publication of Wendy Bacon's 'Barbecue Set' article one day after Rogerson had been served with a summons got the besieged Wran government's nose right out of joint. They reckoned it was in contempt of court. The article implied that Rogerson was 'a murderer, a basher, involved in illegal drug activity and a suborner of witnesses'. Which wasn't far off the mark. Furthermore, they argued that the article would be 'gravely prejudicial' to Rogerson in his committal proceedings and trial. Bacon 'holds a law degree', Malcolm McGregor QC would later intone to the court, implying that she should play by their rules. He omitted to mention that she had been barred from practising in New

South Wales by the old boys' club of the state Bar. They hadn't liked the cut of her jib. Chester Porter QC had, of course, appeared for the Bar Association in the proceedings that stymied Bacon's legal career. The Court of Appeal eventually agreed with Fairfax's view and the matter failed.

Rogerson then decided to have a crack at the prosecution himself via the media. He once said, 'The journalist is a grubby misfit who delights in hounding people.' He then warmed to his subject, saying of the Australian media that it had become 'judge, jury and executioner. I've got no time for the media, the press in particular, especially the *Herald*.' The irony that he himself was being accused of having taken the law into his own hands was obviously lost on him.

Rogerson's public antics from this time would put him squarely in the spotlight.

In the first outing of his press campaign, he found an ally in a very receptive journalist, C. J. McKenzie of the *Sunday Telegraph*. His skills in the witness box transferred smoothly to the media. Obviously, he had a few problems to surmount. At his home in Condell Park, he told McKenzie:

> As you can see I don't have a two storey mansion or a swimming pool and I don't own a yacht . . . I was with the Armed Hold Up Squad for 10 years and there was plenty of overtime and my wife has gone back to work; she works for her father. My wife and I, like any young couple, had a battle in the early days. She stopped work while the kids were young, but now they're grown up she's gone back to work. You don't have to be a pauper to be a policeman.

When asked how he felt on the day he handed over his gun and handcuffs, Rogerson managed a return to form when he replied, 'I feel like a Tooheys or a Four X coming on.' He then added: 'The summons was a shock. But being stood down without pay was a greater shock. This has been a devastating blow to my wife and kids and every other member of our families.' At least his father had been spared. Owen Rogerson had died the year before. It would have been a dreadful blow to the proud old working-class man.

In what was rapidly becoming a very stylish performance, Rogerson cranked up the family values line. His mother Mabel was 'a very religious person', he said.

> She's been praying to God for me every day. She rings me up every day and tells me God will look after me. My wife and the two girls believe in it [religion] and are regular churchgoers. My two girls play the organ and the piano at Sunday school. They are both very talented girls.

Before leaving the subject of God and the family, he added: 'I'm not into religion. I have my own beliefs and a code of living.'

He then commented on the new regime in the NSW Police under Avery, producing a backhander that placed him firmly in the 'old school' of policing:

> I like to see the baddies put in gaol. I like to see the streets clean. I don't buy bullshit about needing a university degree to be able to do the job. I don't accept that we need academics to tell us how to do our job. I believe in catching them [criminals] giving them a whack and charging them.

In closing, Rogerson told McKenzie that he checked his car every morning before leaving home to ensure the car hadn't been 'wired for sound – like bang!' He confided that only his close friends knew his address. In fact, his address was on the electoral rolls, Land Titles Office records, local council records, on the record cards at Darlinghurst Police Station – but Rogerson wasn't one to let the truth stand in the way of a good story.

McKenzie dutifully wrote up the interview, adding that Rogerson's middle name, Caleb, was old Hebrew for 'Bold One' or 'Faithful Brother'. It was a nice touch. Rogerson's mates were quoted as saying that he didn't talk about the people he'd killed. 'It's his job,' one said. 'If he let it get to him he'd be finished. But I can tell you, deep down it tears the guts out of him.'

Rogerson was on a roll, and next tried his hand at radio. He told 2GB's Mike Carlton that he was 'very, very much surprised' he had been summonsed. Two weeks before, Angus MacDonald at CIB Headquarters had told him 'there was absolutely no reason for any charges'.

Rogerson's media work slipped through without even a murmur from the attorney general, the state's legal figurehead, but his career as one of the most powerful men in the NSW Police was finished. The knowledge tore at his guts. Around this time he sought counsel from noted Sydney society psychiatrist Dr Harry Bailey. Bailey's name would later hit the national headlines when his bizarre treatments conducted at the Chelmsford Hospital on Sydney's genteel North Shore became known.

14

FROM 'DETECTIVE' TO 'DEFENDANT'

Chester Porter QC, leading light of the New South Wales criminal bar and no fan of Wendy Bacon, stood up from the bar table at the Local Court in Castlereagh Street, Sydney (now the Downing Centre), on 10 December 1984 and announced that he was appearing for the defendant, Roger Caleb Rogerson. It would be the beginning of a new career for Rogerson as a 'defendant'. Christmas that year was a pretty miserable occasion for the Rogerson family. But 1985 was going to be a whole lot worse.

In February, Rogerson was committed for trial on the bribery charges. He tried to overcome his depression by taking flying lessons. Instead of looking skyward from his Condell Park backyard as small planes clawed their way into the sky from the Bankstown aerodrome, Rogerson could now be one of them. His mate Bill Duff, then of the Homicide Squad, held a commercial pilot's licence. Duff was also under scrutiny for his relationship with Neddy Smith. What better way for two mates to escape their earthly travails? Duff would end up, after getting into a further bit of strife, as licensee of the Iron Duke Hotel in Alexandria, a pub that Smith by then owned in what was a grimy inner-city suburb choked with cars, industry and low-income housing. The ICAC would look into allegations Duff had been using his piloting skills to fly illegal cargo into Australia from Papua New Guinea. There was no truth in the scurrilous rumour that a top PNG minister had swung the prop and wished Duff well.

Rogerson's medical examination for his pilot's licence was performed by the entrepreneurial Dr Geoffrey Edelsten, owner of the Sydney Swans Australian Rules football team, pink helicopters and flashy cars, and proponent of dubious debt collection methods. Edelsten, who was well connected to the police, had hired ex-Melbourne hitman, Painter and Docker, and all-round danger to civilised society, Christopher Dale 'Mr Rent-a-kill' Flannery to collect a couple of debts. It turned very, very nasty. Edelsten ended up in gaol. Flannery simply disappeared on or about 9 May 1985 and hasn't been seen since. The coroner decided that he might be dead, and Rogerson was in the queue of suspects. A bad year for Rogerson, but a worse one, it would seem, for Flannery. The memory of Flannery would return to haunt Rogerson a few years later.

Though suspended from duties and, if a police salary was what he relied on, presumably short of cash, Rogerson continued to party. He lunched regularly with Neddy Smith. Cash didn't seem to be a problem, but hiding it was.

The problem Rogerson faced was what to do with the cash that seemed to be coming his way. For all his abilities, he lacked the financial sophistication to handle the volume. He had no desire to live a 'flash' life. He was, like his father, very much a man of simple pleasures. He was also canny enough to avoid having any paper trail that bore his own name. He and Joy had taken out a mortgage on Gleeson Avenue with the Bankstown Permanent Building Society in 1965 and they were still paying that off. A weekender on the Central Coast, bought in Joy's name the previous April, was also both modest and mortgaged. Financially, the Rogersons fitted the profile of the hardworking cop and his family that he had portrayed them as in the *Sunday Telegraph*. But matters took a turn for the worse when Rogerson did something really stupid.

On 21 May 1985, just a month before his trial for bribery was scheduled to begin, he went into the National Australia Bank in York Street, Sydney. It would be his fifth major error of judgment. With him was Morrie Nowytarger, a sort of successful Arthur Daley character (from the television show *Minder*) with fingers in travel, cars and other business pies. Rogerson and Nowytarger had been mates for a dozen years or more. Rogerson was rumoured to have very quietly become a partner in a club run by Morrie's brother in Bondi. Morrie introduced Rogerson to the manager of the National Bank, Robert Lang, who arranged for Rogerson to open two accounts. Although neither account was in his own name, no questions were asked. The names 'Mike Roberts' and 'Robert Tracey', without any forms of identification, were good enough for Lang, who would later be dismissed for misconduct over the deal.

The initial deposits, from a bag of cash, totalled $14,000. Three days later, Rogerson returned, this time with a bag containing $60,000 in cash. More cash arrived a few days later. Rogerson's annual salary prior to his suspension had been just $32,000 before tax. There was then a brief hiatus in the cash deposits while Rogerson focused on his trial, due to begin on 5 June.

Court 17, Sydney District Court, wasn't one of the bone-chillingly cold and decaying sandstone piles in the Hospital

Road complex just behind the Mint. It was a 'new' building tacked on to the complex and a vivid example of the government architect's stunning lack of imagination in the late 1950s/early 1960s. But at least it was warm on that winter morning, and posed less risk of people being brained by bits of plaster falling from the ceiling.

On the Bench was the chief judge of the District Court, Judge Staunton, a small, feisty, no-nonsense type who enjoyed his lofty position. He had a fierce reputation as a judge who was intolerant of legal tricks, and verbose or ill-prepared lawyers. The appeals list in country circuits diminished drastically whenever Staunton turned up instead of the usual judge. His habit of increasing, rather than decreasing, penalties was well known.

Lurking behind the bar table were the well-respected Crown prosecutor Jack Hiatt QC and, on the other end, Chester Porter QC.

On the second day of the trial, Porter gave Michael Drury everything he had. Why hadn't he reported the bribe attempt at the time it had allegedly occurred? Porter suggested that a normal reaction to the offer of a bribe would have been 'How dare you.' To which Drury replied, 'Perhaps 300 years ago.' Porter told the court that a Melbourne magistrate had earlier rejected Drury's identification of Alan Williams. (Williams was finally 'ex officio' indicted after the magistrate's decision, and went straight to trial for possession of heroin.)

Despite Porter's forensic dissection of Drury, the witness managed to score a few points, telling the jury that Williams was dangerous to be around. He was 'very heavy' and allegedly not very happy, as he had 'paid out a lot of money' to escape prosecution. The jury also learned that drug dealing was a serious business indeed, as one of the figures in the case had been found on the roadside about 80 kilometres from Melbourne with two tightly spaced bullet holes in the back of his head. Another bloke, Frank Avery, had been found dead from a heroin overdose. Avery hadn't been a drug user, Drury told the court. After giving his evidence, Drury broke down and left the courtroom in tears.

It is often the case in criminal matters that the accused doesn't give evidence. Why let the prosecutor have a free kick in cross-examination? However, with a witness like Rogerson, the chance of a free kick was greatly reduced. He could equal, if not best, most of the occupants of the bar table, and he knew it.

Rogerson hopped into the box on 11 June, immaculately and conservatively dressed. With the Bible in his right hand, he faced Staunton and swore to 'tell the truth, the whole truth and nothing but the truth'. Joy Rogerson sat quietly in the crowded public gallery. Rogerson answered the questions put to him clearly, thoughtfully and succinctly. He played superbly to the jury, looking them calmly and unflinchingly in the eye as he responded to questions. He denied the allegations one by one. When Hiatt questioned him about his reaction to Drury's deposition, he looked solemn. 'I wouldn't say I was indignant. I knew he was a very sick boy,' he said. It was a performance worthy of an Oscar nomination, at least.

Christopher Dale Flannery finally got a guernsey on 13 June when Hiatt asked Rogerson if Flannery was a gentleman whose house had been hosed with machine-gun fire and who was believed, at least by his wife Kath Flannery, to be dead. Rogerson concurred. 'Yes. I believe he is dead.' He then confirmed that Flannery had indeed been his informant.

Porter decided to impress the jury with Rogerson's handling of informants by asking him about Lennie McPherson. Rogerson confirmed that McPherson's information had been very useful – in particular, for the Homicide Squad and a special taskforce. With a wonderful modesty, he added: 'There would not be another detective within the NSW CIB who has had the experience I have had in talking to criminals and obtaining information from them.' If only the jury had seen Rogerson at work with Neddy Smith at the Covent Garden Hotel after one of their long lunches – drunk, shirts undone, and slapping each other with wads of cash. A novel way of obtaining information.

Rogerson's stellar performance swayed the jury well into the territory of reasonable doubt. It was an interesting tactic to slide Rogerson's character into the courtroom. In most criminal cases the defence avoids the question of character, because as soon as it arises the prosecution can, if armed, head out on a bombing mission. A common example is a person's criminal record. Usually this can't be mentioned until the person has been found guilty and their sentence is being considered. To bring someone's record up in front of a jury would perhaps bias their decisions. One of the exceptions is when the person's character is introduced by their own counsel, or in their response to a question. For example, if the defendant were to say 'I've led a blameless life', in cross-examination the prosecution may then introduce the person's criminal record into evidence.

In Rogerson's case, Porter had a pretty good idea that despite the smell about his client, this was the first time anything said against him had progressed past rumour. And with a witness like Rogerson, he was on pretty safe ground. Porter led him through their version of the 'truth' and kept it neat and concise. There wasn't much room for Hiatt to cross-examine. However, the Crown prosecutor got his chance on the second day of Rogerson's evidence. Hiatt's best shot was to lead in with Rogerson's relationship with Lennie

McPherson. In particular, he had in mind a 'favour' Rogerson had done for the family in sorting an adjournment for McPherson's son, Craig. Asked if he had intervened out of the 'goodness of your heart', Rogerson replied: '[B]ecause he was a criminal that I had known for some years and it is the kind of thing that sometimes a good detective should do to keep in good with a person like McPherson.'

A little later in cross-examination, Hiatt had the chance to experience first-hand Rogerson's skill as a witness. Unfortunately, it didn't do much for his case. On the matter of the Drury shooting, Hiatt began badly by asking Rogerson about an allegation made to him by Assad Rowda. Rogerson told the court that Rowda had complained that Drury had framed him on a heroin charge. Rogerson, being a loyal bloke, had not reported the matter to Internal Affairs. It's one of the quirks of court matters that this was exactly the same allegation Porter had used to diminish Drury's evidence. Yet, Rogerson sailed through it untarnished. Then the bomb bay doors opened. When asked about the identity of Drury's shooter, Rogerson replied: 'I'd love to know that.' And of Drury himself, he said: 'My opinion is that he is obviously a liar; for some reason he decided to make these allegations . . . From what I have heard he is a man that is corrupt and I have heard information that he is a womaniser.'

Rogerson's hero status was driven home when David Riddell, who had grown up in Gleeson Avenue with Rogerson and his family as next-door neighbours, took the stand. The two had been friends for almost twenty years. Rogerson, in the view of this salt-of-the-earth family man, was one of the finest people he had ever met. He was a highly respected neighbour and member of the local community. He lived modestly in an 'immaculately' kept house. When Riddell's mother had died in 1970, the Rogersons were there to help. When the house had needed a coat of paint, or a bit of maintenance that was beyond the skills of old Bill Riddell, Rogerson was there.

'Did he charge anything?' asked Porter.

'No, it was free,' Riddell replied.

Even Joy Rogerson joined the party, being called by Porter to give evidence attesting to her husband's fine work as a father and provider. The fact that Joy was dragged into the proceedings disturbed Drury, who said: 'I was very upset because his wife had to give evidence at the trial. Obviously she was a very fine lady.'

Porter knew that he had the jury in the palm of his hand, and his summing up was a performance piece – theatrical, bitchy, vicious and eloquent. Two prosecution witnesses, detectives in whom Drury had confided his fears, were dismissed as 'Tweedledum and Tweedledee' whose statements, he said, had been 'written in collaboration using exactly the same words'. This one is straight out of the barrister's text-book but, when dragged out in the closing moments of a trial, it can be quite effective. When two police are involved in the same event, the chances are their statements will look similar, as they will talk about the events and compare statements. There is nothing wrong with that, nothing complicit, unless they are attempting to verbal a witness. The idea was to chuck the scent of collusion into the jury's mind.

As mentioned earlier, Porter's final nail was Drury's reason for not reporting the attempt to bribe him when it allegedly occurred: ' . . . because there was nothing to report,' said Porter, thus chucking the truth out the window.

To give him his due, Judge Staunton, in his directions to the jury, did his best to restore some balance. He told them that while Rogerson was putting himself forward as a man of good character, the Crown didn't accept that. In their view, he was 'a manipulator and a fixer of cases . . . a person who has doubtful associations and acts in suspicious ways'. Staunton was spot on the money. He told the jury that when Drury, a young married man, made his deposition, he was both conscious and lucid but knew that his life was in peril. 'In these circumstances do you think he'd tell the truth about what is troubling him or invent a monstrous charge against a fellow officer who has done nothing to him?' And finally, 'Don't leave your common sense outside the door. Quite clearly in this case one of these two detectives is deliberately lying under oath.'

On 18 June, the jury retired to consider its verdict. As was the practice of the time, Rogerson wasn't allowed bail while the jury was deliberating. As the day drew to a close without a decision, Rogerson's thumb was inked, and his print was applied to the back of the documents that committed him to gaol. He was handcuffed and taken to Long Bay's remand centre, where he spent the night under close guard lest a former client might decide to settle an old score. Next morning he was back into cuffs, and into the prison van for the return journey along Anzac Parade and into the city.

That day, despite the judge's advice, the jury found they weren't satisfied that Rogerson had been misbehaving beyond reasonable doubt. He was acquitted.

Michael Drury went back to work at the Drug Squad, where his colleagues didn't exactly rejoice at his return. Rogerson was reinstated, given a uniform and put on the General Duties roster at Bankstown. He was owed seven months' back pay. His delight at being acquitted was shared with the grubby misfits of the press. Telegrams and champagne had flooded in to what the press described as 'his home in the battlers' suburb of Condell Park'. While he might have been on the verge of losing control, he still managed a deft touch as a spin doctor. He quipped, 'I've got enough grog presents to open a shop. I feel terrific – it's better than being in Long Bay. I've been through a lot of trials, but it's no fun being the guest of honour.'

Rogerson's delight, however, was short lived. As he had been awaiting the nod that the jury was about to return, Joy had joined him in the cell area in the basement of the court building. He had taken that time to do a bit of fessing up to his blissfully ignorant wife. In the event that he was convicted and gaoled, he told her, Joy could find plenty of money at the National Bank in the names of Roberts and Tracey. While his motive in telling Joy had been to guarantee some security for his family, the effect was inadvertently to bring his wife into a criminal conspiracy. For the first time in their life together, Joy accepted that some of the rumours and reports about her husband might have substance. It was a turning point in what had been up until then a strong and unconditional relationship.

Even more unfortunately for Rogerson, his confession was overheard. Details of the conversation were reported to Internal Security, a much more secure and diligent unit than the leaky old Internal Affairs. The lads at ISU got busy, and contacted the National Bank where Rogerson had opened the bogus accounts.

For a detective who had spent ten years in the Armed Hold-up Squad, Rogerson should have known that banks use cameras to record everything that occurs in the banking chamber. Which makes it all the more difficult to understand why, on 1 July, Rogerson walked into the bank and closed the Roberts and Tracey accounts. Did the man think he was above the law? Or did he have a death wish?

He collected the proceeds in bank cheques, and then drove

to Penrith, in the west, where he opened accounts in the same names at a Westpac branch. He was accompanied on the jaunt by a mate, Detective Sergeant Bill Tunstall, who introduced him to the manager, Albert Blatch, as was said at Rogerson's trial. When Blatch asked for an occupation for Mr Tracey, Rogerson replied: 'Motor mechanic.' The total of the deposits was $111,116.18.

Rogerson's pleasure at being footloose and affluent took a tumble when he got wind of the ISU's investigation. Even worse, they were working with the Australian Taxation Office. While he might be able to slip and slide around his fellow police, the Tax Office was something well out of his understanding. Rogerson found himself in uncharted waters, and there were a couple of sharks circling. Control was slipping from his grasp and he found himself with a genuine case of stress.

The situation called for some smart thinking. Legal advice from the ever-friendly Val Bellamy wasn't going to be of much use. The matter was too dodgy to take to a straight shooter like Porter. He needed someone smart, worldly and devious. Luckily, he knew a few people like that.

The boy most likely (front row, far left).

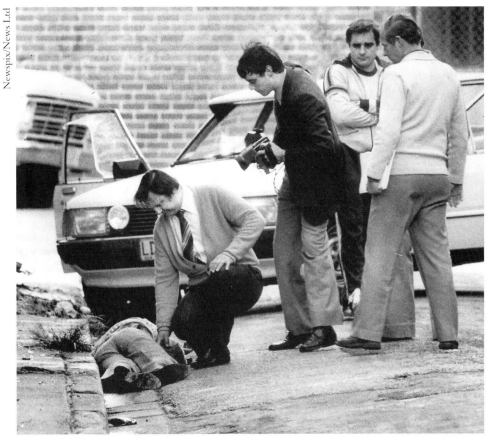

A fateful afternoon liaison. Warren Lanfranchi dead in the gutter of
Dangar Lane . . . Rogerson with his back to the camera.

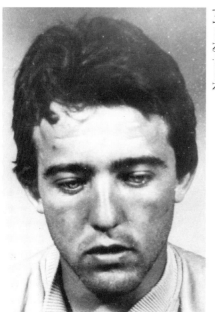

Warren Lanfranchi – beware of
policemen bearing guns.

Sallie-Anne Huckstepp – nemesis.

From Neddy: the life and crimes of Arthur 'Neddy' Smith

A dab hand with an informant – or was that friend.

Newspix/News Ltd

The other life – Roger and Joy at 32 Gleeson Avenue.

Michael Drury – a touch of justice at last.

The disappearing Christopher Dale Flannery.

The safari suit – perfect for all occasions.

A brave face – the Rogerson family, *New Idea*, 1989.

You can take it to the bank! Roger's film debut at the National Australia
Bank in Sydney.

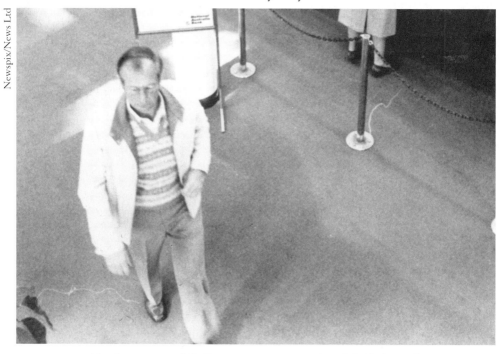

Business over, Mr Rogerson, or was that Mr Roberts?

Roger – never far from the headlines.

In the family business.

NOTICE

Free – for a while, anyway.

15

A MAN NEEDS A HOBBY

Out of his depth and feeling desperate, Rogerson turned to his mates Morrie Nowytarger and Nick Paltos. It wasn't a clever choice. Nowytarger was certainly devious and shifty. But Paltos was a real problem. In his earlier life he had been a migrant success story. One of ten children, he was born in 1940 on the Greek Island of Kastellorizon, a fly speck just off the coast of Turkey. The family migrated to Australia when he was six and settled in Greece's second-largest city, Melbourne. After leaving school, Paltos worked as an electroplater by day and studied at night, finally gaining entrance to university. An exceptionally bright student, he was offered a scholarship to study medicine at the University of New South Wales. Driving cabs and selling flowers kept him in pocket money, much of which was spent at the illegal casinos that were common at the time. He was bright but flawed.

A brilliant physician, Paltos spent twelve years of his career running the casualty department of Sydney Hospital. His work there brought him into contact with many of the police who worked in the inner city. If a copper was sick, hurt on duty or needed a medical certificate to cover a few days off, Nick was your man. If someone had been a little damaged while in custody, Paltos could be relied on to patch them up calmly and discreetly. Politicians, legal eagles, and a smattering of the rich and famous could also swear by Paltos's healing hands.

Unfortunately, his skills as a doctor weren't matched by his skills as a gambler. It was at George Walker's Goulburn Club, a flourishing casino that remained pretty much untouched by police until Merv Beck took over 21 Division in the late 1970s, that he met Nowytarger.

Given his lack of skill, Paltos soon found himself in debt up to his armpits. Nothing legal, aside from a lottery win, would get him out of trouble. He had also had the misfortune to be caught up in an illegal police phone tap back in 1976, chatting to major crime figure, the late George Freeman, who was big in gambling and just about anything else that could turn a quid. He came to very public attention when he was photographed in the members stand at Randwick Racecourse with Freeman and the then chief stipendiary magistrate Murray Farquhar.

In February 1984, Paltos and another inveterate gambler, solicitor Ross Karp, went into business with underworld figure and casino proprietor Graham 'Croc' Palmer to import into Australia $40 million worth of cannabis. Palmer was experiencing severe cash flow problems thanks to Merv Beck and his lads and, more recently, an honest and efficient Gaming Squad. All three men would soon be caught red-handed and collect very long prison sentences.

Rogerson confided his woes to Nowytarger and Paltos. Paltos then chatted to his importer mate, Ross Karp. A bit of legal smarts might come in handy, but, as he assured Karp, it had nothing to do with their drug business. In typical form, business was discussed over lunch, this time at the Bayswater Brasserie in Kings Cross, the dining hot spot of the 1980s. On 21 July, over some of the finest food in Sydney, the lads got down to business. Nowytarger had a plan. He would allege that Rogerson had restored a car for him, and that the car was sold on instalments to Karp. A bill of sale and receipts would be backdated. The cost of Rogerson's work would be 'hobbies' income and thus not taxable. At least, that was the plan.

The car in question was a 1962 Bentley S2 Continental Flying Spur with coachwork by H. J. Mulliner. It was thought to be the only one of its kind in Australia, so the idea of an unskilled tradesman doing work on it borders on the ludicrous. In any case, the car was worth only about $60,000. Rogerson would have to use the hackneyed and utterly discredited explanation, 'race winnings', to account for the balance of the money. Rogerson's skills in commercial matters were definitely not up to scratch. Anyone with half a brain could shoot holes through the story. But after a good lunch, it wasn't easy to be objective.

Karp later reckoned that his mate Paltos had 'prevailed' upon him to help Rogerson. But knowing a cop with Rogerson's reputation could come in handy. After lunch, Karp and Paltos met with Croc Palmer. The cops were listening, thanks to a listening device planted by the federal police in Paltos's car.

> *Palmer*: What did Roger want? You done something for him?
>
> *Paltos*: Fucking oath. Big. The best fucking turn, I tell you.
>
> *Karp*: He got some cash, Croc, right? And he opened up a couple of bodgie bank accounts.
>
> *Paltos*: Morrie's the shiftiest bloke in the world but he's one hundred per cent.

Karp: Opened up two bodgie bank accounts and put a hundred thousand between the accounts. I'm not sure of the exact split up. Right?

Palmer: Yeah.

Karp: What's happened is, ah, Roger's gone to one of the banks to withdraw the money. Right?

Palmer: Yeah.

Karp: In the bodgie name.

Palmer: Yeah.

Karp: Yeah, but they didn't know that the account belonged to Roger.

Paltos: Yes they did.

Karp: No, they found out after they'd photographed him. Well, that's what he told me.

Paltos: Anyway, whenever it is, they photographed him going in to take the money out.

Karp: They recognise him, and they think now that this money is from ill-gotten [interrupted] . . .

Paltos: Drugs. From drugs. Tell the truth.

Karp: Well, he said drugs. Right? OK? Now he went and opened another account at a Penrith bank and re-deposited the money. Right?

Palmer: Right.

Karp: So he's got to explain where the money's come from. Agreed?

Palmer: Right.

Paltos: He comes to me. Somehow, somehow he's got the fucking seventy or sixty thousand dollars he's gotta prove.

Palmer: Right.

Paltos: Right. That's where Rossy comes in.

Paltos then explained in detail that Karp could help, as he

had withdrawn large sums of money on a regular basis that they had used for the drug import business. No one had tumbled to the plan, or so they had thought. Another bloke was restoring a vintage car. What a plan! Another round, perhaps?

Paltos:	I've never seen two happier blokes in my life today, Ross?
Karp:	No, they could have eaten us.
Paltos:	Could have eaten. He said: 'Look, mate, I don't know how to thank you. I just don't know.' I said, 'How the fuck?' He said, 'Take my badge,' didn't he?
Karp:	Yeah.
Paltos:	He said, 'Take me.'
Karp:	No, he said, 'Look, if you were gonna go and rob a bank', and then he says, 'take the badge with you!' [Neddy Smith would have gone green with envy. A green light is one thing, but a green light with a badge was quite another!]

Recollecting Rogerson's gushing thanks caused the merry-makers to tumble about with laughter.

Paltos:	'Take this badge with you,' he says. 'I've got a gun too.'
Karp:	'It might help you.'

On 15 August 1985, just three weeks after the lunch at the Bayswater Brasserie, Palmer, Paltos and Karp were arrested by the Australian Federal Police on drug importation charges. All would plead guilty. Palmer and Karp each got fourteen

years and Paltos twenty. Rogerson's badge and gun would be removed very soon after.

Around the same time, Rogerson's dealings in the banking world became public. He found himself and his business partner Morrie Nowytarger giving an exclusive interview to C. J. McKenzie of the *Sunday Telegraph*. Helping the crime reporter was Will Hagon, the paper's motoring man.

Nowytarger began by fessing up that both he and Rogerson had an interest in the accounts, and the money had come from the restoration and sale of the Bentley. Rogerson, whose vehicle of choice was a Volkswagen Beetle, confirmed that the car was indeed rare, only 61 having been made. Nowytarger had bought the car in the United States and brought it to Australia, they said, where it was restored by the able hands of Roger Rogerson and then flogged to Karp. As for the interest of the Taxation Office, Rogerson said: 'If this matter hadn't involved me there would not have been a word said about it.' This was Rogerson's first outing as a victim, a theme he would soon warm to.

Sydney's answer to Arthur Daley chucked in his two bobs' worth, explaining to the journalists that a similar car had sold a few years before for $109,000, a rather unlikely figure. He went on: the mudguard was damaged and he had been keeping it in his lockup where Rogerson noticed it.

> One day Roger saw the car and said that it was a very valuable piece of equipment to be left lying idle. I said that if he could get it fixed and restored then we'd go halves in it if we ever decided to sell it. Roger has relatives in a panel beating company and he was personally very good at restoring vehicles. I had a couple of quotes and the lowest was about $20,000. Roger said he could get it restored for a lot less than that by doing a lot of the work himself.

Rogerson then said that he had started work on restoring the vehicle in 1978. He had hand-beaten out the damaged area and resprayed the car twice – all while working at the Armed Hold-up Squad, lunching with Neddy Smith and giving the Chapmans a hand. He was unaware of the tape recording that told the real story.

When questioned about the false names on the accounts, Rogerson replied:

> Mine is an unusual name and I've been a high profile policeman for many years. Because of this I checked out just how confidential bank accounts were. I was told they were not very confidential at all; that all sorts of people could get access to them. I thought that until after the trial it would be better to put the money in an account under another name. When I was acquitted we were in the throes of transferring the money into a joint name account – or going back to normal.

McKenzie wrote:

> But what worries him most is the effect the trial and subsequent events have had on his wife Joy, and his two daughters aged 15 and 17. 'My 15 year old was in the 800 metres event for her school on Friday and she ran only about 20 metres and broke down and collapsed on the field in tears,' he said.

Rogerson was likely sincere in his concern for his daughter, but he had no compunction in using the incident to serve his own ends.

*

August 1985 continued to be a rather unpleasant month for Rogerson. Alan Williams, his alleged co-conspirator, faced the Castlereagh Street Local Court, charged with attempting to bribe Drury and, like Rogerson, was committed for trial.

The perceived rivalry between Sydney and Melbourne extended to police work. Exchange duty, extraditions and the sharing of information were quite common, but the Victoria Police perceived the NSW force as corrupt. However, at the Williams hearing, Victoria's image became rather tarnished. Called to Sydney to give evidence were two members of the Victorian Armed Hold-up Squad, Detective Sergeants Paul Higgins and Brian Murphy. (Followers of the recent Melbourne gang wars will recall that Murphy, after his departure from the police force, became very close to Mario Condello, who was gunned down in Melbourne's North Brighton in February 2006.)

Higgins told the court that Williams had denied knowledge of the Drury shooting, but had offered $100,000 to have Drury 'pull up'. When Higgins told Williams he had heard the bribe was only $30,000, 'the expression on his face changed. He said that was his first offer' and that money hadn't changed hands. Higgins said, 'The next thing Williams heard was that Drury had been shot.'

When questioned by Williams's barrister, the sergeant denied that he and Murphy had tried to extort money from Williams. He also denied the scurrilous allegation that 'you and Murphy are basically a law unto yourselves in the Victorian Police Force'.

Murphy was questioned about his status as a favourite target of B11, the Internal Affairs-style unit in the Victoria Police. He dryly observed, 'I wouldn't think I was their best customer but I have had my fair share.'

Rogerson should have been worried about Williams.

Intelligence gathered by Melbourne police suggested that Williams offered $50,000 as the bribe. Drury had been offered $15,000 to $25,000. If true, it meant a tidy profit for Rogerson. But intelligence also suggested that Alan Williams was deeply pissed off at the failure of the bribe and the botched attempt to kill the pivotal witness, Michael Drury. He had reportedly told cronies that he thought Rogerson should be 'whacked', to teach him a lesson. Luckily for Rogerson, Williams's arrest and extradition, and a couple of commissions of inquiry, intervened.

During the course of the Williams hearing, Rogerson's close mate and co-pilot, Bill Duff, found himself in a spot of bother. Duff, like Rogerson, had been a high-profile and well-respected detective attached to the Homicide Squad. Like Rogerson, he was bright and affable, but more of an operator than the hard man that Rogerson was. He had been in the public gallery throughout Rogerson's recent trial.

Duff had become the subject of an investigation by the recently formed Internal Security Unit. Police were subject to a sort of double jeopardy. Criminal charges levelled against a police officer required proof beyond reasonable doubt and thus needed a lot more effort than administrative charges. Then one had to factor in variables such as protracted hearings, potentially negative and long-running publicity, juries, and witnesses who might get cold feet, change their stories, have their evidence rattled or simply disappear. It was much neater, and much quicker, to deploy the *Police Regulation Act* and lay administrative charges. If necessary, criminal charges could be laid later. Likewise, if a cop was acquitted on criminal charges, administrative charges could be laid – for example, for 'misconduct' or 'bringing the force into disrepute'.

Duff had been a cop for twenty years, eight of them at the Homicide Squad. He had a lower public profile than Rogerson, only coming to broad attention in 1978 when he was commended for solving the very nasty murder of a Jerilderie shearer and his wife.

In 1983, Internal Affairs had investigated allegations that Duff was too closely associated with known criminals and had confided to another policeman that he was aware of an operation to import drugs from Papua New Guinea. Whenever police left the country, they were required by the regulations to advise the commissioner of their departure. In October 1980, when he had slipped up to Papua New Guinea on a quick trip, Duff hadn't complied with those requirements. Sums were being done and the scent of rat was in the air. However, Internal Affairs cleared Duff. Ernie Shepard at the ISU decided to use the unit's 'own motion' powers and reopen the file. In the midst of Rogerson sweating over the Williams hearing, his mate was suspended from duty pending an administrative hearing.

In October, the hearing of the charges from the alleged assault on Mrs Pak resumed. As it was a relatively minor matter in the scheme of things, Chester Porter QC wasn't appearing. It would have been like swatting a mosquito with a house brick. Instead, the usual choice of police in strife, John 'Jock' Dailly, was at the bar table. Dailly, who still had the light Scottish accent of his childhood, had spent his formative years as a detective, completing his law degree while at the Fraud Squad. He left the force, but made a nice little earner representing cops. Fortunately for Rogerson and Laurie Burgess, Mrs Pak had given evidence earlier that she couldn't identify Rogerson as the man who had slapped her. The prosecution went downhill from there, and Rogerson and Burgess would soon walk from the court as free men. However, further trouble was just around the corner.

In November, Internal Security laid an 'information' for three counts of 'goods in custody' relating to Rogerson's bank accounts. (An information is something sworn after which a summons may then be issued.) He would have to prove where the money came from.

By Melbourne Cup day that year, Rogerson was back on the couch, though not the couch of Dr Harry Bailey. The Chelmsford scandal was breaking, and Bailey would later take his own life. Rogerson was now under the care of the respected Dr William Metcalf, who found his patient to be depressed, distraught and suffering from very high blood pressure 'for a man of his age and fitness'. It wasn't surprising, considering the year Rogerson had just been through. His career was in ruins, his family wondering just what he had been up to, he had no power to speak of, a chunk of hard-to-explain cash had been seized, income both legitimate and illegitimate was hard to come by, and perhaps even worse, he had lost the respect of the public and his colleagues.

16

A CAREER IN TATTERS

Misery comes in many forms. For a crook in Sydney during the 1970s and 1980s, it was being in the District
Court for trial or sentencing and finding yourself in Judge
Barry 'Thumper' Thorley's court. The nickname dated back
to his days as a fine rugby player, but was quite appropriate
for his courtroom. Police loved Thorley, because he was
tough, fair, and didn't take any nonsense from the barristers
and solicitors appearing before him. He and Judge
Cameron-Smith were the CIB's favourite judges. If one of
your charges appeared before either man, they could be
assured of a punishment that fitted the crime – at least from
the police point of view. The appearance of either of these
gentlemen on the Bench would see a flurry of last-minute
applications for adjournment by defence counsel, but neither
judge fell for that sort of nonsense. In 1986, Barry Thorley
found himself heading the Police Tribunal.

January got Rogerson's year off to a bad start when Alan
Williams pleaded guilty to attempting to bribe Michael
Drury. He got a 'good behaviour' bond. It wouldn't be the
last that Rogerson would hear of the Drury matter.

In February, at the tribunal's instigation, Bill Duff was

dismissed from the NSW Police Force after he was found
guilty of 'improper associations' with criminals. One criminal with whom he improperly associated was Neddy Smith.
Rogerson reached for another handful of the antidepres-
sants he had been prescribed by Dr Metcalf.

It was Wendy Bacon, in the *National Times* on 14 March 1986,
who made public the news that Rogerson was again in strife. He
was soon to be charged over his relationship with Smith, she
wrote. After Rogerson had beaten the charges of bribery, and of
assault against Mrs Pak, these latest charges were 'a last ditch
attempt to rid the force of Rogerson who became Internal
Security's number one target'. Tapes of Rogerson and Smith discussing 'whacking up' the money from Harvey Jones would
form part of the evidence. The deal with Karp, Paltos and
Nowytarger would also be covered.

Rogerson was on sick leave for stress. However, Bacon
upped the ante when she wrote: '[S]enior police have not
been prepared to allow some of those under investigation
their traditional option of an invalid pension and have
insisted that inquiries continue to their conclusion.' Avery's
new broom would ensure that Rogerson wouldn't follow
Fred Krahe into pension-land.

Four other senior police would join Rogerson in the ISU's
firing line. Among them was aspiring commissioner Nelson
Chad and Darlinghurst's John Openshaw. Openshaw's trou-
bles would also be slated back to Neddy Smith. Drinks at the
Gaslight in Darlinghurst would prove to have been a very
poor idea.

The activities of Internal Security offended the entrenched
old guard at the CIB. Like Rogerson, they hadn't quite
sensed the winds of change in time, but unlike him they had
very sensibly kept a low profile. Allegations of ISU misconduct would fly. Utterly disreputable 'businessman' Frank

Hakim alleged soon-to-be-Commissioner Tony Lauer and his mates had planted heroin on him. Investigations, including one by the ICAC some years later, exonerated Lauer and his fellow police. Time and public opinion had moved on, and Internal Security emerged the victors from the mud flinging. The public would be fed a bit of spin about black knights versus white knights brawling for control of the police. It sounded cute but had no basis in fact. Police were seldom black or white, just varying shades of grey.

Following the *National Times* lead, John Dowd joined the fray. In Parliament, the shadow attorney general attacked the police force and government for allowing the 'obvious associations that Rogerson has had and who bring contempt upon the entire police force'. He said that Neddy Smith was 'a heavy criminal for years and is now a senior middle-ranking drug trafficker'. Poor Neddy, he always thought he was top rank. That Rogerson was still a member of the police was 'a concern of many members of this Parliament and many people in the community'.

Rogerson had been acquitted of all the charges brought against him up until that time, and so in real terms was an innocent man in the eyes of the law. Although political game playing had supplanted proper legal process, the shadow attorney general would soon be proven correct. Police normally remain tight-lipped when publicly attacked, but Rogerson had come a long way from being a normal policeman. His response to Dowd was poised and supremely confident. 'I have no regrets I telephoned him. I am quite pleased the transcripts have gone to Internal Affairs because once the commissioner or Internal Affairs see it they will realise I was in no way intimidatory.' He was proven correct.

Dowd did, however, get it right when he told Parliament that Rogerson was 'carrying on the tradition of Freddy Krahe and Ray Kelly', though not when he said the police force 'is probably cleaner now than it has been for a couple of decades'. He obviously hadn't met Larry Churchill, Trevor Haken and 'Chook' Fowler, all serving police at the time, who would star a decade later in the Wood Royal Commission, or the lads at Manly and their nemesis, the Police Integrity Commission, a few years later.

The Rogerson response to all this was to fight. No surprise there, and it was no surprise that he chose the 'grubby misfits' of the media as his main weapon.

On 1 April 1986, Roger Rogerson was the lead story on Channel Nine's *Willesee* program, just after the national news. Ray Martin introduced Rogerson as 'Australia's most controversial cop'. By the end of the interview, everyone around the country knew about Roger Rogerson.

Unfortunately for Roger, he wasn't what television hacks call 'good talent' on this outing. The man who had seduced tabloid journalists and juries looked shifty. He sounded like a liar. He evaded some of Martin's rather pointed questions. He claimed, very stupidly, that he 'didn't know of one crooked cop'. This was a swipe at Assistant Commissioner Bob Shepherd and the remark he had made at a conference held at Curzon Hall in Sydney. Shepherd had managed to offend both the NSW Police and the government when he said that, in his opinion, New South Wales had the most corrupt police force in Australia, 'if not the world', and that the New South Wales government was 'the most corrupt in Australia'. Luckily for Shepherd's career, that government would soon get the boot. Later in the interview, Rogerson contradicted himself by saying that he thought one of his colleagues was corrupt.

Martin switched tack and gave Rogerson a decent workout

on the Warren Lanfranchi shooting. When Rogerson said that Lanfranchi had been armed, Martin, who was aware that Lanfranchi had been wearing skin-tight pants, quipped: 'You couldn't hide a packet of cigarettes let alone a revolver.' Rogerson said the reason for the hullabaloo over the shooting was that Lanfranchi and Sallie-Anne Huckstepp had got their heads together before the meeting. Rogerson was a victim of their collusion, he said. However, his story didn't sell.

Martin asked Rogerson if there came a point 'where a policeman becomes part of the criminal world'. Rogerson replied, 'Well, I can imagine that happening, but I can certainly say that it hasn't happened in regards to myself.' His conversion, however, was close at hand.

During the interview, Rogerson did something that was very out of character. One of the hallmarks of his career was his implacable silence on the activities of his colleagues and mates. Even today, Rogerson remains mute, though his testimony on the activities of others could have mitigated his sentence. On *Willesee* he broke that silence, stating that he believed Michael Drury to be corrupt and that he would produce evidence that would 'involve other people'. It was the first step in a potential defence, by the sound of it. That 'evidence' has never seen the light of day.

He then named Neddy Smith as his 'informant'. A comment like that could be very dangerous for an informant's health.

The interview with Ray Martin coincided with a piece that appeared in the *Daily Telegraph*, a safer medium for Rogerson. In it, he alleged that the misconduct charge, which still hadn't been laid, was 'trumped up'. He further alleged that Internal Affairs had been leaking to the media. He would be charged to 'cause further embarrassment', because he had complained to the ombudsman about aspects of his prosecution in the Drury case. He also took a swipe at Bob Snape, the head of Internal Security, and John Dowd for 'rubbishing' him in Parliament.

Rogerson's spirited defence didn't work, and he was charged the next day with misconduct arising from his chat with Neddy Smith in 1983 about Val Bellamy's coins. He was given seven days to decide whether he wanted to have the charges heard by the Police Tribunal or Commissioner Avery. His decision wasn't too hard to predict. He followed the charging with an impromptu press conference. Nattily dressed in the CIB's favourite informal uniform of light grey trousers, blue blazer and white shirt (no tie), he reiterated: 'It's a trumped-up charge. I'm innocent.' Warming to his subject, he said: 'This incident allegedly happened in 1983. The Police department has a habit of putting things on the shelf and pulling them out when they want them . . . My career is finished, I know, but I'm going to battle this one. I'm doing it on principle. I want the full facts to come out . . . I have opted to have the charge heard in public by the Police Tribunal. I will be calling evidence and subpoenaing witnesses.' Very brave, very arrogant, very deluded.

While Rogerson was downtown sorting out his mounting problems, Neddy Smith was in a spot of bother himself. Blame for the bother could be slated back to Rogerson's admissions on national television.

That same day, 2 April, Smith left his Iron Duke Hotel in Alexandria to walk to his car parked about a hundred metres away. As he walked across the driveway of the Camberg's Carpets store, a car mounted the footpath and ploughed into him from behind. Smith hadn't heard or seen it coming. He later reckoned the driver had been waiting for him outside the pub. He scraped himself up just in time to dive out of the way of the car as it then attempted to reverse over him.

Smith went for his gun, only to recall that Bill Duff had borrowed it earlier. Smith reckoned he caught sight of the driver and recognised him. He said, 'It hit me like a ton of bricks; I knew the guy well and I realised I'd been set up by that mongrel Duff.'

He made it back to the pub, where he collapsed. He had received six broken ribs and a broken left leg. Neddy had some cold comfort when 'that mongrel Duff' ended up with a three-year sentence for supplying heroin.

Though Neddy was down for the count, Rogerson was pressing on. In the *Sunday Telegraph* that week, he said: 'If I go down, I'll go down swinging.' With his usual lack of irony, he offered: 'It [the charge] is a load of rubbish. There is no way they will fit me with it. You have got to have the evidence to fit people.' (One might have thought that if you have the evidence, then a fitting isn't necessary.) He continued: 'They won't accept the umpire's decisions. They tried to fit me with the Drury thing and failed and they failed again with the assault charge against me.'

He also showed little compassion for his battered 'informant'. When told that Smith was very unhappy about being named as an informant on national television, and about the attempt to run him over, Rogerson growled: 'No, I'm not Neddy's fucking keeper, but he's okay. He knows I've always been fair with him.' When asked if he thought Smith was safe, Rogerson said: 'I'd say he's not safe at all.'

No good should pass without acknowledgement, and so Rogerson's helpful on-air comments about Michael Drury and Neddy Smith were repaid, with interest. The Police Tribunal charge list swelled with three new matters arising from the interview. The list already covered his relationships with Smith, Paltos and Karp, the shonky bank accounts and a few porkies he had told Internal Security. He was suspended without pay. In between court matters and lunches with Neddy, who – despite having been outed on national television – still considered Rogerson to be a mate, he tried his hand at a career he had managed so far to avoid. His father would have been chuffed to see his son wielding an oxy torch, building security grilles and flogging used safes. A bloke had to make a quid.

Rogerson's new career in the security business was great fodder for the rumour mill. While there was nothing to suggest that his businesses – Statewide Security Systems Pty Ltd and Bullion Engineering Pty Ltd – were anything other than a bloke trying to make an honest living, rumours began to circulate about some 'consultancy' work Rogerson was doing in the Kings Cross area. Among his new colleagues was Louie Bayeh, who had taken a firm grip on the drug trade in the Cross. Rogerson had the skills Bayeh needed to resolve some business matters. He was the thinking man's Tim Bristow.

Rogerson wasn't alone in facing charges before the tribunal. On 27 March 1986, suspended or soon-to-be-suspended detectives Mike MacDonald, John Brown, Rod Moore, John Openshaw and Nelson Chad met with Rogerson for lunch at the Balmain Rowers Club to plot a last-ditch attempt to derail the prosecutions. They discussed establishing a 'fighting fund' to make an application to the High Court to exclude the taped evidence. Though some of their pockets were deep, nothing came of the plan.

By June, the tribunal was in full swing. One of the early cabs off the rank was Nelson Chad. Like Rogerson, he'd had a flirtation with Dr Nick Paltos. Paltos, it seemed, had been a little too close to Robert 'Aussie Bob' Trimbole, one of the leading lights of international drug trafficking. It was a relationship that didn't do Chad much good. The Commonwealth Police were all over Paltos, and Chad was collateral damage. Again like Rogerson, he found it all damned depressing. However, before his prescription pads and liberty were taken away from him, Paltos had referred Chad to a psychiatrist. Midway through the proceedings against him, Chad reckoned the game was over. He would rather resign, he said, than linger in a career that was moribund. A line was drawn through his name in the studbook.

On 23 June, 'Thumper' Thorley called the Police Tribunal to order. Counsel assisting, the petite, bearded and Jaguar-fancying Ric Burbidge QC, outlined the case against Rogerson. The next day, the court enjoyed a video presentation of Rogerson – or 'Mike Roberts' or 'Robert Tracey' – doing a bit of banking.

It got worse. Ross Karp was brought in for a visit from Long Bay. He refused to take the oath or to answer questions, so a record of interview between him and Eric Strong of Internal Affairs was tendered. In it, Karp asserted that he had been told by Paltos that the money in the dodgy accounts 'most probably' had come from drugs. Given Rogerson's associates, that assertion was credible. Of the purchase of the Bentley, he had said: 'I was to prepare the contract which was to be appropriately backdated and then a detail of payments was to be drafted establishing the method of payment.' The contract was dated 22 September 1983.

Neddy Smith, naturally enough, got a few mentions. However, his name was suppressed, and so he became 'Mr X'. His anonymity lasted until John Fairfax Limited persuaded Justice Michael McHugh, then sitting in the Court of Appeal, to lift Thorley's suppression order. Smith got his name in print again.

Eric Strong gave evidence of his investigations into the car debacle. Jock Dailly, again representing Rogerson, wrapped by asking him: 'Without going through all of these comments such as polished performer, outstanding overall appraisal, an extremely enthusiastic worker, outstanding potential, an outstanding detective, those comments are fairly consistently seen throughout the appraisals going back from 1984?'

Strong: I would agree with that.
Dailly: Very high assessments in anyone's language.
Strong: Yes.

Unlike at his trial, Rogerson didn't feel the urge to give evidence to the tribunal. It would place him 'at great risk', Dailly decided. Not even a witness of Rogerson's skill could turn black into white. Instead, Dailly offered Dr William Metcalf, who spoke of Rogerson's mental state. It was more mitigation than defence.

In his summing up, Dailly hauled out a contemporary version of the Nuremberg defence. It was a dud for the Nazis, and it hasn't improved with age and use. The police hierarchy had known of his associations with underworld figures for years and had approved of it, he said. Police, 'particularly in the higher echelons', were encouraged to associate with criminals because of the information they could supply. Rogerson had even been given money to pay for information that had led to major crimes being solved. He omitted to mention the major crimes that had been green-lighted or simply ignored. Rogerson was an outstanding detective partly because of his special ability to communicate with some of Sydney's top criminals. His character and reputation had been attacked in all sections of the media.

On 27 June, the last day of the hearing, Dailly told the tribunal that Rogerson would resign from the police force 'whatever the outcome from his hearing before the Police Tribunal'. 'However,' he added, 'if there is a determination on any matter against him, a recommendation [will] be made that he be allowed to resign from the force.' This would entitle Rogerson to benefits such as holiday pay and superannuation, and to avoid having to admit to being sacked.

On 28 July, the tribunal found Rogerson guilty on three charges of impairing the efficiency of the force by naming Neddy Smith and Lennie McPherson as informers, and labelling Michael Drury as 'corrupt'. He was found guilty of improperly associating with Ross Karp and Nick Paltos, and for his operation of the two bank accounts. The tribunal recommended he be sacked. There was to be no soft exit. Rogerson wasn't there for the final blow to his career; he was on sick leave. His high blood pressure and depression were taking their toll.

Commissioner Avery took Thorley at his word and sacked Rogerson. The gun and handcuffs had been handed back some time before. The pension, superannuation and entitlements went down the gurgler. It put a few runs on the board for the commissioner. Rogerson could now devote his time to safe sales and metalwork. His career of 27 years, most of which was covered in glory, was over; Roger Rogerson was now 'disgraced'. 'Notorious' would soon follow. His subsequent appeal, despite the dexterity of his counsel, Frank 'Dancing Man' McAlary QC, was rejected by Justice Perignon.

The criminal career of Neddy Smith didn't falter with the findings against Rogerson. In the period from 26 September 1985 to 3 November 1988, Smith was responsible for nine armed robberies, yielding a booty of over 750,000 tax-free dollars. Rogerson may have gone, but his touch could still be felt.

With Rogerson's sacking, his travails were far from finished. Things were just warming up. He was now the very public face of everything thought to be wrong with the NSW Police. Justice, if only in name, must be seen to be done.

17

SETTLING SOME OLD SCORES

Since the death of Warren Lanfranchi in 1981, Sallie-Anne Huckstepp had continued to be very vocal about her belief that Rogerson had murdered her lover. She had pointed the finger in the print media and on Channel Nine's *60 Minutes*. Along the way, she had also found herself embroiled with other coppers not involved with Rogerson. It was indeed a dangerous life she was leading.

At around midnight on 6 February 1986, while the suspended Detective Sergeant Roger Rogerson was breasting the bar with a few cronies in Sydney's west, that dangerous life ended. At 8.45 the next morning, a jogger found Huckstepp's body floating in Busby's Pond near the Robertson Road entrance to the lung of Sydney, Centennial Park. A park ranger notified the NSW Police Tactical Response Group, who were training in the park, and her body was dragged to the shore. Her car was found in nearby Martin Road. She had driven to the park to meet someone, it would seem, sometime after the park gates had been closed at around sunset.

The initial investigation wasn't handled with any degree of dexterity. It took until 19 February for the cause of death to be established as 'a result of drowning due to asphyxia by manual strangulation and associated narcotic intake (morphine)'. Heroin is formally known as diamorphine. There were marks on her back consistent with her being dragged into the water. There was another mark on her back that suggested a foot had been firmly applied. Busby's Pond was quite shallow. The suspect list wasn't short, but prominent on it was Roger Rogerson.

Eleven days after the murder, the tall and patrician-looking former police prosecutor, Inspector Austin (though everyone called him 'Ossie') Prescott, arrived at 32 Gleeson Avenue, Condell Park. When questioned regarding his whereabouts on the night of the Huckstepp murder, Rogerson was reminded by Joy that he had been out at a regular drinking session with Mal Spence and a few others at the Merrylands Bowling Club. He had arrived home in the early hours of the morning a bit the worse for wear. 'Joy jogged my memory,' he said, 'and I have forgotten it since. I got home about one or one thirty, maybe a little later.'

'Did you speak to your wife when you arrived home?' Prescott asked.

Roger replied, 'Yes, I did. In fact she did most of the talking.'

Mal Spence was yet another mate of Neddy Smith. For a while, anyway. As a police prosecutor, he should only really have consorted with criminals in the confines of a courtroom. However, that wasn't the case. Spence was everyone's 'pal', and 'pal' was what he called everybody. He was well liked by the older magistrates and was known by the more 'flexible' criminal lawyers and detectives as a bloke with whom 'you could do business'. The rule of thumb was that if Spence was prosecuting and you had loaded or verballed a crim, let him know. 'She'll be sweet,' Spence would say. He was vain. A man born to wear white shoes.

Mal Spence had entered the orbit of Neddy Smith – according to his story, anyway – one day when he had been drinking at the old Lord Nelson Hotel in The Rocks. He had seen 'a very large man walk into the hotel with a detective I knew'. The large man was Smith, and the detective was Rogerson's pal from Darlinghurst, John Openshaw. Spence would later enjoy a beer or two at the Nelson with Smith and other friends, including Bill Duff and Roger Rogerson.

At his 40th birthday party held in July 1985 at the King Arthur's Court Hotel, then a low dive on William Street near the Cross, the guest list was a curious mix of coppers and hardened crims. Things would later turn a bit nasty for Spence. On 15 December 1988, while he was having a beer at the Lord Wolseley Hotel in Ultimo, another of Neddy Smith's favoured drinking spots, he got into a fight with 'Abo' Henry, Smith's former partner in crime. It ended badly, with Henry stabbing Spence in the stomach and leaving him in the gutter to die. Henry was convicted and given six years in gaol.

Henry alleged that he had paid Spence a bribe of $50,000 to run dead on a murder charge against Smith. The charge in question was the murder of the tow-truck driver for which Smith is still serving time. Spence, according to Henry, took the money and did precisely nothing. The stabbing was a falling out among thieves.

In sentencing Henry, Justice Badgery-Parker put up a barrier to Spence's career prospects. He said, 'This offence, committed by a man with an extensive criminal record, who is an associate of notorious criminals, had its origins in the fact that the complainant, Spence, also has very questionable associations with persons of criminal bent. What the precise nature of those associations may be, I know not, nor do I need to consider, but it is obviously desirable that the proper

authorities should give very close attention to that question.'
The authorities did.

Spence was asked to pop into hearings held by the ICAC
a year or so later. Mal, who had been getting some psychiatric counselling himself, decided he was too sick to attend
and admitted himself to the Sydney Clinic, a private mental
health clinic in Waverley.

Ian Temby, the ICAC commissioner, didn't take the compassionate view that Spence had been hoping for, or that
history would suggest he could have expected. Temby reckoned that Spence was 'lying doggo' (hiding). He issued a
warrant and Spence was dragged before the commission.
Temby noted that Spence gave evidence 'in an apparently
competent fashion'.

Spence would also be an apparently competent witness
when he attested to Rogerson's whereabouts on the night of
Sallie-Anne Huckstepp's murder. The inquest into her
death began in April 1987. Rogerson's numerous court commitments were playing havoc with his new security business.
Giving evidence at the inquest was clearly not something he
was keen to do. After a bit of argy-bargy, Rogerson, through
his lawyers, agreed to present himself at the Coroner's Court
on Parramatta Road, Glebe on 4 May 1987.

Prior to his day in court, the coroner had been told that
Rogerson and Warren Richards, the incarcerated former
heroin-dealing associate of Neddy Smith, had arranged to
meet with Huckstepp the day before her murder. Richards
told the coroner he didn't know anything that could help and
then refused to answer questions. One of the coroner's reasons for calling the two was that they had allegedly been
caught on tape chatting about police involvement in drug
importing. This was at a time when Huckstepp was plying
her trade in the Madam Lash room at the Kingsdore Motel in

the Cross, an establishment operated by the late and unla-
mented Peter 'The Black Prince' Farrugia. Sallie-Anne was a
dab hand at disciplining some of Sydney's kinkier gentlemen,
it seemed. As with many of the allegations made against
Rogerson, this one wasn't vigorously pursued. For Richards,
it was at least a day out of Parklea Gaol and a chance to chat
about old times.

On hearing the allegations, Rogerson popped up again on
Channel Nine, saying: 'Today's allegations are an absolute
joke and it's news to me. I will be consulting my legal people.' Huff, puff and not much else, considering the evidence
was given under the protection of the court.

When called to the witness box, Rogerson took the opportunity to take a couple of swings at his detractors. He began
by declining to give his address. 'There are people in this
court who I would not like to have my address,' he told the
packed room. It added even more drama to the proceedings.
Of Huckstepp, he said: 'She rubbished me and caused a lot
of harm. I knew what sort of person she was.' He told the
court that while he would rather not have had her around,
he wouldn't resort to having her killed.

Then it was time to settle a few scores. Rogerson told the
court that he had received information that the journalist
Wendy Bacon was responsible for the murder. She had had
a lesbian relationship with Huckstepp that had gone bad,
he said. He had heard that Bacon had hired convicted criminal Stephen Sellers to do the job. Those with an interest in
Sydney's underbelly recalled that Bacon had put up $10,000
some years before to bail Sellers. She had forfeited the bail
when Sellers had failed to turn up to answer the charges
against him.

It all made for great theatre, which was lapped up by an
appreciative audience. However, the coroner, Greg Glass,

wasn't too happy. He later wrote that Rogerson's remarks had 'brought discredit on himself and in doing so [he] was guilty of disrespect to this court'. Rogerson and many in the police simply found it a bit of malicious fun. Payback is an old NSW Police habit.

The next day, a statement by Bacon was read to the court:

> I state that there is no truth in the contents of the alleged conversation referring to me which Roger Rogerson described in the evidence he gave to the City Coroners on the 4/5/87. At the time of her death I had not seen or spoken to Sallie-Anne Huckstepp for several years. I only knew her in the context of work of a journalist interested in the issue of Police corruption.

A little over four years later, on 22 February 1991, Coroner Glass agreed with the original cause of Huckstepp's death. He noted that it was inflicted by a person or persons unknown. Loose lips, rather than brilliant investigation, finally put an identity to that unknown person.

In 1994, Neddy Smith was enjoying the balmy breeze and swaying palms of the 'Matraville Motel', also known as Long Bay Gaol. Smith had grown a bit garrulous after his years behind bars. This would prove to be a serious error, as the prisoner sharing his cell was a police informant wired for sound. Smith's bragging about murdering Huckstepp was caught on tape. On 22 January 1995, the *Sydney Morning Herald* had a lovely scoop: 'I killed six: Neddy Smith – confessions rock police'. One of the six was Huckstepp. According to the report, Neddy had told his cell-mate he murdered Huckstepp 'because Roger Rogerson had said she was taping police who were supplying heroin to the drug trade'.

Tapes, while handy, are not necessarily reliable evidence,

particularly when one is dealing with someone like Smith, a braggart desperate for an audience. He was subsequently charged with the murder, but the jury wasn't convinced and found him not guilty. Huckstepp's murderer remains at large, or not.

During the hearings against Smith, it emerged that a palm print had been found on the boot of Huckstepp's car. It was that of a male, and a male whose prints weren't on record. When the evidence of the print was introduced by a Detective Quinlan, the decidedly feisty and usually entertaining Winston Terracini SC, who was acting for Smith, asked a question that caused a stir: 'Was Rogerson asked to provide a palm print?' He went on: 'Was Rogerson fingerprinted when he was charged with a series of offences in the eighties?'

'No, sir, he wasn't,' replied Quinlan.

'So despite being charged with a number of serious offences and being convicted of one major offence, Rogerson has never had his palm print taken?' asked Terracini. 'That's correct,' replied Quinlan.

It is common practice these days, when joining the police, for recruits to have their fingerprints and palm prints taken, first to ensure that they don't have a record, and second to be able to identify and eliminate those prints if they are found at a crime scene. However, at the time when Rogerson joined the force, only fingerprints were taken. It still hasn't been explained why his palm prints weren't taken when he was arrested. On looking into things further, I ascertained that Rogerson's palm prints were in fact on record as the result of another matter and that a diligent copper had done the hard yards. The print found on Sallie-Anne Huckstepp's car wasn't Rogerson's.

*

The best police force money can buy can also just be the best police force when it puts its mind to the task. In July1987, Taskforce Omega was formed under Detective Inspector Doug Kelly. It followed Taskforce Zig Zag, which had been formed a few weeks before to look into the activities of Neddy Smith.

Kelly's detectives were seasoned investigators who didn't bring with them the taint of a squad's 'inner circle'. Their target was Roger Rogerson. Kelly later commented that 'Rogerson didn't have much faith in us; he said we were B-graders, couldn't track an elephant through the snow'. It was bravado on Rogerson's behalf.

The police were cleaning up their act, and a very high profile scalp was needed to show the public just how serious they were. The stench around Rogerson, even though he was no longer on the force, was still pervasive. Kelly and his men were unleashed.

The timing of Taskforce Omega was lousy for former Detective Sergeant Rogerson. The media campaign started by the *National Times* into corruption in general, and Rogerson in particular, had stimulated the more serious players to join the bandwagon. Corruption was well and truly on the agenda, and the public were becoming very well informed. Perceptions were changing, and questions were being asked. Neville Wran, after a record term as premier, departed the New South Wales political scene, leaving the state in the hands of the cardigan-wearing Barry Unsworth.

It was a government on the nose, and one of the more unpleasant odours was coming from the NSW Police. Unsworth would get the flick a few months after Omega's formation. Nick Greiner and his Police Minister, Ted Pickering, would stand squarely behind Commissioner

Avery and his efforts to capitalise on the groundswell of opinion and give the NSW Police a good spruce-up.

Police who had formerly been a little on the edgy side of honest would find themselves being born again as scrupulously honest. Dodgy pasts would at least be forgotten or buried if the chance arose. Capable and honest officers would have a much better chance at being promoted. Rogerson would find that his 'mates' had become elusive. Calls weren't returned. Lunching opportunities would wane. Favours could no longer be called in, unless he had 'the wood' on them and even then it would take a serious nudge.

Rogerson was now too 'hot', and it was a career killer if you were caught on tape or video with him. The police culture is a wonderful thing when you are on duty and in the line of fire. When you are 'ex', you're on your own.

The detectives assigned to Omega were far from B-grade. Under Doug Kelly, and spearheading the taskforce, was Geoff Hoggett, who had worked briefly with Rogerson at the Motor Squad at the time when Rogerson had been anointed for a spot on the inside. Hoggett had spent a chunk of his career at the CIB or involved at the sharp end of some very serious special investigations. He was honest, smart and highly experienced. The taskforce was in a very safe pair of hands.

Among the group of seven detectives was Clive Small, who came to prominence when he headed the investigation that saw Ivan Milat convicted in 1995 of The Backpacker Murders in the Belanglo State Forest, in the Southern Highlands. He had been working in Commissioner Avery's policy unit at Headquarters in College Street, along with soon-to-be Deputy Commissioner Jeff Jarratt, and Christine Nixon, daughter of Assistant Commissioner (Crime) Ross Nixon and today Commissioner of the Victoria Police. Small, with his long experience as a detective and rather forthright views, had been annoying the others who were more bureaucratic than operational. Omega presented them with a chance to take a break from Small, and to give Small a break back on the streets. Terry Campbell, Chris Olin, Bill Smith and Ewan Hreszczuk were equally capable and experienced detectives.

Behind Rogerson's bravado was a large chunk of unease. When the government or police commissioner announces a new taskforce, the public is led to believe it has been put together carefully and is well supported. In reality, taskforces are frequently formed in haste, often as the result of a 'policy on the run' doorstop interview with a politician. They are cobbled together using whoever is available at the time. As for infrastructure, make it up as you go. Omega was lucky to find some very good detectives who were coming back from leave or from specialist duties outside their normal slots.

Given that they were investigating the former golden boy of the CIB, it was unfortunate that it was decided to locate Omega at the CIB, on the same floor as the Duty Office, in the Remington Centre. News of the arrival of the members of the taskforce spread quickly and their reception on the first day was decidedly lacking in warmth. Although Rogerson was 'ex' and on the outer, the detectives investigating him were shunned in the lifts and common areas, and in the pubs around the CIB.

The detectives spent the first few weeks rummaging through, reviewing and collating the various piles of paperwork they had inherited. There were bits and pieces from Internal Security, Internal Affairs and the Police Tribunal, court transcripts and briefs, as well as the limp investigative efforts of 'Black' Angus MacDonald following Michael Drury's naming of Rogerson in his deposition made in the early eighties. There were the running sheets that were the blow-by-blow record of everything that happened in the investigation of the Drury shooting. Who did what, when, where, why and what happened.

The taskforce were looking for lines of enquiry that only emerge once there is a firm grip on an investigation. While popularly supposed to 'hit the ground running', most of the running is initially done from a chair, with a pile of papers to be gone through. All investigations are the same: reading, analysing, kicking ideas about, arguing, applying the benefits of a few lifetimes of experience, and finally the leads emerge from the soup of words. That's when shoe leather, hard work and a sprinkling of inspiration can lead to a shouted 'Eureka!' when a lead pans out.

The initial focus was on Rogerson's alleged involvement in the Drury shooting. The bribery aspect had already been dealt with and the double jeopardy rule protected Rogerson from further charges being laid on that matter. Not so with the allegation of conspiracy to murder; that was still very much on the cards. Kelly and Hoggett, at the insistence of Commissioner Avery, hopped on to a Qantas flight bound for Los Angeles to chat to Drury, who was working temporarily at the Australian Consulate there before heading back to duty in Sydney. No revelations came from the interview, but it was a chance to see for themselves what Drury was like, and for them to bring a fresh eye to his evidence.

In reviewing the files, it soon became obvious that the motivation, and much of the plotting, for the shooting had occurred in Melbourne. What was also obvious was that about 80 per cent of the inquiries in Melbourne either hadn't been done, or hadn't been followed up when flicked to the Victoria Police. Cooperation between the states wasn't a hallmark of the investigations into the shooting.

Under pressure to get an early result, and with the obvious

problems of pushing a murder inquiry that was going to be a hard slog, Omega gave some of the detectives assigned to the taskforce the job of looking at the Rogerson/Karp/Paltos entanglement. The efforts of Internal Security and the Police Tribunal had put some runs on the board. Converting that work to a respectable brief of evidence was clearly possible with the resources available to Omega.

The taskforce strapped up the brief against Rogerson, and at 7 am on 29 September 1987 they tapped on the door of 32 Gleeson Avenue. At the same time, detectives were also knocking on the door of Morrie Nowytarger's place in semi-rural Oxford Falls, in the hills behind Sydney's Northern Beaches.

Joy Rogerson came to the front door, but didn't open it. She initially denied that Rogerson was at home. It didn't work. Curiosity got the better of the ex-detective, who was spotted poking his head out of a side window as he tried to see what was happening. He remained reluctant to come out of hiding until it was pointed out to him that the detectives had no intention of leaving without him. They would break down the front door, if that's what it took, they told Joy.

Doug Kelly would later deny that he yelled, 'If he is not fucking out in five minutes we're gonna smash the fucking door in!' In Kelly's version of events, Joy Rogerson said, 'He's not coming out. You've been picking on Roger for years. This is only another effort on the Police Department's part.' To which, Kelly says he retorted, 'Don't be silly. Tell him to come out.' I know which version I'd put my money on.

Kelly reckoned it took Rogerson 25 minutes to emerge from the house. After asking what the warrant was for, he said he wanted to ring Val Bellamy.

Rogerson was placed in the back seat of the unmarked police car and driven to the Remington Centre for an interview. It wasn't a long process, as he wasn't doing much chatting. Next, it was off to the then new Sydney Police Centre, where he was charged with conspiracy to pervert the course of justice, arising from the Bentley episode. Nowytarger suffered the same fate. Both men were given bail and told to appear at the Castlereagh Street Court, now the Downing Centre, on 20 October.

October 20 was the first of many lousy days in court for Rogerson, who was represented by Bellamy. A standard police quip of the time was that if you were a criminal who had Val Bellamy (or a few other Sydney legal practitioners) appearing for you, you must be guilty of something. Bellamy wasn't too fussy provided his clients paid up, but he wasn't a livewire advocate. Things got worse when Ross Karp, by that time serving a lengthy sentence for the dope importation, and who was representing himself, became determined to plead guilty. In fact, he was very perturbed that the Crown wasn't ready to proceed. He wanted to get it over with and get back to serving his sentence. He didn't intend to spend his time dealing with lingering court matters. The case was adjourned until 30 October.

Appearing for the Crown that day was Alan Saunders QC, who had had dealings with Rogerson in the past and didn't like him. If a judge has a bit of a past with a defendant, most will immediately stand down and hand the case over to someone else. Not so with prosecutors. This was a case Saunders would approach with vigour. The matter was adjourned for committal, the first step towards a hearing in a higher court, on 9 May 1988. Rogerson remained on bail, despite the Crown muttering darkly about his potential to interfere with witnesses.

With the conspiracy case under way, the focus of the

taskforce switched back to the hard slog of the Drury attempted murder. As usual, the Victoria Police weren't going out of their way to be helpful. The only ray of sunshine down there was some help from Peter O'Halloran, who had a brush with infamy recently when accused, and later acquitted, of sex offences while on secondment in Sierra Leone. Digging around the activities of Alan Williams, Christopher Flannery and their associates, mates and enemies, many of whom were old-style Painters and Dockers types, wasn't an easy task. It got more complicated when it became apparent that the allegedly squeaky-clean Victoria Police might not have been so clean after all. The inquiry was digging up connections that were on the nose. The men of Taskforce Omega were very pleased to get back to Sydney.

18

FROM THE FRYING PAN INTO THE FIRE

The break in the Drury inquiry finally came the task-force's way on 15 February 1988. Alan Williams had moved from the metaphorical heat of Melbourne to the real heat of remote Katherine, in the Northern Territory. The move marked the end of his career in crime that had begun at age sixteen when his parents separated. A short term in a boys' home got him off to a bad start; four years in prison for armed robbery was his 'finishing school'. Armed robbery obviously had its limitations, but drugs were fairly safe to traffic and very profitable. His big error was using his own product.

He finally got the message, however, and in August 1987 Williams went to Katherine to clean up his act and find a little safety. He had 'lived in the fast lane' until March 1982, when 'the rot began to set in; it was one mistake after another'. Rogerson and Drury loomed large as those 'mistakes'. Of his departure to Katherine, Williams said: 'I must state my main reason was people were trying to kill me. I believe it stems from the Drury matter.'

What brought him undone in that remote part of Australia was being pulled over by a local cop. He was unlicensed and riding a motorbike. A routine check by the diligent copper revealed that New South Wales detectives were very keen to chat to him over the Drury shooting. News of his arrest quickly made it to Sydney, where some of the lads from the taskforce were enjoying a Chinese New Year celebration with their families. Clive Small and Bill Smith were soon on a plane to the Territory. Williams was extradited back to Sydney four days later, and they couldn't shut him up. He readily agreed to plead guilty to a charge of conspiring with Rogerson and Flannery to murder Drury.

Breaks like this don't happen often. Williams, for a career crook, was in the rather odd position of finding that the best way to protect himself was to tell the truth. The missing – and believed dead – Flannery must have weighed heavily on his mind. Years later, during a coroner's inquest into his disappearance, it would become obvious that people had been queuing up to bump off Flannery.

Back in Sydney, the paper went into the typewriter. The result was a record of interview that Williams was happy to sign. He told Small that he had met with Flannery just before Christmas 1983. Flannery told him the go-between was Roger Rogerson, who was 'sweet' and had made an offer to Drury to run dead on the case. Drury was thinking about the offer. Williams told Flannery to tell Rogerson to up the ante to $100,000 or an open ticket. Whatever it would take.

In February 1984, Williams had booked into a Sydney motel using the name 'Harvey'. Rogerson and Flannery had turned up for a chat about his progress. Rogerson collected a copy of the transcript of Williams's committal proceedings and a wad of cash 'for his time'. In May he was back in Sydney where he lunched at a seafood restaurant in York Street, in the city, with Rogerson and Flannery. Rogerson gave Williams the bad news. 'I have spoken to Drury again and basically he said he is too committed to change his evidence.' Williams told Small that Rogerson had then left the room and Flannery said to him: 'Do you want me to kill him [Drury]?'

Williams: That's a pretty big step.
Flannery: That seems to be the only alternative.
Williams: If that's what's got to be done, you do what you think best. Do you trust Rogerson that much?
Flannery: Yes.

When Rogerson returned to the table, Flannery told him the only way to solve Williams's problem was to make sure that Drury didn't make it to court. 'Alan wants Drury killed,' Flannery said bluntly.

Williams said he couldn't recall whether it was Rogerson or Flannery who said, 'It will be done.' The topic of money then arose, with Flannery requesting his 'usual' fee of $50,000, half up-front, half on completion. When Williams asked Rogerson if he required his palm to be greased, Rogerson simply told him that if questioned, he would keep quiet. Keeping quiet went both ways. Rogerson later said to Williams, 'I think everything will be sweet as long as everybody keeps their mouths shut.'

Back at his hotel, Williams, a little concerned about Rogerson's lack of interest in money, asked Flannery again if he really trusted him. After all, cash in Rogerson's hand would tie him in game, set and match. Flannery replied, 'Yeah, I do, but just on the off-chance, it won't be done unless he is with me.'

Williams's evidence was both credible and detailed, and given without the promise of an indemnity. Aside from its legal value, it indicated that Rogerson was interested more in power than in money. He had always wanted to be a player, and the biggest in the game.

Doug Kelly contacted Rogerson and asked him to come in for an interview. He duly arrived at the Remington Centre on 24 February with solicitor Val Bellamy in tow. Kelly was surprised when Rogerson agreed to answer questions. Allegation after allegation was put to him, with Hoggett feeding questions to Kelly, and Hreszczuk taking notes on the old manual typewriter. Rogerson answered the questions and denied any complicity. He stood by his story that on 6 June 1984, at shortly after 6 pm, he wasn't standing beside Flannery in Drury's driveway in Chatswood. He was driving home from a day's toil at Darlinghurst Detectives, he said. Shortly after he got home that night, he said, Joan Morey, wife of his old mate and sometime Hold-up Squad boss Noel Morey, had rung to ask if Rogerson had been with her husband or knew where he was. There was a flap on and Jim Willis, another senior detective, was looking for him. A detective had been shot, she said. It was a very memorable night.

Omega's digging around in Melbourne and chatting to Flannery's wife, Kath, had raised a couple of questions. Kathleen Flannery had spoken to the investigators about Rogerson's close association with her husband. It had been closer than the usual police–criminal informant relationship, she alleged. In particular, Kath alleged that she saw Rogerson with her husband at around 7.15 pm on the night of the shooting of Michael Drury.

Rogerson recalled, somewhat coyly, 'I don't know about the time, but I recall receiving phone calls from Flannery at the Darlinghurst Detectives. He was in a flap about something. I can't recall what it was. He asked me if I could see him. I told him I was busy at that stage, but I could see him after work on my way home. I think it was at the Arncliffe Scots Club, which was just up the road from where he lived. That's where I met them, that is Flannery and his wife.' Rogerson's response, whether the truth, a lie or somewhere in-between, dovetailed neatly with Kath Flannery's observation and his phone conversation with Joan Morey. The chances of putting him at Flannery's side in Drury's driveway were about zero.

On the evidence, heavily supported by the interview with Alan Williams, Rogerson was arrested at the conclusion of the interview and charged with conspiring with Flannery and Williams to murder Michael Drury. Bail was refused by the police. At the time, Flannery was missing and presumed dead. 'Flannery was a complete pest,' Rogerson would later say of his luncheon partner. 'The guys in Sydney tried to settle him down, they tried to look after him as best they could but he was out of control. Maybe it was the Melbourne instinct coming out in him, but he didn't want to do what he was told.' It's my belief that Rogerson was simply one of many reasonable suspects for the disappearance of Christopher Flannery. As in the case of Warren Lanfranchi, sympathy was something in short supply around the CIB.

The next morning in Central Local Court, Magistrate Kevin Waller considered the charges against Rogerson and an application for bail. Because of the 'chilling gravity of the allegations and the possibility of interference with witnesses', bail was refused.

Rogerson was taken downstairs from the dock and into the complex of cells attached to the police station in which he had once worked and where many of his conquests from his toil at the CIB had been charged. Long Bay was the next stop. The hunter was now mingling with his former quarry. Any police officer in gaol can expect to get a hard time from the inmates. Payback time begins. You can't turn your back or let your guard down for a moment.

The remand section of the Long Bay complex of prisons is a lower-security part of the gaol housing people who are protesting their innocence. It's a mixed bag of unpleasantness, with anyone from those arrested for failing to pay parking fines, and serving time in lieu, through to those accused of terrible crimes.

During his stay, Rogerson was harangued regularly by his fellow inmates, and death threats were almost mandatory. Although housed in a special protection unit, he was still gravely at risk. On one occasion, he was playing cards with an inmate, when another inmate on a level above tipped out some boiling water that narrowly missed Rogerson. Rogerson later quipped, 'Lucky it was hot water and not acid.' His sense of humour, if black, was still intact.

Rogerson escaped meeting a nasty fate in gaol, thanks to Justice Adrian Roden of the NSW Supreme Court. Roden had been a rather feisty advocate, despite his small physical stature. He had represented some fairly hard crooks over the years, including a few Rogerson foes.

I recall seeing Roden for the first time at the bar table in Central Court in the mid-1970s. He was representing a heavy crim in committal proceedings. Security was tight just in case the crim decided to try his chances at escaping. On the Bench was Lennie 'The Glove' Nash, considered by police to be hard, but fair, and by crooks and their lawyers as just hard. Nash was a beak who looked as comfortable on the Bench as he did in his Northern Beaches backyard, with barbecue tongs in one hand and a 'cold gold' can of Tooths KB lager in the other. Roden was lecturing Nash, who interrupted him and pointed out that his argument was pointless. 'Note where you're sitting, Mr Roden, and note where I'm sitting.' Roden didn't flinch and continued his lecture.

Roden took the view that Rogerson wasn't a grave flight risk, and that he would be in danger if he remained in gaol. He also took the chance to take a swing at the prosecution brief, which was rather outside his remit, stating that he was 'unimpressed with the Crown case' as it relied heavily on the evidence of a 'co-conspirator' – a view that wasn't shared by the magistrate, who subsequently committed Rogerson for trial, after hearing the evidence of the co-conspirator.

Roden put bail within Rogerson's reach. A surety of $250,000 was required, which would be forfeited if Rogerson did a runner. The family home at 32 Gleeson Avenue was the surety. A caveat was registered to the title on 2 March 1988.

Rogerson walked from the court at 6.30 pm on 26 February, and strolled into a throng of waiting members of the media. He stepped on to the front foot over the ensuing weeks, telling the eager press that he was now merely a humble factory worker. This wasn't quite right, given that he was in the safe and security business, but it was a good line. His stay in gaol had been 'nasty and horrible', he said. The secure family home was now on the line. It was another blow to the marriage that had become shaky after the revelations of the dodgy bank accounts.

The old ego was back in control when Rogerson told the press he was thinking about writing a book, or maybe a movie script, of his life. 'The bottom line is completely commercial exploitation,' he said. 'When I left the police force, I walked away with peanuts as far as superannuation and long service leave is concerned.' Warming to his subject, he said: 'If you analyse what I've lost, I'd say it was somewhere between $300,000 and $400,000 and I'm now more or less unemployable. But I have a lot of time on my hands and I've been thinking about this for some time. The time is now right for me to write a piece and tell a side of police work which hasn't been told before.' The press conference at which he made known his literary and film plans came complete with a photo opportunity of Rogerson in the definitive detective's summer safari suit.

Omega's response to the Rogerson publicity machine was to add two charges of conspiring to supply heroin to the list. The supply was tied to the charges facing Rogerson over the bank accounts. After all, the money had to come from somewhere, and the chronology, the backbone of any investigation, was compelling. It was neat work by the B-graders.

In the midst of all this hullabaloo, Alan Williams faced Justice Maxwell in the Supreme Court of NSW and pleaded guilty to conspiring with Christopher Flannery and Rogerson to murder Michael Drury. He was remanded in custody for sentencing on 1 June 1988. He got fourteen years with hard labour.

It was back to court, this time the Coroner's Court in Glebe, on 9 May for the committal proceedings on the car and bank accounts. It was one of the few available courtrooms for what would be a long hearing. Appearing for the Crown was David Rofe QC, and for Rogerson, the decidedly colourful Patrick Costello. Having Costello as your barrister was like having Val Bellamy as your solicitor, an indication that you might well be as guilty as hell, whatever your plea. Costello's core business was representing drug importers and sellers – a very lucrative one, as his clients seldom had a problem finding his fees and Costello wasn't troubled about the source of the cash. He didn't win all that often, due mainly to the usually overwhelming evidence against his clients, rather than to any lack of skill on his part. Costello would later die of natural causes, despite talk of 'settling up' by some of his former clients who weren't too happy with him for pocketing a large share of their ill-gotten gains.

One rather unwilling witness called at Rogerson's trial was bank security manager Anthony North, a mate of Rogerson's who had given him a character reference at the bribery trial. When asked if he would repeat what he had told the jury at that trial, he said: 'You put me on the spot, sir. $110,000 is a lot of money in the accounts. Roger never had that kind of money when I knew him, sir; it's a lot of dough.'

A little drama was added by the arrival of mystery witness 'Miss Jones', who was a protected witness with an indemnity from the federal attorney general. She alleged she had flown to Sydney on 14 May 1985 and exchanged bags with Rogerson at Sydney airport. The bag Rogerson handed over contained about 2.5 kilograms of heroin, she estimated. The bag she swapped for it contained around $100,000 in cash. Chronology is the lifeblood of an investigation, and the timing coincided with Rogerson's banking exploits.

'Miss Jones' told the court she was a former prostitute from Melbourne. She had regularly bribed Paul Higgins, of the Victoria Police, she said. (Higgins ended up in Victoria's Armed Hold-up Squad and was well acquainted with Alan Williams.) The witness then alleged that while she was giving evidence, she had seen Rogerson mouth the words 'You're dead' three times at her.

Listening to the slew of sordid allegations were Joy Rogerson, and Melinda and Gillian whenever their studies allowed.

Just down the corridor, State Coroner Greg Glass was presiding over the inquest into the death of Sallie-Anne Huckstepp. The name 'Rogerson' was also uttered regularly in that venue. Matters became even more exhausting for everyone, particularly the Rogerson family, when the committal ran way over time and was adjourned. The adjournment was so that Rogerson's committal for the conspiracy to murder Michael Drury could get under way. The venue this time was the Glebe Local Court.

On the Bench was the rather saturnine Peter Miszalski. Gerald Dempsey appeared for the Crown, and Greg James QC, later a Supreme Court judge, appeared for Rogerson. Chester Porter QC was busy elsewhere, running, among other things, the unsuccessful defence of Manly hotelier Andrew Kalajzich who was charged with conspiring to murder his wife, Megan. Porter would soon be giving the NSW Police a fair serve when representing former senior detective Harry Blackburn at a royal commission to find out why he had been wrongly charged with a series of rapes. It was one of the greatest investigative 'oops' in Australian history.

Michael Drury gave evidence, reliving the events that led up to the attempt on his life. James, in cross-examination, trod the same path as Chester Porter in the bribery trial. Why hadn't Drury reported Rogerson's overtures, he demanded? The passing years had taken some of the rawness from Drury's recollection. He told the court he had been too frightened. 'Rogerson had unbelievable connections and a lot of power within the Police Department,' he said. 'There would have been a cover up.' Blabbing would have done to his career what the bullets failed to do to his life. No one had wanted to hear the unpalatable truth in 1984; but by 1988, people were starting to believe that the accusations against Rogerson may have been true. James tried to have the reporting of Drury's evidence suppressed, for fear the media would go into a feeding frenzy and damage Rogerson's chances of a fair trial. Miszalski declined the request.

James also had a fair crack at Alan Williams, the star of the Crown's case. In his submission he gave details of Williams's career as a crook, and stated that by giving evidence he was simply serving his own ends. The irony that Williams had pleaded guilty and was doing fourteen years' hard labour eluded the learned counsel. Miszalski, however, gave James a little slap, pointing out that Rogerson was on record as being an advocate for the use of criminal informants. Rogerson had said that 'criminals often made the best informers'. He noted that Williams looked uncomfortable in the witness box, but found that understandable given he was a criminal giving evidence for the Crown. He said, 'Criminals do give evidence on behalf of the Crown.'

Despite the eloquent and expensive pleas of both of Rogerson's counsels, the magistrates in both cases decided that Rogerson should stand trial. On his way out of the committal for the conspiracy to murder, Rogerson's famed cool slipped and he spat at Clive Small.

19

TRIAL BY JURY

In the year following his committals, Rogerson was uncharacteristically quiet. His only outing was a puff piece in the supermarket potboiler *New Idea*: 'Joy Rogerson: Living with fear'. It came complete with a picture of Roger, Joy, the girls and the family's pet basset hound and was taken on the lawn at Gleeson Avenue. 'We've had letters from people saying what they're going to do to him in there if he gets convicted – and what they're going to do to us,' Melinda was quoted as saying. 'It wears you down when you constantly see the name Rogerson in the papers.'

It was certainly wearing down the resolve of the loyal Joy, who told the magazine: 'I mean should we all curl up and be shaking on the bed 24 hours a day? But when we walk past and hold our heads high, people can see we're still coping. We're living our lives as we think we should.' What she didn't let on was that the news of piles of money deposited in bogus bank accounts, the dreadful allegations that were racking up, and the loss of control over the family home as a result of Rogerson's bail, had badly shaken her faith in her spouse.

Having to sit through the hours of courtroom testimony,

and the constant reminders in the media, had been very wearing on the entire Rogerson family. But most unsettling for Joy was her growing concern that at least some of the barrage of allegations were accurate. The good father, son and husband might just also be 'Australia's most notorious detective'. Loyalty could take one only so far. Gillian Rogerson, when she was asked by a fellow student about 'that cop', replied: 'He's my father.' Roger's brother, Owen, was also finding that the name 'Rogerson' was proving somewhat of a liability in his career in the Licensing section of the NSW Police.

Rogerson's trial for conspiracy to murder Michael Drury began in October 1989. The usual suspects were brought into court and gave their evidence. Greg James QC for Rogerson did his bit. Prosecuting was Chris Maxwell QC, despite attempts by NSW Police to secure an 'outside' prosecutor, a barrister from the private bar. First choice had been the current director of public prosecutions, Nicholas Cowdery QC, but the police had lost the argument. On the Bench at the Central Criminal Court in Darlinghurst was Justice Allen.

On 2 November, Rogerson was called to the witness box by James. The case needed a star turn, and Rogerson was it. Drury had been emotional while giving his evidence, just as he had been at the bribery trial. Much play had been made by James of Williams's track record. Rogerson's role was to put the boot into both, and to do it with his customary poise. He didn't disappoint. Seizing on Drury's obviously emotional state, he very neatly said that Drury had been 'befuddled' in his recollections. Rogerson had offered 'to help' Drury and he wasn't 'greatly concerned about what was happening in Melbourne'.

With Flannery not around to give evidence, James asked Rogerson about their relationship. Did it go outside the police–informer relationship, he asked? 'No, never,' Rogerson firmly replied. Though Maxwell's subsequent cross-examination did little to dent the Rogerson performance, he did bring up one curiosity which, if nothing else, gives a further insight into Rogerson's personality. In response to Maxwell's probing about the so-called police–informer relationship, Rogerson offered that many criminals he trusted had his unlisted home telephone number. He said, 'I had gained a reputation for being able to talk to these dangerous criminals ... and Flannery was included in this group.'

After Flannery had disappeared in May 1985, Kath Flannery had called Rogerson. 'Mrs Flannery contacted me after he had gone, saying his boy was in a very bad way,' Rogerson said. 'It was school holidays and we were going to the Georges River at Revesby with my kids for a picnic with the neighbours. She brought the kids over.' He went on, 'I always made a practice of being nice to the wives and families of persons I had arrested. If I could help them I would. This is how I was successful in gaining the confidence of those people, because it was unusual for a policeman to be pleasant to the wives of some of these criminals.'

In January 1985, when Rogerson had been suspended pending the outcome of one of the many investigations, Flannery's house had been machine-gunned. Rogerson visited the family. 'I was interested to see how lucky they were,' he said. 'I was concerned about his kids. It seemed amazing to me that they'd escaped.'

Rogerson then denied being a friend of Flannery's. Nor was their relationship that of police–informer. It is tempting, then, to speculate whether, at the core, Rogerson still had a shred of concern for others; some remnant of the values that had been drummed into him as a kid. Or perhaps it was purely ego, after all, and the need to exercise a degree of control over all those around him, whether it be through a show of benevolence or malevolence.

Once the evidence had been presented, it was time to sum up. Maxwell took the tough line, suggesting that Rogerson's performance was just one of 'artful pretence of a skilled witness'. The jury wasn't buying it, he said. Of Williams, 'quite clearly he is not lily white', and 'it is not a fantastic scenario plucked from out of nowhere . . . [T]here is no reason for Williams to falsely nominate the accused person [Rogerson].' Williams had known Flannery for twenty years, Maxwell told the jury, and regarded him as 'a man of violence . . . a killer'. On the money. You would certainly think twice about offending these old members of the Painters and Dockers Union.

Greg James countered with a very punchy address, tough and uncompromising. Drury, he said, had gone to great lengths to prepare himself for cross-examination and was 'emotionally involved'. One might have thought the first advisable and the second understandable, but James was able to undermine Drury's credibility in the eyes of the jury. When he asked Drury why he hadn't reported the attempted bribe, the question was left hanging in the air. Williams, James told the jury, was a 'cunning man who will not only stoop to foist off his own guilt onto others but a man who will not scruple from doing so'. Williams was 'a liar, a drug pusher, a criminal, a manipulator who will stop at nothing to achieve the best result for himself'. Call me old-fashioned, if you will, but Williams's admissions made without the benefit of a deal or an indemnity, and which resulted in a plea of guilty and fourteen years' hard labour, is hardly a 'best result'. Of course, there is a rather large gap between 'justice' and the 'law'.

In his summing up, James had neatly moved the status of victim from Drury to Rogerson. His client was the victim of a crafty plotter, he implied. And the jury shouldn't buy the prosecution's angle.

Justice Allen, in his directions to the jury, took a case that was by then wobbly, and killed it stone dead. He removed the only link between Rogerson and Drury when he told the jury it would be 'dangerous in the extreme' to convict Rogerson on the basis of Williams's testimony. 'Look at Williams's motivation to lie,' Allen told the jury. 'He had been told that there were tapes of recorded telephone conversations that he'd had where he'd made admissions about his role in a conspiracy to murder Detective Drury. What would this Melbourne heavy do? A deal with the only people left to deal with . . . the Police.' Allen didn't sit often in the criminal jurisdiction, and if he had I suspect that the then Corrective Services Minister Michael Yabsley would have had his hands full making prison guards redundant.

Allen went on, 'It would have to be a big deal and he would have any motivation, you may think, to do the biggest deal he could. Was the deal better than to give the Police Rogerson?' He added a few points to 'balance' his directions, but the jury had a pretty fair idea of what they were going to do.

The jury retired to consider its verdict on 20 November 1988. After three weeks spent hearing the evidence, they took less than three hours to deliberate before reaching a decision. It was barely time to enjoy the lunch provided by the sheriff's officers.

'Not guilty,' announced the foreman.

Roger Rogerson walked out into the afternoon traffic of

Oxford Street a free man. But unlike when he was acquitted on bribery charges, the lads from Darlinghurst Police Station weren't there to celebrate with him.

Doug Kelly, who had been sharing his time between Omega and his day-to-day police work, said the team were 'shattered' by the result. Michael Drury had to be helped from the court by friends.

Rogerson, of course, was very quickly out and about with his new best friends, the media. He claimed that he had been 'fitted' by a 'new breed' that had taken over the police force. 'Thumper' Thorley and the Police Tribunal copped it as well, being described by Rogerson as a 'kangaroo court'. He rejected claims that Angus MacDonald was an old mate, saying that he was simply a colleague with whom he'd had the 'odd picnic or two when the kids were little' and an occasional beer. Any senior detective would have known him, he said. Moving on to the front foot, he called for an inquiry into allegations that the investigation into the Drury shooting was flawed.

The centrepiece of the performance was, yet again, putting the boot into Drury. Twice he had been tried on Drury's testimony, he stressed, and twice he had been acquitted. As for the Omega Taskforce members and their superiors, Rogerson said he thought Commissioner Avery was out to get him. 'It just seems to be some of these high ranking police officers are so inexperienced in court matters. I don't think half of them would know where the District Court was and most of them wouldn't know what it was like to arrest someone.'

Val Bellamy joined the chorus, writing to the attorney general and demanding an independent public inquiry into the charges against his client. 'The present situation is completely unsatisfactory,' wrote Bellamy, 'and is aggravated daily by further publicity even including remarks by the Premier as to "the forces of evil" and the paranoid pronouncements of the Police Board as to some illusory conspiracy.' It was eloquent, but baffling. Bellamy was trying to get a bit of spin from the Blackburn inquiry, which was grabbing most of the headlines. Harry Blackburn, a former senior detective, had been charged with 25 sexual assaults on women. The cases against him were thrown out of court on 11 October 1989 and the investigating police later found to have ignored evidence that would have exonerated him. The debacle cost the New South Wales taxpayers over 2 million dollars in compensation. Bellamy added, 'Such an inquiry should not occur until after the present royal commission into the charging of Blackburn has been concluded.' It was a nice attempt to keep Rogerson, who had another trial waiting in the wings, firmly in the victim's seat.

The attorney general in the new Greiner government was John Dowd, a man with a long memory. Bellamy's plea fell on very deaf ears.

Geoff Hoggett wasn't a gentleman with a penchant for rushing to the media. A very quiet and private bloke, I reckon he would rather gargle Drano than hold a press conference. But in the storm of publicity and accusations that followed Rogerson's acquittal, Hoggett's superiors shoved him into the limelight. If he was good, then they would bask in his success, and take credit for it. If it went pear-shaped, the problem was his. When the burdens of command become heavy in New South Wales, the notions of the Westminster system are thrown to the four winds. 'Cover your arse,' is the literal English translation of the police motto *Culpam poena premit comes*, or something along those lines.

Hoggett flatly denied that Omega had been set up to 'get' Rogerson. 'We came in with completely open minds,' he said. 'We always ran straight down the middle. We realised that we in turn could be investigated. It was a completely fair investigation. There was no skulduggery. We never did anything to try and prefer a charge.' In response to Rogerson's assertions that Avery was behind the charges, Hoggett said: 'I would never have accepted that. Our charter was to investigate the Drury shooting. All I knew about the case before was what I'd read in the papers.' He expressed the thoughts of most NSW Police when he added, 'We didn't want to think one of our own could have been responsible. It was a terrifying thought.'

Of the often-maligned Alan Williams, Hoggett said: 'We were not prepared to bargain with him in any way. The only guarantee Williams asked for was to be protected. He is terrified of Rogerson. I think it is a relief for him.' Williams had just wanted to get out of the whole mess by fleeing Melbourne for the Northern Territory.

There was no Merry Christmas, nor any chance of a happy new year, as 1989 became 1990. Rogerson's trial was looming, and at home he had been found guilty of letting down his wife and children. Given the pressure cooker that had been the Rogersons' lot since the Lanfranchi shooting in 1981, it's a testament to Joy and the girls that the family stayed together as long as it did.

By the time Rogerson joined Morrie Nowytarger and Nick Paltos in the dock at the District Court in Darlinghurst, cheek by jowl with Central Criminal Court where he had appeared in the dock a few months before, the Rogersons were formally 'estranged'. Divorce would soon follow.

When the trial began before Judge Shillington on 30 January, Rogerson's elderly widowed mother, Mabel, was present in the courtroom to support her son. Also sitting unobtrusively in the public gallery was Anne Melocco, the next Mrs Rogerson. Like Joy, Anne was a local girl. She was a handsome woman some thirteen years Rogerson's junior and lived only a few streets from what had been the Rogerson family home. She worked as a personal assistant for a printing business in nearby South Strathfield. The relationship between Melocco and Rogerson would be well and truly under way by 1991, and they would marry in 2004.

As usual, Rogerson was impeccably turned out, though the trousers of his court suit were becoming a little shiny. Prosecuting him this time was the distinguished senior Crown prosecutor Bill Job QC. David Dalton was appearing for Rogerson. The detectives from Omega had done their job thoroughly, and there was a parade of witnesses. Early on was Rogerson's accountant, Robert Gamble, who testified that the first he had heard of the pile of money in the dodgy bank accounts was when he received a tax assessment notice from the Australian Taxation Office. He'd asked Roger about the reason for the assessment. Rogerson had explained to Gamble that he was involved in a court case and may have needed the money. Gamble, who had done the family tax returns for years, wisely didn't ask about the source of the windfall.

The Crown also beat the defence to the punch by calling evidence from one of Rogerson's neighbours, Gwyn Josephs. Though overseas at the time of the trial, Josephs had given a detailed statement to the investigating police. The jury missed hearing his lyrical Welsh tenor voice. In his statement, Josephs said that Rogerson had stored a 'rusty biscuit tin' in his safe. Rogerson had told him it contained the family passports, insurance policies and other documents. Though Rogerson had come for the tin on several occasions over the three years it had been in the safe, he thought it a little odd that in April and May 1985 Rogerson had taken it out twice in a matter of a few days. This, of course, tallied with Rogerson's banking exploits.

Josephs used the safe he kept in his modest Gleeson Avenue home to store pistols. Contrary to the sensational media reporting of the time, Josephs wasn't a gun dealer. He was an expert competitive pistol shooter, and the safe was a legal requirement of his pistol licence. In his spare time, he was a dab hand at writing poetry. He maintained that he would always think of Rogerson as a reliable friend and a good neighbour.

Ross Karp, who had already pleaded guilty to the conspiracy, came in from Long Bay Gaol. Despite his conviction for this crime and his involvement in drug importation, he brought with him a glimpse of the integrity he had displayed in his former career.

The struck-off solicitor told the court of the lunch at the Bayswater Brasserie with Rogerson, when the Bentley motored into the plot. He recounted Rogerson's story of the problem with a pile of cash in bank accounts under false names. Karp said, 'I thought I responded by asking do you need to explain how the money arrived in the accounts?' He said that Rogerson replied, 'Yes, I am renovating an antique motor vehicle and could you prepare a contract of evidence for the sale.' Karp then said to Roger, 'How much do you need to explain?' Rogerson replied, 'Between $60,000 to $70,000.'

Karp said he had prepared the documentation of his sham purchase and renovation of the car, leaving the dates and amounts blank. He later gave them to Rogerson to fill in the blanks. Karp told the court, 'I've never paid them one dollar' and had only seen the car at Nowytarger's office. When asked why he agreed to the conspiracy, he said: 'I did it because Nick Paltos wanted to ingratiate himself with Rogerson at the time.' It also covered Karp's withdrawals from his own accounts. When asked what he had spent his cash on, he admitted that it may have been used for illegal purposes. The subsequent tape recordings of Paltos, Karp and 'Croc' Palmer were heard by the jury, but Shillington warned them to disregard the content.

'Miss Jones', still a protected Crown witness, turned up and reprised her allegations of swapping heroin for cash with Rogerson at Sydney airport. She was more poised on this occasion, and Dalton's cross-examination didn't rattle her. When he tried to shake her by asking about her psychiatric treatment in Melbourne's Queen Victoria Hospital, she was candid. Yes, she'd had hallucinations while using heroin. Then came the sting. On the day of the airport meeting she hadn't used heroin. 'I wasn't hallucinating when I went to Sydney,' she said. 'I wasn't hallucinating about who was there – I know who was there.' With the usual benefits of hindsight, it wasn't a good question to have asked her, but Dalton was fast running out of good news opportunities.

Witnesses for the defence weren't thick on the ground this time, and so on 19 February, Dalton's best bet entered the witness box, took the Bible in his right hand, faced Judge Shillington, and again swore to 'tell the truth, the whole truth and nothing but the truth'. The judge asked him to take a seat. He turned briefly to acknowledge the jury, and then it was down to business. After all these years, the best defence witness they could muster was the accused, Roger Rogerson.

His evidence ambled back over familiar ground, such as

boating with the Flannerys and the allegations by 'Miss Jones'. Dalton decided to bite a few bullets along the way. He canvassed Joy's ignorance of the dodgy accounts and the pile of cash in them, and Rogerson's relationships with informers in general, and in particular with 'Mr X' (Neddy Smith's name was again suppressed), Lennie McPherson and Bobby Chapman. It was all the usual police–informer relationship, Rogerson told the jury. Detectives received an 'informants allowance' to pay for entertaining them, he said. I was a detective at around the same time as Rogerson's career was dazzling his colleagues. The 'informants allowance' ran, to swipe a phrase from politician Amanda Vanstone, to covering 'a hamburger and a milkshake'. It wouldn't have gone further than paying for the entrée at Dimitri's, Eliza's and the Bayswater Brasserie. But Rogerson was on a roll, telling the jury that in the Drug Squad alone there was a 'huge fund'. Informants were encouraged so that they 'just rang you up freely'. The jury might just have been wondering where their tax dollars were going. Bill Job asked Rogerson why, if this encouragement was all above board, he had been captured on tape telling 'Mr X' (in regard to the Bellamy gold coins) to 'be careful on the phone'. Val Bellamy must have begun to feel uncomfortable around that time.

Job turned to Rogerson's daily diary, which the methodical detective kept in addition to his formal police notebook and duty book. Unfortunately, the diary had fallen into the hands of Omega. In particular, Job was interested in a couple of entries around the times of the visit by 'Miss Jones' to Sydney airport. 'I have been through your little book and I show you exhibit number 6 from May 1985. Two days in a row you had done some whiting out . . . Why?' asked Job.

'No reason,' Rogerson replied.

Job continued, 'What have you written under the white-out?'

Rogerson's normally brilliant memory failed him, as did his credibility as a witness.

What really nailed the Crown case was the ex-Armed Hold-up Squad detective being caught on a security camera in a bank. There are times in an investigation when a suspect 'walks right out of the description'. Rogerson walked right out of the still photograph taken from the security video. It couldn't have been anyone else.

David Riddell was then called to the witness box. He reprised the character reference he had given at the bribery trial years before. Rogerson was 'one of the best men I ever met,' the retired company director told the court.

Neighbour Neville Ashdown also made it into the box to talk about the Flannery boating adventure. He wasn't as vigorous as Riddell, and his evidence started badly as he was keen to have his name suppressed. Being a mate of Rogerson's wasn't something he wanted on his CV. He gave evidence that his son had written in his diary that on 15 May he had 'been out all day on Uncle Roger's boat', thus providing an alibi for Rogerson at the time he was supposed to be at the airport. The problem was that 'Miss Jones' reckoned she had met Rogerson at the airport on the 14th. Ashdown compounded Rogerson's growing problems by saying:

> My wife and I had a bit of an argument over this [the boating trip] because Roger had gained a bit of notoriety over the Lanfranchi case . . . [A]fter some discussion we decided we would tell Roger we wouldn't be going on the picnic and also we'd like to disassociate ourselves a little

243

bit . . . [A]s much as I respected Roger . . . the publicity
and everything he was getting wasn't the type of publicity
I wanted to be involved in.

The Ashdowns later moved to nearby Georges Hall.

At the end of February, after a month of evidence, the
trial moved into its closing stages. As was the custom, the
prosecution had first crack at summing up. Job told the jury
it was 'perfectly clear' that Rogerson had relationships with
crooks long after he had been sacked. When he got to the
nub of the allegations, the car plot, as told by the defence, he
said: 'The story is so improbable that you just can't accept it.
They had to come up with a story very quickly . . . this was
the best they could do with it and they stuck with it.' The
traditional defence of a 'few wins at the races' would have
been more credible.

Dalton didn't have much to add. He said that the Crown
was portraying Rogerson as a corrupt policeman and heroin
dealer, but that he 'had absolutely nothing to hide'. Rogerson
was an 'exemplary man', an 'extraordinary policeman' and
simply the victim of a 'mud rake'. The old 'make him a victim' trick.

On 2 March, after Judge Shillington had added his two
bobs' worth and just in time for lunch, the jury retired
to consider their verdict. It wasn't a protracted affair. At
8.15 pm, as Rogerson faced the prospect of a night in the
cells of his old stamping ground while awaiting a verdict,
the jury returned.

The forewoman announced that the Crown had won
the trifecta. Rogerson, Nowytarger and Paltos were all
guilty.

*

Rogerson was knocked flat. Any vestige of power he may once have enjoyed was completely gone. He was a 49-year-old ex-cop looking down the barrel of a solid prison sentence. His past had caught up with him, and he had little to show for it. The power he had brawled, lied, manipulated and shot people for was now gone. The cash in the bank had been seized. There were no blocks of flats, investment portfolios, or pots of gold sitting in tax havens. The closest thing to fine German engineering his driveway had seen was a Volkswagen. Stylish lawyers and long trials don't come cheap, so any ill-gotten gains he had managed to stash away had been absorbed during his numerous trials. (In the late 1980s, Ian Barker QC, the darling of the criminal bar, was charging $8000 a day, and that was without the cost of a junior barrister, solicitors, their minions and the dreaded 'disbursements'. A law degree can be more effective in generating cash than a gun and a balaclava.)

Joy Rogerson was keeping her distance but was fearful of the effects of the verdict on their two daughters. And Rogerson's former police friends and 'informants' were either in gaol, being prosecuted, or keeping themselves at arm's length lest they be dragged into the mire along with Rogerson. He was on his own.

Doug Kelly and the men of Taskforce Omega were elated. Almost three years of hard work, and the flack they had received from their fellow officers, had been worthwhile. Outside the court, Kelly told the media scrum that Rogerson was an evil and charismatic man. In a later interview, he said that Rogerson was 'obviously a highly intelligent person, [who was] able to manipulate people and they certainly were prepared to do things for him'.

The media were very keen to hear a comment from Michael Drury. It was dignified, but with a justifiable element of mongrel satisfaction. 'In view of the result, I imagine many people would feel this is an occasion for me to respond. I have had to sit back now for many years without making any comment because it was my firm belief that I should never attempt to influence anyone outside the guidelines of our legal system. But I would take this opportunity to make a promise to Roger Rogerson that I, God willing, will be able to go on for many years as a proud member of the NSW Police. With all my energies I will serve this community to allow Roger's wife and two little girls each night to sleep safely in the comfort of their home. This is something Roger failed to guarantee my wife and two little kids.'

On 9 March 1990, Rogerson was back in the District Court after having spent a very tense week at Long Bay. It was a surreal experience for him to appear in the dock of a courtroom outside of which he had paced frequently over the years, waiting to be called to give evidence. The usual practice in sentencing matters is for the arresting police to give the prisoner's antecedents – details of his schooling, family, the fact that 'he was a good boy who loved his mother', his work history, sports played, social bits and pieces – and, of course, his criminal record if there was one. Rogerson found it bizarre to hear, this time, his own antecedents read out to the court.

After hearing submissions on the penalty, including a request by David Dalton for something non-custodial – 'the type of life he can expect in prison would be of the worst possible nature' – Shillington said that Rogerson's behaviour was such that it would 'undermine the police force and the morale of its members'. He gave him eight years' hard labour. He would be eligible for parole in March 1996. Nowytarger got four years, and Paltos had two-and-a-half years added to the sentence he was already serving.

The public gallery was crowded for the sentencing hearing, and included Howard Lanfranchi, brother of the slain Warren. One of the few supporters was Rogerson's mother, who, despite her son's insistence, had attended the hearing accompanied by her two granddaughters. Joy hadn't attended. The dignified elderly woman was a rock. She told reporters, 'I'm his mother. He would never be guilty of those charges that they brought against him because he's a very honourable man. [H]e showed that even when he was a child. If he did something wrong he admitted it . . . I don't think he deserves it,' she concluded. 'The truth will always show up in the very end. That's what will happen with my son. One day we'll be able to prove that he's a good man.' Hers was a lone voice. The truth had taken a while to surface, but it had finally shown up.

The only good news Rogerson would hear for a while was that the Crown would be dropping the heroin charges. Justice had already been done.

Later that afternoon, Roger Rogerson was handcuffed and placed into the prison van with the rest of the day's unsuccessful clients and taken to Long Bay. He would spend his first day in the prison hospital under close watch for his own safety, prior to being classified. His past would make his safety somewhat of a challenge for the Department of Corrective Services.

Rogerson's full-time membership of the prison population would reunite him with Neddy Smith.

20

BACK IN LUCK

As Roger Rogerson was driven off down Anzac Parade, Val Bellamy was strapping up an appeal against the conviction. His application for bail failed.

Rogerson's luck didn't kick back in until 11 December 1990, when Justice Lee of the NSW Court of Criminal Appeal quashed the conviction. He threw in a bonus, saying the charge hadn't been established and the case shouldn't go back for a new trial. Lee and his fellow judges focused on the meaning of the word 'justice' and the need to define it so that Rogerson and his mates could then be convicted of conspiring to pervert its course. It was an interesting decision, given that there had been committal proceedings, which are supposed to root out fundamental failings such as there being no substance to the charge, followed by a review by the Crown to file the bill to prosecute, then a month's worth of trial. As a bit of an each-way bet, Lee indicated that he would allow appeals. Nowytarger and Paltos also had their convictions kicked out. In one of those legal quirks, Karp, who had pleaded guilty, didn't get a mention.

A rejuvenated Rogerson immediately held a press conference. 'I've always been innocent,' he said. 'Finally justice has been done. I'm not bitter, but I'm much lighter. It's been difficult at times with the trouble in the gaols, but we've survived it.'

It was wishful thinking when he said, 'They have tried and I think this will have to be the last chance they will have. There is nothing else that I can possibly imagine they can do to try and keep me behind bars.'

He provided a glimpse of the old Rogerson when he added that he had 'dazzled' prison staff by designing and building grilles for the prison vans. 'The authorities had been quoted too high a price for the job. I did it for the cost of the steel, and of course my lodgings.' He had avoided 'going around the bend', he said, by using the metalworking skills that had endeared him to his neighbours in Gleeson Avenue by sprucing up the old gaol. In his spare time he had 'chewed the fat' with a fellow prisoner under close protection, John Wayne Glover, 'The Granny Killer', who had murdered a number of elderly women on Sydney's North Shore from 1989 to 1990. Not a bad bloke, Rogerson thought.

Rogerson was a practised spinner of good yarns. He told the rapt reporters, 'Work and exercise kept my mind active. Every morning I'd wake up at 5.30 am and run on the spot for 30 minutes, then do 100 sit-ups and 100 push-ups, and I did that religiously.' The years spent training with SWOS weren't wasted. 'For the first two months I just sat in my cell [in Cell Block B of the prison hospital]. That was the most difficult period, adjusting to the shock of the conviction and the sentence and just being in prison. And I was apprehensive about going inside. On the first night I was placed in the Metropolitan Remand Centre Program Unit for ex-police and protected prisoners, and there were prisoners above and below us screaming out abuse at me. I learned quickly to switch off to that but there was still a fair bit of abuse when I was moved to the hospital. There was one prisoner telling everybody in the hospital that he'd been shot by me and he used to show some scar he had to the other inmates. I said to him, "Look, mate, the people I've shot don't end up in hospital, they go straight to the morgue" and that seemed to quieten him down a bit.' Then it was time for a beer with old mates, including Bill Duff.

He popped up, almost inevitably, on *A Current Affair*, telling Australia: 'I don't feel lucky. I feel that justice has been done.' Judge Shillington should 'eat his words', he said.

When Rogerson went home that night for the first time in nine months, it wasn't to Gleeson Avenue. His first night as a free man was spent with his mother at the old family home. During his time in gaol, Joy had divorced him. Rogerson hadn't contested it, but it had knocked him about. The divorce, he reckoned, had come as a surprise. 'I don't see her at all,' he said. 'We should never have divorced.' However, he wasn't alone for long. Anne Melocco, who had been in the background during the trial, was waiting when Rogerson was released. He was uncharacteristically quiet about the blossoming relationship. He didn't want to hurt his daughters, it would seem, who had been regular visitors while he was in gaol, and still believed in their father.

Judge Shillington didn't get the chance to dine on his words. The director of public prosecutions didn't think much of Justice Lee's view, and took up his offer of appealing to the High Court. The appeal would take a while.

In the meantime, Rogerson went back to work, wielding a welder wherever he could pick up work. His consultancy career continued. With his reputation, even muttering the name 'Rogerson' could be an effective tool. If he turned up in person to discuss a problem, few problems would remain unresolved. Louie Bayeh wasn't backward in letting everyone know that Rogerson was a 'mate'. It provided a bit of cash on the way through.

On 7 August 1991, the Independent Commission Against Corruption started poking about in the relationships between police and their informers. One of the star turns in this investigation was Neddy Smith. He had an indemnity to protect him from prosecution for offences committed by him with police officers, except for any murders. The relationship between Smith and Rogerson had been on the decline since Rogerson had decided to out Neddy as a police informant on national television. Smith had later been arrested when about to rob the Botany Council payroll and he was pretty certain the police had been tipped off. The list of suspects wasn't too long.

While in gaol, Smith had been talking to fellow felon, the soon-to-be-late Roy Thurgar. Thurgar would last six months back in circulation before being murdered by a single shotgun blast while outside his laundromat in Alison Road, Randwick. Suspects for the murder included a few NSW Police.

Thurgar had been chatting to the ICAC about the activities of some police and encouraged Smith to do the same. Years of bribes had got him nowhere, and police promises to look after his wife and children had been empty. The ICAC was a chance for payback. Rogerson was collateral damage.

Rogerson, still waiting for the High Court to decide his fate, got wind of Smith's chats with the ICAC. He visited him in gaol and wrote him regular letters. The two men would maintain a friendly relationship up until mid-way through the following year. Rogerson tried to buoy Smith's spirits. 'Anyhow mate, I haven't forgotten you. I know you are in a pretty horrible situation,' he wrote. In one letter, he suggested that Smith's newly acquired typing skills might be handy in a new career. He wrote, 'When you get out and are completely reformed you might be able to get a job at the Armed Hold-up Squad typing out unsigned records of interview.' At least Rogerson still had his sense of humour.

With a problem in the wind, Rogerson decided to do a bit of PR himself. As usual, he used his talents to put himself on the high moral ground. This time he didn't go for the tabloid style of television, choosing instead the doyenne of Australian current affairs, *Four Corners*. He told Australia that loading up criminals was 'a cult' in the NSW Police. 'You were doing a community service . . . it was all done in the interests of truth, justice and keeping things on an even keel and keeping crims under control,' he said. Loading was just a way to control crims who were stepping over the line. 'In the old days the safe blower was the smart crim . . . so they always feared getting a couple of sticks of gelly found in their cars or in their possession . . . The crims accepted it. If you stepped out of line you were asking for trouble and someone would tap you on the shoulder or come knocking on your door and you'd be given a present.' Rogerson was right on the money.

On *A Current Affair*, he said: 'Verbals are a part of police culture. I think they still are.' When later asked, 'You are telling me that police lying under oath was part of the police culture?' he replied: 'Yes.'

Rogerson's candour rattled a few cages. Tony Day, president of the Police Association, said: 'I believe those people have gone. Those older type police for some reason thought they had to go around loading up people. It is definitely not the case with the greater majority of police in this force. They've been weeded out,' he said. The Wood Royal Commission and the various travails of the Police Integrity Commission were just around the corner. Rogerson had put the unpleasant habits of some police squarely in the public eye. However, his PR didn't do him much good. In Neddy Smith, the ICAC had found manna from heaven. Informants like Smith come along only once in a career, if that.

In late 1991, the ICAC started dragging witnesses before it. Among them was the former Rogerson mate Aarne Tees, then an inspector of police and soon to head off to the Bar. Aarne put the boot in squarely, telling the commission that Rogerson's PR was the act of a man 'obviously round the twist' and he was 'degrading' himself. Heaven forbid if Rogerson should decide to tell the truth.

Although it wasn't well intentioned, Rogerson did take heed of Tees's comment and kept his head out of the limelight. It didn't last long. On 17 June 1992, the High Court in a three-to-two majority ruled that the jury and Judge Shillington had been right. There was sufficient evidence to sustain the conviction. It was back to the NSW Court of Criminal Appeal for yet another round in the saga. The only good news was that Rogerson wasn't immediately thrown back into gaol. He continued working as a welder.

When the appeal hearing began again on 6 October of that year, it was with more limelight than Rogerson could have imagined in his worst nightmare.

21

THE RED LIGHT

All hell broke loose in mid November 1992 when Barry Toomey QC gave the Australian public a taste of the antics of the NSW Police. His informant was Neddy Smith.

Toomey had a finely tuned sense of the theatrical. With his opening address he intended to put the ICAC squarely on the front pages of the nation's newspapers. In doing so, he dragged Rogerson, unwillingly, with him. Rogerson 'looms large in this investigation as he has done in the examinations of corruption in the NSW Police Force throughout the decade,' he said. Rogerson was 'in on police crimes worth millions'. He then segued into a potted version of the numerous and saucy allegations made by Smith.

On day two, Toomey put the boot into the former assistant commissioner (crime), Ross Nixon, who had once candidly remarked, after one too many schooners, that he 'wasn't up to the job' as assistant commissioner. Displaying a remarkably poor memory, Nixon declared his disgust at 'learning senior police were associating closely with A-grade criminals'. He was horrified to learn that information had leaked from Taskforce Zig Zag to Neddy Smith, while he [Nixon] was assistant commissioner. Rogerson was 'a disgrace to the NSW Police Force'. However, he had also been 'an excellent detective and the life and soul of the party'. When he heard of Michael Drury's dying deposition and its allegations against Rogerson, Nixon said: 'It became incontrovertible to me . . . he'd crossed the line.'

Rogerson, as might be expected, provided a star turn himself when called to give evidence about his relationship with Neddy Smith. Toomey wasn't the only interrogator. Representing 'Abo' Henry was the pugnacious, brawling and very entertaining Winston Terracini, a barrister once described as not being out of place in a Palermo court giving stick to the mafia. When he asked Rogerson if loading and verballing had been rampant in the old CIB, Rogerson replied: 'I don't think it was in the past tense.' However, he conceded that many officers, including himself, had lied to courts. No one in the court seemed surprised by the admission.

Rogerson told the commissioner, Ian Temby QC, that since his dismissal from the force he had been suspected of committing every type of crime, from the murder of Federal Police Commissioner Colin Winchester through to the persecution of Jesus Christ. As expected, he denied all the allegations of skulduggery.

But the inquiry took its toll. A few days after giving evidence, in a last-ditch attempt to save some face, Rogerson appeared on *A Current Affair* in an interview with Jana Wendt. Unlike his previous appearance on the program, which had been a catalyst in his downfall, Roger Rogerson now appeared all but beaten. The bravado and certainty were gone. Wendt introduced him as 'Australia's most notorious detective'.

Rogerson told Wendt that he was on the dole and living with his mother. He accepted that he was now in disgrace. 'I would have to accept that. Another one is "notorious"; I get that all the time too.' He admitted that his once-prized credibility was 'pretty low'.

When asked if he thought Neddy Smith was evil, he told Wendt: 'Well, he's now admitted all these robberies and he has been convicted of this murder. You'd have to say he was evil, the same as people can think of things to say about me.' Wendt pressed him further: 'Well, some people think *you* are evil,' to which Rogerson replied: 'Sure. I've got to accept it. What can I do? I have my circle of friends and my relatives and they believe me and I just leave it at that.' Tellingly, he admitted for the first time that he was 'good mates with Neddy'. He told Wendt he had hit rock bottom. The saving grace was that his daughters had remained loyal, he said. He looked a truly sad man.

On 16 December 1992, the Court of Criminal Appeal brought down their decision on Rogerson's appeal. Justice Lovegrove told the court, lest there be any confusion, that where Rogerson had gone wrong was creating a false story and documents to 'frustrate or deflect possible criminal proceedings against him'.

Two years after the court had sprung him from gaol, they sent him back, albeit with his sentence reduced to a maximum of three years. Before he was taken off to the cells, Rogerson told the media pack, 'I have never had any faith in the justice system and this is a good example of it.' Inevitably, there was no trace of irony in the statement. Rogerson was completely knackered. There was nowhere left for him to go but to gaol.

This time, his new home wouldn't be beneath the swaying palms of Long Bay, but Berrima Gaol, in the bucolic Southern Highlands. Located just off the old Hume Highway, the gaol specialises in historic tours and well-known inmates who need to be protected. It has been home to crooked coppers, lawyers, politicians such as Rex 'Cuckoo Clock' Jackson, Tim 'The Retired Gangster' Bristow, and a nasty pile of paedophiles. But if you must do time, you could do it worse than in Berrima.

Rogerson proved himself rather creative on the potter's wheel. However, his time at Berrima wasn't without incident. In March 1993, he was summonsed to appear at the Downing Centre for using an expired rail ticket at Town Hall Station on 30 October 1992. Val Bellamy did the honours on his behalf.

Just before his release, he was taken to Glebe Coroner's Court to give evidence in the inquest into the disappearance of Christopher Dale Flannery. Rogerson was one of many people who had been considered as possibly being involved. He would make a few more appearances at the inquest, though his heart certainly wasn't in it. 'If criminals go and murder themselves it doesn't worry me in the slightest,' he later told the court. 'I don't care at all. I don't care about this inquest and I don't care if you don't find out anything about Flannery at all.' He had had enough. The case is still unresolved. However, the coroner did find that if Rogerson didn't murder Flannery, then he certainly knew who did. Rogerson's summing up was concise: the coroner was a 'jerk' and the report 'bullshit'.

Roger Rogerson walked free (aside from fifteen months of parole), and with no court matters pending for the first time in about a decade, on 15 December 1995. The Wood Royal Commission into the habits of the NSW Police was, however, keen to chat. For his re-emergence into the outside world, Rogerson had chosen a snappy blue pinstripe suit. This time, there was no press conference. As he slipped into the back seat of a waiting Mitsubishi Magna, he told the waiting journalists he was off to have a beer.

22

A GREAT DETECTIVE BUT A LOUSY CRIMINAL

Neddy Smith's evidence to the Independent Commission Against Corruption, and its subsequent report in 1994, made Rogerson a very unhappy man. Around the same time, Smith, assisted by the respected Melbourne journalist Tom Noble, produced a book called, not surprisingly, *Neddy*. Unlike many 'kiss and tell' publications by criminals, *Neddy* was both a great read and a chilling insight.

Neither the book nor the ICAC report showed Rogerson in a good light. Both confirmed his status as 'Australia's most notorious detective'. Edited highlights of the dirty details of their 'professional' and 'social' lives were laid out for the public to savour. For the first time, the nation had the insider's view and it was disconcerting in the extreme.

These endeavours were one of the catalysts for the Wood Royal Commission, which kicked a lot of goals with serving police up to no good. (Who could forget the video footage of 'Chook' Fowler's crotch while he negotiated bribes with Trevor Haken?) Unhappily for Rogerson, the Drury matter got a mention, with former Omega Taskforce member Detective Inspector Bill Smith not mincing his words: 'As I and other investigators on Omega were doing this [the investigation], it became blatantly obvious that the initial investigation was an absolute cover up in relation to Roger Rogerson. It became blatantly clear as each stage progressed that Rogerson was the lynchpin and organiser of the shooting of Detective Drury.' Even this strong assertion, however, failed to provoke another long, hard look at the Drury shooting. There was more chance of reviving a dodo.

Thanks to Rogerson, Smith and their supporting cast, the shenanigans of the police had gone from 'Don't ask, don't tell' to part of Australians' daily news diet and a base for entertainment in the form of *Blue Murder*, which screened in all Australian states except New South Wales in 1995. (In New South Wales, Smith had yet another slew of murder trials awaiting him, and it was considered potentially prejudicial. The show would be screened in that state some years later.)

The writer of *Blue Murder*, Ian David, created a piece of film terrifyingly close to reality. I watched a pirated copy sent from interstate. It looked and felt all too familiar. There was also a strong physical resemblance between the lead actors and the characters they were portraying. Rogerson wasn't a fan of the programme. '*Blue Murder* was quite bloody stupid, even though it was a good action movie. About 90 per cent bullshit. None of the scenes happened exactly as they were portrayed,' Rogerson said. 'The first time we saw *Blue Murder* I was sitting with my wife [Anne], watching it. We'd both had a few drinks and about halfway through it she said to me, "You know, when you were a young fella, you were quite good looking." I said, "Listen you jerk, that's Richard Roxburgh. That's not really me." That's how authentic he played the part.'

The content was pretty authentic as well. At one point during the filming at Gleeson Avenue, a neighbour leaned over the fence and said to Roxburgh, 'Where's the lawn mower I lent you, you bastard?!'

Never one to let an opportunity pass, Rogerson added: 'I must admit a lot of the guys have said, "What a great movie, mate. It's a pity you're not doing it again, out there with your shotgun." Ha, ha, ha.' I suspect it's a view held by quite a few people. Any chance that Rogerson had of resuming a reasonably normal existence was now out the window.

The split between the two former mates became very public at Neddy Smith's committal proceedings for murder, held in March and April 1996. The venue was Central Local Court, and on the Bench was Pat O'Shane, probably the least favourite magistrate of active police officers over the past two decades.

There was a spot of sartorial role reversal in court, with Smith dressed in a well-tailored 'State Department' grey suit and silk tie. Rogerson turned up sporting casual clothes, a windbreaker and with no sign of a tie. In another interesting reversal, he had been called by the prosecution. Prosecuting was his former tormentor from the conspiracy to murder case, Chris Maxwell QC. Smith was represented by Winston Terracini.

Rogerson got off to a flying start, telling the court that his woes were the result of a vendetta by senior police. He wasn't corrupt, he said in answer to repeated badgering by Terracini. The cross-examination quickly descended into chaos, with Rogerson shouting at Terracini, whose low regard for the witness was obvious. 'I'm getting frustrated,' Rogerson complained to O'Shane. The clashes continued for two days, with Terracini repeatedly accusing Rogerson of lying, and Rogerson repeatedly denying it. 'I'm not lying. I'm not certain,' he complained. 'I'm being careful not to say anything under oath that could be twisted by you!' At one point he rose from his chair in the witness box and, theatrically brandishing a copy of the *Evidence Act*, accused Terracini of harassing and intimidating him.

Rogerson wasn't the only one waving documents in court. Terracini held up a copy of *Neddy* open to a photograph of Smith and Rogerson, drunk at the Covent Garden Hotel. They were stripped down to their underpants, and were flashing handfuls of dollars at the camera. Rogerson was furious. 'I'm doing nothing wrong!' he yelled. 'I'd left the police force and I can see nothing wrong with having a beer like this.'

Terracini raked through Rogerson's past, destroying any credibility the witness had left. Finally, Terracini asked him, 'Do you feel harassed?' Rogerson replied, 'Yes I do, and I believe it's contrary to the *Evidence Act*.'

'Look,' said Terracini. 'You're a convict, not a lawyer. You've got a hide like Jessie the Elephant!' After being suitably admonished by the magistrate, Terracini said: 'That's it.' Rogerson then left the court. Neither he nor Neddy Smith came out a winner.

For almost two decades, Roger Rogerson had been both apprentice to and then master of the universe, albeit an Australian universe. He wielded power that was literally one of life and death, both physically and socially. He could help make someone wealthy, or he could see them locked up with the key thrown away. He was above the law. And then the world changed and he became the target of the system he had manipulated and, finally, a guest of the government.

With all his experience and intellect, he hadn't got the message. Turning straight would have been a good idea, but one of Rogerson's greatest weaknesses was letting his ego interfere with his decision-making. He just didn't get the message that the game was up.

Rogerson's public face became one of a reasonably successful small businessman who had learned his lesson. Finally, he was on the straight and narrow. In 1997, he began Scafco Scaffolding Pty Ltd and Re-Con Holdings Pty Ltd, both businesses supplying the building trade with scaffolding. He was supported by his partner, Anne Melocco. In August 1998, the couple celebrated their new life by handing over $385,000, with a mortgage to Citibank, for their new home at 22 Churchill Drive, Padstow Heights. It was close to his elderly mother and not far from his old digs in Condell Park. No fibro this time, but instead a very smart brick-veneer home. In typical Rogerson style, it was meticulously maintained inside and out. In the driveway was a far from new, yet still very stylish, Daimler sedan.

The only problem was that if one probed a little deeper, things weren't quite as genteel as they appeared. Doing the poking this time was the Police Integrity Commission and the ICAC. Lurking in the background was the Australian Taxation Office.

Rogerson was again keeping lousy company, and using some business methods that were rather unsporting. Sadly for him, it was no secret. As 1998 drew to a close, his former mate Louie Bayeh proved that there is no honour among thieves. He had come unstuck during the Wood Royal Commission and started babbling to try to save his own skin. He told the ICAC that Rogerson, a frequent visitor to Bayeh's home and to his nooks and crannies in Kings Cross, had threatened him not to tell the truth about the murder of Christopher Flannery. Rogerson wasn't the only one. Stan

'The Man' Smith, a particularly nasty thug, and Lennie 'Mr Big' McPherson had done the same thing. Nice company for Rogerson to be placed in.

The tag team player, the Police Integrity Commission (PIC), was soon in on the act, giving Rogerson yet another chance to appear in the witness box. The questioning opened with his association with Kostas Kontinarakas, another royal commission favourite, and Alan Chara. These gentlemen, among other things, operated the Eros Cinema in Goulburn Street, in the city, which featured 'live' shows featuring well-worn strippers. Private shows were readily arranged, and punters could also buy a beer despite the Eros not having a liquor licence. It was a less than savoury establishment frequented by plastic raincoat wearers and drunk punters out for a night with the boys.

Rogerson began by denying he knew anyone as sleazy as Kostas and his mates. 'I'm too busy working to socialise with the likes of Con,' he said. Unfortunately, he had been caught by a surveillance camera collecting a large wad of cash from Chara. He was just doing a bit of work on a horse float for Chara, Rogerson told the commission. 'It was all done under the old mateship act.' Nice friends, and the price of mateship was estimated at around $10,000.

Rogerson had also provided a loan of $40,000 to Chara to give him a hand after Kostas had been gaoled. He denied that Chara was paying protection money. 'You tell me how I could protect him,' he growled. 'You tell me what senior police officer would be prepared to cop a quid off Roger Rogerson. All they want to do is run me in!' he claimed. As usual, he also put in the boot, making the suggestion that the commission was a 'kangaroo court' and a 'star chamber', and that its investigators, rather than serving him with a summons to attend, should have popped out to Cabramatta and 'witnessed some real crime'. It was becoming a familiar refrain.

Among Rogerson's mates was Laurie Burgess, his former co-defendant in the alleged assault against Mrs Pak at the Korea House and now an ex-copper who had departed under a cloud; 'Bandido' Arthur Loveday, with a healthy list of convictions for violent crimes; Ray 'Chopper' Johnson, a former cop of substantial proportions; and Boris Link, a former New South Wales deputy sheriff who had spent some time as a guest of Her Majesty for dope cultivation and distribution and also hadn't learned his lesson. While Rogerson denied being in the protection business, one could be forgiven for thinking he wasn't being entirely truthful.

Neither Rogerson, nor Anne, nor the lads knew that the ICAC and PIC had some very sophisticated listening devices, and 22 Churchill Drive and the Long Jetty weekender were wired for sound. It was all quite legal this time as well. Some 154 conversations would be recorded.

Dave Frearson, counsel assisting the PIC, had a field day. Rogerson had been caught discussing a potential marijuana crop up at Peats Ridge with Boris Link. 'Chopper' had popped around to tell Rogerson that Laurie Burgess had been told Rogerson was under investigation for some behaviour to do with Liverpool Council tendering. 'It's going to blow out there,' he told Rogerson of the council inquiry. He and Anne were taped talking about the council investigation. Rogerson told her to clean the computer of 'all those double quotes'. Later, he was heard to say: 'We should get rid of this stuff, wipe the whole lot.' Rogerson's response to the taping was, 'It's an absolute invasion of privacy.' It was, but it was also abundantly clear that while Rogerson had been a great detective at one point, he made a lousy criminal.

His grief with Liverpool Council came courtesy of

another mate, Liverpool Council official Sam Masri. Masri looked after purchasing and had done some business with the printers where Anne worked. Rogerson's companies and affiliates were beneficiaries of the council's largesse for scaffolding and excavating contracts. Rogerson was a great small businessman, according to Masri. 'If contractors wouldn't go out and quote, I'd ask him to do it so we could get the work done. We drank at the same place. We were just friends and grew up in the same area. I had greyhounds at the back of his mother's place.' To get past the tender process, and in the interests of efficiency, Masri would ask Rogerson's companies and affiliates to put in dummy quotes to satisfy the three-quote requirement. Rogerson got the business, but Masri never asked for a kickback. Rogerson denied ever offering a kickback, but couldn't remember if Masri had asked for one.

Rogerson had forgotten about the tapes, and in particular his conversation with Anne about putting 10 per cent aside from the jobs as 'commission' for Masri. This outing in court would eventually see both Rogerson and Anne standing in the dock.

At around the same time, Owen Rogerson appeared in court at the Police Integrity Commission, courtesy of Roger. Owen was fourteen years younger than Roger, rather bald, with some similarity of facial features to his brother. He was a 'straight shooter' with an unblemished record. Owen had spent most of his career in Licensing. He had been called on to appear so that he could be asked whether or not he had leaked information to Roger. 'I don't think there's too many other people in the service with a problem similar to mine,' he said. He told the commission: 'This has been going on for many years and I've had to live with that and my family's had to live with that.' He wasn't his brother's keeper, he said. He didn't associate with the people his brother did, and he would never divulge police information. He had been horrified to hear that the violent Loveday was a mate and that Roger had gone to his wedding. Of his relationship with his brother, Owen said: 'Believe it or not, I try to distance myself.'

Rogerson corroborated Owen's testimony accidentally when he was caught on tape. He had said, 'I would never compromise him because of – my mother would – I'm sure would just die of a broken heart', and later: 'I wouldn't fuck him up for anyone . . . he's doing a good job.'

Unfortunately for Owen, Roger didn't need to 'fuck him up'; the name 'Rogerson' did that for him. The sins of his brother proved to be a career killer. The two brothers were not close, initially because of their age difference. Roger's notoriety drove them further apart. Owen commented, 'The pain and suffering the whole family, including his daughters, have undergone has been quite extraordinary.' Owen's pain and suffering were heightened when he found his career had stalled. He left the NSW Police in 2001 on medical grounds and began legal action against his former employers.

When he was recommended for a job at the PIC, he was turned down. He wrote to the commission, saying: 'I am writing out of a sense of despair due to the impact that this event has had not only on myself but my family, which I say is at least humiliating and depressing.' The commission replied that it was 'entitled and indeed required to carefully vet persons who are proposed to be given access to its premises'. Justice for Owen Rogerson seems to be a genuinely elusive thing.

23

THE GOOD, THE BAD, OR THE UGLY?

Roger Rogerson's reputation was now shot to pieces. Many of his criminal and/or other dubious mates were either in gaol, in court or under suspicion. His solicitor, Val Bellamy, was fighting off bankruptcy and was about to be locked up, owing Rogerson a chunk of cash. The ATO was demanding its slice of the dodgy funds he had been caught banking, and the Australian Securities and Investments Commission was prosecuting him for managing two companies within five years of his release from prison. What was he to do?

Rogerson took to the stage, after signing up on a two-year good behaviour bond for the corporate law problem. He joined up with the likes of the former footballer Warwick Capper (famous for his short, tight shorts) and the large and energised Mark Jackson to tour the pubs of the nation. The show was occasionally called 'Wild Colonial Psycho'. Rogerson was the replacement for the very unsuccessful criminal-turned-writer, Chopper Read. Chopper needed a break from the arduous performance schedule to be with his pregnant wife. Rogerson, for some reason, seemed to be the natural replacement. The bad guy becomes a good guy, and the good guy becomes a bad guy. When asked if he was the good, the bad or the ugly one of the trio, Rogerson quipped: 'I'd have to be the bad, wouldn't I?'

In promoting the show, Rogerson told the world he was 'just a normal guy' with 'seven grandkids and two wonderful daughters'. Rogerson, it seems, was working hard in his late middle age to reinvent himself as a lovable old rogue. Provided you forgot his recent past, of course. He was reminded of that past when the lads were touring South Australia in 2004. On 11 August, the local police collared Rogerson for the offence of 'abuse of public office'. He was allowed out on bail and the show went on. Rogerson reckons he was just helping a mate. The matter is still in the lists of the criminal division of South Australia's District Court.

In September 2004, the reinvention came to an abrupt halt when, aged 63, Rogerson suffered a mild stroke and was taken to hospital. His family were on hand. The timing was lousy. Hovering over both his and Anne's heads were charges arising from their having lied to the PIC about Sam Masri. For the first time in his career, Rogerson put his hands up.

Anne was sentenced that October to two years' periodic detention. In mitigation, her psychiatrist, Dr Thomas Clark, told the court that she had acted out of 'a sense of misguided loyalty' to her husband, and that she was 'totally under her husband's influence'.

Rogerson's trial was delayed after he was admitted to a psychiatric hospital suffering, allegedly, from deep depression. His doctor, again Thomas Clark, told the court:

> Mr Rogerson is normally coherent but [on Monday] he was confused, expressing suicidal thoughts, but he hadn't done anything . . . [H]is confusion and paranoias were quite pathological. He was nearly psychotic but he was in a delirious psychosis rather than a permanent one.

The doctor added that there was a possibility Rogerson was faking his condition.

By 17 February 2005, Rogerson had recovered sufficiently to stand before Judge Berman of the District Court. The judge considered his guilty plea, his age, evidence of good character provided by mates who were of good character, and his prospects if the sentence was the maximum of five years. The judge remarked that Rogerson's performance at the commission was 'not some spur of the moment decision which he immediately regretted'. He gave him two years with a non-parole period of one year.

Outside the court, solicitor and former New South Wales detective Paul Kenny said, 'Roger used to be a tough guy. These days he's just a broken down old man, completely broken by the system.' It was the same system that Rogerson and his inner circle had wrapped around their little fingers for many years.

Rogerson served his sentence mainly amid the trees and fresh air of the Kirkconnell Correctional Centre at Sunny Corner, near Bathurst in western New South Wales. Kirkconnell housed prisoners who needed considerable pro-tection, including disgraced ex-cops, sex offenders and, briefly, the disgraced former HIH director Rodney Adler. Rogerson worked as a storeman and was a model prisoner until his release on 17 February 2006. He didn't hang around to chat to the waiting media. A cold beer with some mates was his first priority. Reuniting with Anne would have to wait. She was still doing weekend detention.

Ironically, although he denies it, Roger Rogerson is now suffering from Parkinson's disease, the same disease that is afflicting Neddy Smith, who remains in Long Bay. The future looks bleak for the two former mates.

EPILOGUE

'Get him around a lunch table, and he's the life of the party!' was a comment made frequently by Roger Rogerson's mates when I asked them about him. I didn't encounter any serving or recently departed NSW Police among his 'mates'. Even his old friend and mentor Noel Morey apparently is no longer on speaking terms with Rogerson.

Despite his chequered past, his non-police friends and acquaintances all remember Rogerson as a charmer and the focal point of any social gathering. They shake their heads when reminded of the allegations levelled at him, and the charges proved in court. The man of whom they were fond was a very different bloke from the one who ended up with a bikie as an acolyte and up to no good on tape. As he had done with his family, at least for most of his career, he had kept both lives separate.

I wrote to Rogerson when he was still at Kirkconnell Correctional Facility. I received a polite and well-written letter in return. The prison, he said, wasn't keen on the media communicating with the inmates. In any case, he said, he wasn't 'in the mood to talk to anyone such as yourself at the moment'. He thought he might catch up with me following his release, but expected that he would be rather busy.

At the time of finalising this book, I haven't heard from him. Even if he had decided to tell his story, one could be forgiven for wondering where fiction might end and the truth begin.

Roger Rogerson was the product of a noxious culture that had lost touch, if it ever truly had it, with the community. The notion that the police were doing what the public expected was about half-right; however, the public was a bit of a mushroom. Politicians, the media and the judiciary didn't do them too many favours. It was a culture that even a very straight and honourable upbringing had trouble countering. The line became so blurred that it became difficult for Rogerson to distinguish right from wrong. They blended, and that could, at least in that unhealthy culture, be accepted as 'doing the job' and 'getting results'. The end justified the means.

Rogerson's greatest problem was his own ability. He was a gifted investigator who combined that special skill with charm, wit and magnetism – and a huge ego. Money wasn't the motivator for Roger Rogerson. For him, the aphrodisiac was power: power over someone's liberty; the power to bend the legal system to achieve the result he wanted. Playing the game was engaging, but Rogerson had to be the winner, and for years he was. He had seen what his mentors could do and he bested them.

Rogerson was so busy getting away with blue murder, he missed the scent of change on the breeze. And he wasn't on his own. In 1995, the Wood Royal Commission showed the country that a slew of New South Wales police, particularly detectives, hadn't learned from the travails of the 1980s. But even then, some didn't learn, and in 2001 the Police Integrity Commission again showed the public that the education of the NSW Police had a long way to go. The Armed Hold-up Squad got special mention.

As my favourite philosopher, Maxwell Smart of TV's *Get Smart*, once said: 'If only they'd used their powers for goodness and niceness.'

INDEX